SHORT WAY UP

Other books by Steve Wilson include:

Down The Road
Genuine Mileage on Classic Motorcycles

British Motor Cycles Since 1950
Volume 1: AJW, Ambassador, AMC (AJS and Matchless) and Ariel
     roadsters of 250cc and over
Volume 2: BSA, Cotton, Douglas, DMW, Dot, EMC, Excelsior and
     Francis-Barnett roadsters of 250cc and over
Volume 3: Greeves, Hesketh, Indian, James, Norman and Norton
     roadsters of 250cc and over
Volume 4: Panther, Royal Enfield, Scott, Silk, Sunbeam, Sun and
     Tandon roadsters of 250cc and over
Volume 5: Triumph Part One: The Company
Volume 6: Triumph Part Two: The Bikes; Velocette and Vincent-HRD

Practical British Lightweight Two-Stroke Motorcycles

Practical British Lightweight Four-Stroke Motorcycles

Triumph T120/T140/Hinckley Bonneville

When Rosie met Anneka
A White Horse Mystery

(with Garry Stuart)
Harley People
Voices from the real Harley-Davidson scene

SHORT WAY UP

A classic ride through Southern Africa – 5,000 solo miles on a 1950s Ariel

Steve Wilson
Foreword by Ted Simon

Haynes Publishing

Dedication

This book is for Rosemary Angela Bonhote Wilson, with love

First published in June 2011

A few accounts in this book have appeared in *Real Classic* magazine.

A catalogue record for this book is available from the British Library

ISBN 978 1 84425 685 3

Library of Congress catalog card no 2010927385

Published by Haynes Publishing,
Sparkford, Yeovil, Somerset BA22 7JJ, UK
Tel: 01963 442030 Fax: 01963 440001
Int.tel: +44 1963 442030 Int.fax: +44 1963 440001
E-mail: sales@haynes.co.uk
Website: www.haynes.co.uk

Haynes North America Inc.,
861 Lawrence Drive, Newbury Park, California 91320, USA

Designed and typeset by Dominic Stickland

Printed in the USA by Odcombe Press LP,
1299 Bridgestone Parkway, La Vergne, TN 37086

CONTENTS

ACKNOWLEDGEMENTS

With grateful acknowledgement to S.W.A.T. (Steve Wilson Assistance Team). They were, in order of appearance: Bruce Kirby, Graham "Corkie" Corke, Tony and Lorna Lyons-Lewis, Tony and Verna Barlow, Darryll Moresby-White, Melville Price, Mike and Rialet Wood, Tony Connolly, Roy Cartvel, Stewart Fergusson, Ginty and Kate Melvill, Andy Legg, Cholo, Martin and Daniella Haenz, Rob Clifford and the Nkwali workshop crew, Jo Pope, Peter Mastert, Jimmy Young, Karsten and Linda Nielsen, Jimmy Whyte, Bryan Hunter, Pierre Cronje and Tys Pottas. Heartfelt thanks to all.

Also to the S.W.A.T. folk (Still Waiting At the Third deadline) at Haynes Publishing: Mark Hughes, Flora Myer, Darryl Reach, Dominic Stickland and Peter Nicholson, with thanks for all their skill and patience.

And to Julie "Flaming Jubblies" Taylor, who came from Rhodesia, and typed and typed and typed.

FOREWORD
by Ted Simon

Round-the-world motorcyclist and author
of "Jupiter's Travels" and "Dreaming of Jupiter"

Among the more common words of wisdom addressed to me when I came back from my *Jupiter's Travels* journey was, "If you'd known anything about bikes you'd never have started." The level of confidence in the reliability of British bikes seems to have been at an all-time low. And it's true that everything I knew about my bike when I left in 1973 was what I had learned in three hours at the Meriden plant and what I could glean from my mimeographed copy of the workshop manual.

Being supremely ignorant of the anatomy and history of bikes in general, and my Tiger 100 in particular, I was blissfully confident. It was a new and modern bike and I assumed that as long as I didn't crash, it would run happily for ever. There were so many other things I knew nothing about that the bike was a long way down my list of worries. I knew I could run into all kinds of trouble, and I gave myself a 50-50 chance of survival. So it came as a great surprise to me when, after four years, I returned the bike to Ivor Davies, who did the PR for Triumph, and he told me that at the outset they'd been far more concerned about the bike surviving than about my ability to ride it.

In this respect, if no other, Steve Wilson was far braver than me. He knew how to ride motorcycles, and he also knew just about everything there was to know about what could go wrong with the old Ariel he had chosen to ride. And yet, being by his own admission "not mechanical" he was rather poorly equipped to do anything about it.

In the event, of course, both of us had plenty of troubles and both journeys became immeasurably richer because of them. None of our breakdowns was terminal, and they all provided connections and insights into the world around us. Both bikes took us there and brought us back. Aside from that, our journeys could not have been more different, because every journey is the story of the traveller finding himself. And the moral of this story is that in the end it's not the bike, or the planning or the intentions that matter: it's who you are, and how you tell it. Steve tells it well.

MAP OF THE JOURNEY

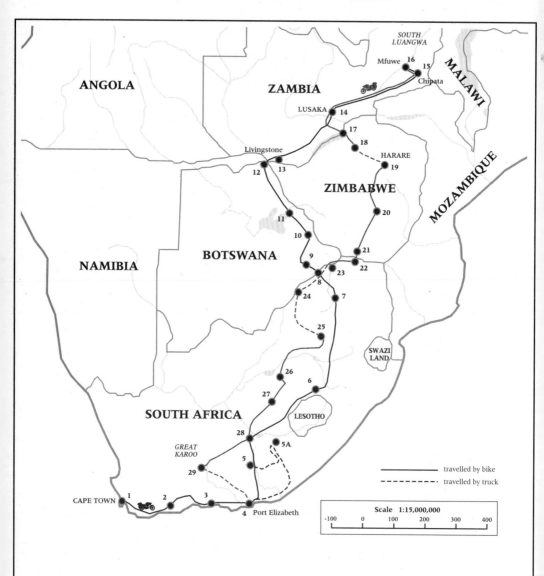

ANGOLA

ZAMBIA

MALAWI

SOUTH
LUANGWA

Mfuwe 16
15
Chipata

LUSAKA 14

17

18

HARARE
19

Livingstone

12 13

20

ZIMBABWE

MOZAMBIQUE

11

10

9

21

22

23

8

24

7

25

NAMIBIA

BOTSWANA

SWAZI
LAND

26

6

27

SOUTH AFRICA

LESOTHO

28

5A

GREAT
KAROO

5

29

6

CAPE TOWN 1

2

3

4 Port Elizabeth

—————— travelled by bike
- - - - - - travelled by truck

Scale 1:15,000,000

-100   0   100   200   300   400

JOURNEY UP 🏍

South Africa		**Botswana**	
1	Cape Town	9	Palapye
2	Swellendam	10	Francistown
3	Knysna	11	Nata
4	Port Elizabeth	12	Kazangula Ferry
5	Cradock		
5A	Sterskstroom	**Zambia**	
6	Clarens	13	Livingstone
7	Mokopane	14	Lusaka
8	Groblers Bridge/	15	Chipata
	Martin's Drift	16	Mfuwe/Nkwali

JOURNEY DOWN 🏍

Zambia		**South Africa**	
17	Chirundu	22	Musane
		23	Alldays
Zimbabwe		24	Lephelale
18	Marongoro	25	Benoni
19	Harare		(Johannesburg)
20	Masvingo	26	Welkom
21	Beitbridge	27	Bloemfontein
		28	Colesberg
		29	Richmond

Author's Foreword

This book is about a 5,000-mile trip which I undertook on a classic motorcycle in 2009, the year I turned 66. I rode from Cape Town in South Africa to the north-eastern side of Zambia, and back, on my own.

So it is a motorcycle travel book and, because old bikes can go wrong, there may be a little more technical detail than the general reader might welcome. But then again, there were dimensions to the journey, and the reasons for undertaking it, that go a bit beyond the "one-man-and-his-bike" narrative which rider readers will expect.

Thus I have to ask for patience from both the special interest and the general reader. Hopefully the latter will be able to skim over the sprocketry and discover something about growing old disgracefully, and about some of the extraordinary men and women, and children, that Southern Africa has bred.

And for the old bike enthusiast, before long there are plenty of specifics, and excitements, as the far-from-perfect old Ariel nevertheless pulls off some real feats of endurance, and carries its short-winded old rider out of a couple of tight spots.

At the very beginning, though, there were no motorcycles at all...

"A book must be the ice-axe for the frozen sea within us."
Franz Kafka

"We call them British bikes, but in a sense they aren't British at all. They are Greek, in the classic dramatic sense, like the men and gods in Homer. Beautiful, spirited, heroic, flawed, and full of fateful games that measure hubris against honour, and seek to test our tenacity and sense of adventure. They are here to see what we are made of, not to be our friends."
Peter Egan, *Leanings 2*

PROLOGUE

Africa gets into you.

Everything in Africa appears the same, but it is different, more extreme. The landscape in the Zambian bush – trees, shrubs, broken red earth – is recognisable. Yet viewed from a hill with the sun sinking ahead, that red earth seems to go on forever. Those magnificent trees – African ebony, Cathedral mopane, the sausage tree with dangling pods weighty enough to concuss or kill you, the baobab, like a giant ancient dalek, and the flat top umbrella tree, the typically African one, layered out horizontally like the sunset itself – those fine trees might be fighting to the death with the strangling limbs of parasite figs, or have their roots engulfed in termite mounds. And the bushes, however blunt or innocent-looking, will cut or snag you, every time.

The life and death struggle is everywhere – from the death-throes of a fallen impala, trapped in the intent, almost-loving choke-hold of a leopard, as the big cat lies along it in the dust, teeth locked to the throat, embracing the prey tightly from behind to avoid its final, spasmodic kicks – to the ant-lion's tiny circular holes in the sandy soil, their steepening sides inextricably sliding an ant down into the pit where the predatory insect waits to suck it dry.

From your front door you watch the wide river below, the Luangwa, bending lazily, and listen to the basso profundo *chortle of a hundred hippos glistening in the brown water; but you go carefully around the edges, where the motionless basking crocodiles are ever vigilant. Even from within the cocoon of an upmarket safari operation, there is no escaping this truth: behind the beauty of the African world is a relentlessly unforgiving environment, where life proliferates but where the weak will not last long. Where only the strong survive.*

PARADISE LOST

In July 2007, my wife Molly and our 13-year-old daughter Rosie went on a safari holiday for 12 days to Africa. Not just any old safari, but an eye-wateringly expensive one involving a week with the legendary, award-winning Robin Pope Safaris (RPS) in Zambia, and then a long weekend chilling out at Mumbo Island on Lake Malawi. It had been Molly's initiative, largely because Rosie was animal-mad and, practically since she had been a baby, an acute observer of the natural world. But it was also something of a last-ditch attempt to save our marriage, which had been in poor order for the last several years.

Painfully expensive, yes, but in this life, more often than not you get what you pay for. Every day with RPS remained etched in all our memories. We started out in their main camp at Nkwali, just across the broad river from the South Luangwa National Park game reserve. The park was vast: 9,050 square kilometres, that's 2.25 million acres, or over twice the size of Gloucestershire. Playing the motoring journalist card to do an article on the Series I Land Rover which Robin Pope had personally restored (and it drove sweetly, despite having been immersed up to the top of its engine in the floods earlier that year), we briefly met the man himself. A significant figure in Southern African conservation, Robin had turned out to be a bespectacled, friendly, but essentially taciturn individual. His wife Jo, the country's first qualified female walking guide, as well as a formidable administrator and businesswoman, had famously proposed to Robin five times before being accepted.

But our main man at Nkwali had been Kiki (real name Keyala Phiri). It later turned out that he was the head guide, and he looked after us exclusively. Kiki was so relaxed, so self-effacing and above all so funny and full of the joy of life, that it took a little while to realise the depth of his knowledge. It was Kiki on the game drives, us with our cameras and binoculars, perched on bench seats on top of the adapted Toyota Land Cruiser, who taught us to distinguish among the herds of antelope (a generic term), between Impala (elegant with black-striped bums), Puku (chunkier, chestnut-coloured, warning whistle), and Kudu (hump and horns); and who showed us how Impala and Puku would mingle with baboons, due to the monkeys' barks and screams of early warning against predators. It was Kiki who stopped me wandering off to pee behind a particular patch of thorn-bushes, pointing quietly to the fresh tracks of leopard paws there; Kiki who, on a night drive (South Luangwa was one of the few National Parks in Africa which allowed operators to go on spot-lit night game drives), identified a spotted hyena from half-a-mile away just by the shape of its eyes in the reflected light. It was Kiki who when we drove around the corner and startled an elephant 20ft away with no way out, when it flared dangerously, talked the animal calm ('sorry mate'), waiting for long minutes before it was safe to drive on.

Above all, it was Kiki who could conjure and interpret the whole interrelated world of the bush out of the minutest scraps. One morning we made a tea-stop (always very welcome, and accompanied by delicious old-fashioned cake or biscuits baked in camp) under the shade of a tall, tall tree. Rosie had been amusing herself with the hole of a lion-ant, one of the Little Five, the insect equivalent of the better-known Big Five (lion, elephant etc). Then she spotted, in a heap of vegetative debris, a tiny frog, although in this 'winter' dry season we were a mile or so from the nearest bit of the river. Kiki explained: the vegetation was Nile water cabbage and it had arrived on the back of one of the river's abundance of hippos. These creatures might weigh two tonnes and cause more human casualties than any of the other wildlife, but they carry their weight on dainty trotters, their tracks significantly smaller than buffalo, and their skins are so sensitive that they must immerse themselves for most of the day, and come out, mostly singly, to feed at night, ranging out from the river and creating the broad churned-up trails that Kiki called hippo highways (as opposed to zebra crossings). On night drives we had seen them lumbering purposefully across in front of the vehicle.

The cabbage also contained water-snails, and Rosie then found a fish skeleton and the desiccated remains of a snake. But these, said Kiki, related to the tall tree. It was a winter-thorn, which the elephants loved for its orange pods. Their feeding resulted in nitrogen fixing and fertilised soil, but the tree had another role. Its height made it a vantage point for birds of prey like Zambia's national emblem, the magnificent fish-eagle, and a safe place for them to eat – hence the fish skeleton and snake. In a quiet and unexceptional spot, Kiki had made us see how everything connected.

Molly and I were also pleased because, without his making a fuss, we could tell that Kiki appreciated how Rosie was observant, lively and deeply engaged with the natural world. Which was not always the case with visiting kids: we once passed a safari vehicle where one child didn't look up from the book it was reading, despite the elephants all around, and another was lying down asleep on its parent's lap, with its head under a blanket.

And it was Kiki who one morning on a drive saw, unusually, a leopard moving in daylight, and then traces of blood and fur in a deep gully, and a hyena circling the meadow in the distance. And shortly afterwards we saw the kill, an impala lodged up a tree. We felt very superior when we met another safari vehicle (a rare occurrence in South Luangwa, unlike the Masai Mara etc), whose occupants said proudly, "We've seen three hyenas!"

After a day's drive, we returned to that meadow at 4.30-ish to check for the hyena, and couldn't believe it when we spotted the leopard coming back towards the gully, clearly making for the tree that harboured the kill. Kiki got us parked in the shade with a view of the tree, and we waited. A male impala had placed himself about 50 yards from the tree, facing away from it and giving the warning cough continuously. The leopard, a male, arrived, went gracefully up the 8ft to 10ft of bare trunk, and was soon in the fork where the kill was lodged. Kiki drove forwards steadily until we were right by the tree and then stopped, the westerly sun shining straight at us; not ideal for taking snaps, but we could see the leopard very clearly, less than 25ft away. Then Kiki without a word drove slowly to the other side of the tree, perfect for photographs.

We watched the leopard eat for a bit, licking the flesh rather horridly to scour off hair, then fanging down with a terrific crunching of bones – a leg was dangling loosely, and briefly I imagined it coming off and dropping into the vehicle, with the leopard jumping down after it. Then the beautiful cat decided to take the carcass higher up the tree. Clamping its neck in his jaws, with the dead impala, which was larger than the cat, between him and the trunk, he pulled himself and his prey, by sheer strength of shoulder and claw, fluidly up another dozen feet of bare trunk, and entered the foliage above. We thought that might be it, but then the leopard's head emerged along a higher branch, gazing west with a bloody muzzle as the sun sank towards the horizon.

After a good time had passed, we drove off on the track, soon meeting the other vehicle we had encountered that morning. Kiki magnanimously led them back and right up to the tree. "O – My – God!" came a voice from that Cruiser. It was a moment to savour and laugh about over supper, delicious as always, round the fire outside our quarters, the large and luxurious Robin's House, by the bend in the river. Susannah Sullivan, our personal and personable young American hostess, who had greeted us with hot towels, presided at the lamp-lit table, with the food appearing, after being solemnly announced, out of the surrounding circle of darkness.

Kiki capped that day's story with one about the time when a walking safari he had been leading in the same meadow had accidentally separated a lioness from her cubs in the gully. Kiki and the Scout with .375 rifle were on one side, and the walking party on the other. The Scout had drawn a precautionary bead on the angry lioness and someone in the party was shouting, "Don't shoot! Don't shoot!" whilst someone else, as they formed a protective circle, was calling, "Hold hands! Hold hands!" It might not have been that funny at the time, but we were helplessly convulsed by Kiki's telling of the tale, and his mighty roars of laughter.

Later when he and I were sitting alone I said to him, "I'm not a brave man", at which he nodded imperceptibly, "but I haven't felt a moment's anxiety for me or the family when we've been out. But then we haven't met a lion yet." Kiki said, "Lions in the end are just big cats. If you stand up to them, they will run away. But buffalos, when they start to charge, there is no stopping them."

Afterwards in my mind I returned to that tiny nod of agreement, not in an aggrieved way that Kiki had taken a formal remark of protestation at literal value, but in recognition that, without fuss or judgement, once again he had seen into the way things really were. I had never been fundamentally physically brave, or graceful under pressure, despite a series of smokescreens like parachuting, motorcycling and fast driving, and a sometimes rackety bohemian life with plenty of sex, drugs and rock 'n' roll. Though fascinated with war, and suffering from a tendency to hero-worship, I could now be grateful for the accident of history that had led me to escape the wars which I and my generation had been educated to prepare for, and in which my flaw might have been exposed. With age, I had eventually partially accepted that a sensitive nature, once seen as a curse, and now mostly cauterised into a graceless, thoughtless insensitivity, had been a prerequisite for anything of value that had emerged from my life as a jobbing writer (I had never considered any other course). To paraphrase David Copperfield, I might at least have turned out to be the anti-hero of my own life. But by now, the wife didn't see it that way.

Within a day we were enchanted with Luangwa's wide, croc- and hippo-infested brown river, its bush-buck and baobab trees, the marks of a baboon's claws in the dust on the windscreen of Robin's Land Rover, the arabesque of a lizard frozen on the white wall of Rosie's bedroom and, for me above all, the close proximity to usually unconcerned big herds of wild elephants.

But the RPS literature said that if we spent a day at Kawaza village, half an hour's drive away in the bush, it would stay in our minds even longer than the animals. Given the recent leopard experience, we wondered about that, but went anyway, dutifully, but not without foreboding. The culture shock of the drive from the local airstrip had been considerable for all of us. I had once travelled through South America, Molly had visited Goa in India, but for Rosie this was a Third World first, and the poverty, the one-room shack housing, the bare feet and ragged clothing, and the burning, angry eyes of the women wood-cutters with their heavy burdens of sticks and their hand-made axes, as we drove by on our high perches, had struck us all silent.

On the fourth morning we set out for Kawaza; still on Nkwali land, we saw bush-buck (dots and stripes) and then a bunch of banded mongoose, running with baboons. We passed the landmark big baobab tree on the way out, with its thick trunk rising in a narrow taper to stumpy branches like a dalek's shooters. A baobab contains between 40 per cent and 75 per cent water, so elephants love its bark for the moisture; fruit bats live in the hollow at its base (one flew out as we passed), and antelope eat its flowers. We were told that the trees were between three and five thousand years old.

As we drove out of Nkwali, passed the hand-painted sign for "WEMY'S

AUTOWORKS, for all your quality auto repairs", and turned off onto the side track towards the village, I was in some apprehension. Exotic trees were easier to deal with than unknown social situations – my head filled incongruously with Pink Floyd's mournful song, *Wish You Were Here.*

Amos, an assistant from the camp, came with us to see his family, as Kawaza was his village. Except it was not quite that simple. The village consisted of around 300 outlying settlements, each housing an extended family, and the centre 'village' we would visit was principally a show construction, though people did live there. So just after we had negotiated a steep approach and crossed a clear, shallow, sandy-bottomed stream, with women on the far edge pounding clothes on stones, Amos pointed to a cluster of huts off to one side; that was where he had grown up. It was hard to suppress the patronising reflex of surprise, because young Amos – smart, highly articulate in English (a second language for Africans) and well on his way to passing the extremely testing exams to qualify as a wildlife guide – had evidently come a long way.

At a corner further on, around another collection of huts, were raised thin fences to above head height, consisting only of strings, with rags soaked in old diesel and chilli-juice tied into them. The floods earlier that year had affected the vegetation which the elephants fed off, and they were moving further from the Park, seeking the villagers' crops and melons. And elephants, we were told, couldn't stand the smell of the 'pepper fences'. It seemed a flimsy front-line to protect the food that fed these families. The crops were almost all they had – we did see a very few cattle with lyre-shaped horns, but keeping livestock that close to the park couldn't really be done, due to the lions.

We stopped first at Kawaza School, which was administered by RPS, specifically under the supervision of the formidable Jo Pope. They and other safari operators in the area plough back a percentage of their profits into schools and clinics. This was enlightened self-interest, for unless the locals became, and stayed, convinced of the benefits to them of the camera-safari and hunting tourism, the wildlife we came to see in the Park would quickly be eroded by poaching, for money, meat, and a more robust self-defence than those pepper fences (though later we were told that a fringe-benefit had developed from the fences, as farmers sold chillis in the market for a modest profit). The threat was real: since the Seventies, poachers had killed

75 per cent of the elephants in the National Park, and in the Eighties, allegedly partly due to government corruption and complicity with the poachers, black rhino had been wiped out in South Luangwa, before the tide had been partially turned by the RATs (honorary Rangers Rapid Action Teams) and the Scouts of the South Luangwa Conservation Society. Even so, buffalo had declined by almost 50 per cent since 1998.

Our visit was not all plain sailing. We went first to the headmaster's small dark office (briefly raising shades of skool), where busy but serious and articulate David Mwewa laid out the school's mission statement and its problems – though my eyes kept being drawn guiltily to a newspaper clipping pinned up on the board, emphasising the need for pupils to respect their teachers, and how difficult that was when they saw them being taken home drunk in a wheelbarrow. Some 700 pupils were educated here, despite shortages of books and everything else, on a government-encouraged gender-equality basis, so that girls were no longer so likely to be hauled off at the age of 12 for domestic servitude or early marriage; there was also an adult literacy scheme in the evenings. Afterwards I presented David with a copy of the little book I had written for Rosie, for the school library, but he took it away himself; he and I laughed that he was perhaps checking to see if it was suitable.

Then without preamble we were led into a large, dusty classroom with 50-plus pupils, and introduced to them and the broadly smiling teacher who, when we turned around, had disappeared – we were the entertainment for the next 30 minutes. We were each with a different group, and it was hardest on Rosie, as they couldn't understand why at her age she wasn't married. I tried showing my lot a photo of our dogs, but they weren't interested, so I took a photo of them which went down better, with some major posing by the boys. Some of the students, boys and girls, were quietly getting on with their work: the Amos-figures of the future, you hoped. But it was a long half hour.

The village visit also had its quota of excruciating moments: Rosie, a young 13, narrowly missed having to spend time with a voluble gang of women, full of back-chat, who with long logs were pounding flat the floor of a hut under construction. They had threatened to tell her women's stuff she would need to know when she would (soon, they thought) get married. Rosie shrank visibly at the prospect but mercifully the women decided that none of them spoke English well enough. The round huts were impressive, neatly constructed with walls to shoulder height and a substantial gap above them before the reed thatch roof began, which kept them cool and airy in the heat of the day. In one built for guests there were no beds or bedding. "We don't need that," they said. I had spent enough uncomfortable nights under canvas on foam mats to really be struck by this, a major physical difference.

Before lunch we were driven off around the many outlying clusters of huts, each with their quota of grinning kids running after the Land Cruiser. We were accompanied by a somewhat glib and self-satisfied village representative. Bumping along the network of tracks, he explained that the hollow logs slung horizontally by cords in the stands of trees near the huts were beehives; and in the compounds, the square little box-houses mounted up on 8ft poles were hen houses – both constructions aimed against predatory honey-badgers.

Aside from a few small patches growing cotton, which was the sole cash crop, all the cultivated areas were for subsistence farming. We saw a patch newly burnt-off prior to cultivation beside one of the many makeshift chapels and churches, and the grinning kids there were waving small things as we passed. They were mice, our guide explained, a valued protein source. It was a quiet index of the people's hunger. The process of rooting the mice out after the burning was not without hazard. A couple of days later at Nsefu, another RPS camp, our guide, Sebastian, told us how as a boy he had been doing that when he had disturbed a spitting cobra. The reptiles project their venom high, to maximise the chance of getting it in your eyes. Sebastian would have gone blind, but nearby his older sister was nursing her baby and had used breast milk to wash out the poison. Not because breast milk had healing properties in this context, but because it was the only uncontaminated fluid for many miles around. We were reminded of all this on the way to Lilongwe Airport to fly out of Malawi; boys vending food by the side of the highway held up kebab sticks on which were skewered small but strangely familiar shapes. "Mice," the driver confirmed laconically.

Our last stop was at the village clinic. The exhausted and frustrated male nurse, with the nearest hospital 40 miles away, told us sombrely that malaria rather than HIV still caused the majority of (entirely preventable) deaths. The average life expectancy in Zambia was 38 years. Everywhere on our route, women and children walked gracefully with the crushing burden of 20-litre water cans on their heads, due to the (absolutely remediable) lack of wells.

Then it was back to the village for lunch in a cool round-house. The food was guilt-makingly good: chicken and *nshima*, a sort of savoury maize-based porridge, somewhere between mashed potato and polenta, though I suspect we were enjoying a de luxe version of it. Molly had a question for the representative. We had seen the women pounding the floors and building huts, washing clothes, cooking the food and now serving it, but apart from one guy working on a bore-hole, we had seen no men at work. Her question was: what did the men in the village do? After some hemming and hawing about heavy work at harvest time, the rep concluded grandly, "But mostly, you see, they take more of a *managerial* role ..."

And sure enough, it was the women, the same ones that had been building and cooking, who now had to turn out and entertain us with a display of tribal dancing to drums, as we sat cringing on a line of chairs like a royal party. To be fair, some of the youngest ones put their whole souls into strutting their stuff, and the older ones got into it too, but it was hard to dodge the question: did they really need this one further call on their time and energy, to entertain us? We should have joined in, of course, but were far too English for that.

The literature had got it right: we did remember the village visit for a long time. *Wish You Were Here*?

They had also been right that, after a week of getting up in the dark, roused by quiet drums to drink tea and eat porridge round the fire that flavoured the food, in the glowing minutes before dawn; and the night drives; and all the emotional impact, the wonder and the learning – we were knackered, and really did need those few days on Lake Malawi to regroup and chill. We three were driven back to the modest air strip, grandly titled Mfuwe International Airport, and walked out not to the regular twin-engine passenger plane we had arrived on, but to a single-engine Piper Cherokee (yes!). On take-off there was just enough of a cross-wind for things to be interesting without being sick-making. As we rose away into the blue, droning over the burning land and its perpetual columns of smoke, low enough to see the red dirt roads running through the bush and converging at lonely crossroads, a plan hovered in my head. My thought was: I'll have some of that.

Nearly 50 years previously I had left school and taken my first major two-wheel trip, down through France and Italy to the ferry for Greece. I had ridden round that still quite primitive but beautiful country with a mate, often on dirt roads, and then alone back up to Blighty. This transfiguring trip had as many highs, lows and doldrums as they always do, but overall it took me straight out of beastly boarding school into a world of colour and light, Mediterranean wine and food, companionship and movement; an experience – yes, it has to be the F-word – a freedom, which I'd been attempting to recapture ever since. OK, I did the journey on the new silver Vespa GS 150 scooter bought for me for getting into Oxford. But it did get me the 4,000 miles there and back without even a puncture, and permanently imprinted on me that Travel is Good, and that two-wheel travel is the best of all.

Since then I'd ridden all around the UK, Europe and Morocco, on Norton, BSA and Moto Guzzi twins. Travel, as I once told my best pal, was for me a kind of violent rest; and right at this moment, like Captain Willard in *Apocalypse Now*, I needed a mission, a journey, and I wasn't thinking about the sickening metaphorical kind that psychobabble and politicians fall back on so frequently these days. My age had started with a six for the past few years, so if I was ever going to do one last really good ride to book-end that first one, it would have to be sooner rather than later. How about combining that with fundraising for Kawaza School and Clinic? Sure, the school visit had not been a comfortable experience, but encountering those unfailingly cheerful people and their heroic under-funded efforts to improve their lives had, as the organisers predicted, got under my skin. Education represented the only way out from the subsistence farming trap, and if the locals saw the benefits to them of tourism, the wildlife had a better chance too. And with the Popes administering the money directly, I knew that any funds I raised had the best chance of actually getting to the projects.

So, we did get what we paid for. The holiday changed our lives. From then on, Rosie abandoned her previous goal of archaeology, becoming passionate about conservation and bending her educational efforts to begin qualifying as a zoologist.

But sadly, there was one thing the trip did not do. It didn't save the marriage.

PART ONE

PREPARATION

"[After World War 2] the only customers for motorcycles were the young, the poor, and a sprinkling of older men with psychological problems."

L.J.K. Setright

Chapter 1

ISLAND OF DREAMS

Later in 2007, with separation pretty well decided upon by Molly and me, I went for the first time in my life to motorcycling's mecca, the Isle of Man. I had not been before because I did not follow motorcycle sport, or like crowds, and the TT races in June were a circus involving plenty of both. But the more laid-back Manx Grand Prix in late August/September, with various classic-oriented races, was something else. I flew over and stayed with biking friends, John and Jane South, who had moved to the Island, and John lent me one of his collection of thirty-odd machines, a 650 BSA A10 which he called Black Betty and rode to work. I owned an A10 of my own, but John's was the Super Rocket version, so a little quicker. I was also the guest of a large Vintage Motor Cycle Club (VMCC) group visiting for the Manx, and as such got to ride, with a pack of vintage and classic machines, the hallowed 37.7 miles of the Mountain Circuit, on roads with no speed limit and closed to traffic after race practice – so with nothing coming the opposite way.

The organisation and marshalling were tight, as on the final day of that year's TT tragically there had been three deaths, a rider and two spectators, and two marshals were seriously injured; this had happened at the tail-end of the last race when the rider had lost control at speed. Modern race bikes can reach speeds of up to 200mph. John, who was marshalling the MGP races, despite his left shoulder and arm still suffering from a tumble he'd taken a couple of years before, knew that I was far from a fast or competitive rider like himself and many of his pals. But on his mobile he told Jane, as I thundered by him above Glen Helen, "I think Steve's all right. He just came by on Betty, and he was smiling, and overtaking someone". I loved everything about the Island, and even the famously fickle weather stayed mostly OK.

John travelled extensively to the Middle East and Hong Kong with an IoM-based IT company, and had taken to delivering motivational talks to employees (sometimes as a prelude to down-sizing, ie just before they lost their jobs). Accustomed to people at a crossroad in their lives, he said one evening that he would ask me a question and I should answer without thinking about it. "If you were free to do anything at all with the rest of your life, what would it be?" I didn't have to think. "Have another go at writing fiction, and do one more big trip on two wheels."

It was Royce Creasey, the Bristol-based guru of Alternative Biking, who coined the phrase The Cosmic Exchange Company, to indicate serendipity – the way in which a spare part or contact which a person involved with old motorcycles needed, seemed so often uncannily to turn up for them at just the right time.

After another excellent morning's run with the VMCC lads, through rural lanes twisted up like intestines to fit inside the Island's modest 32-mile long by 13-mile wide dimensions, I was waiting for tea at Mouragh Park in Ramsey, where our bikes were all parked up. The accent of the rider in front of me in the queue suggested he was from South Africa, and I told him I had just been in Zambia, and was contemplating a return journey on two wheels. This was Gary Brown from outside Durban. When we met up at the same spot the next day for the Ramsey Sprint, he introduced me to another rider from Southern Africa, Ginty Melvill, a short, sardonic ex-South Rhodesian/Zimbabwean, now living outside the Zambian capital of Lusaka. "The last ones we had through," said Ginty, "were that Ewan McGregor and his mate."

Ginty later wrote that Gary had told him about "this grey-bearded, white-haired old bloke... My first impression of this well-known writer of many books and bike magazine articles was that he would be better suited to standing next to a tall desk, ink-well at his side and a quill in hand, while he pondered his next move. He admitted his mechanical skills were non-existent, so I doubted he was serious over the whole plan... only a fool would envisage such a trip unless he were a dab hand at bike mechanics." Ourselves as others see us, eh? But we exchanged e-addresses, and in the coming months Ginty could not have been more helpful with routes, maps and contacts.

However, now for the shameful admission, though it's one which, as

Ginty's remarks indicated, I have never tried to conceal: I am not, and never will be, "mechanical" – an odd phrase, conjuring donk-eared Bottom in *A Midsummer Night's Dream*, but we all know what it means. I had grown up largely without my father present to teach me the way of spanners, and even if he had been there he never even learned to drive a car, and claimed to be unable to change a light bulb. I discovered early on that it could be positively dangerous if I tried to be mechanical, even in minor ways. Back in the Sixties, running a 500 Norton twin with a fully enclosed rear chaincase, I noticed that one of its bolts was missing and went to Gus Kuhn's for a replacement. I didn't tell them which bolt, and they didn't ask. I bolted in what they sold me, rode across London, stopped and parked up, and then noticed a deep gouge, down to the canvas, in the left hand wall of the rear tyre, where the wrong, over-long bolt had been ripping into it.

But I had become fixated on British motorbikes, and found that I could bring something to the two-wheel table. With a degree in modern history, I became interested in building up a picture of what had produced the objects on which I was fixated: in the British motorcycle industry. One thing led to another, and ten years later I had written and had published a six-volume work both describing the background of the British motorcycle companies, and cataloguing their products year by year, from 1950 on. By the time I was finished, so was the traditional industry. People found the books readable and useful, and despite the lack of engineering background I was able to relay the technical information I had researched in a sufficiently clear and accurate way. But that didn't make me any handier with the spanners. So I was in the contradictory position of knowing quite a lot about British bikes, but not being able to do much in practical terms with that knowledge.

Being non-mechanical, you often end up relying on the kindness of professional strangers. Where old British motorbikes are concerned, this is frequently in short supply. Not surprising, really, when mechanics are working every day by the hour, and you come in with your depression and your worn, imperfectly-designed old machinery displaying poorly delineated or intermittent problems, and hope that they will resurrect your mood, nay, your *life*, and Make Everything Right. Ain't gonna happen. The bottom line – usually unspoken but quite clear, and bred of a largely working-class culture in a time when people simply could not afford to go to garages – was that if you were going to be involved with the things then you should be able to adjust and mend them yourself. But over the years I have been lucky enough to build up relations with a handful of skilled mechanics who restored and serviced the Brit bikes which in the main served me well on the long journeys I loved. And that was what I was hoping would be the case for this run through Africa.

Still, with the youngest traditional bike by then 30 years old, and a wealth of more practical machinery available from elsewhere, why was I still pursuing the Impossible (Brit bike) Dream? It was not quite patriotism (we were all caustic about Sixties' build quality, worn-out production machinery etc), and not quite nostalgia (although a big component was that the familiar, simple and strong Brits in some circumstances contrasted well with the unduly complex, though much more reliable, rice-burners). In the end it got down to quasi-religion: that for some of us, the Brits were just the Righteous Path. And for a writer, a trip on one certainly made for a better story.

Back on the Island, the one thing that Gary Brown, Ginty and his pal Alan Obst all insisted on was that doing the African trip on one's own would be unwise in the extreme. So the next steps were to select a mount, and then find a companion.

Chapter 2

HOUSE OF THE HORSE

The way I came to do the ride on an Ariel was as long and eccentric a tale as the rest of the saga. Late in 2005, with a bit of cash in hand, I had looked around for a winter bike to replace a much-loved, well-sorted BSA M21 side-valve 600 single that had gone (sob!) to pay for half a new kitchen. I'm a bit of a BSA nut, but when I looked again the prices of BSA singles had ratcheted up a notch and they no longer qualified as cheap classics (if there is such a thing). The only really economical candidates were AJS/Matchless Heavyweight singles which, as the adjective suggested, were on the ponderous side, or their Ariel equivalents. I had not been too impressed with the tail-end handling of a friend's 350 Ariel I once tested, but the marque had a good reputation – and from 1943 they had become part of the BSA Group (though it hadn't done them much good).

Since an Ariel single is one of the central characters in this story, perhaps a little history is in order. Ariel are in danger of becoming one of the forgotten marques on the British post-war classic scene. Dominated by the big boys – Triumph, Norton and BSA – who managed to keep on into the Seventies and beyond, today's enthusiasts tend to overlook the smaller, second rank (but not second-rate) marques like Douglas and Ariel, "The House of the Horse". This is unjust, as from their base in Selly Oak, Birmingham, the company produced machines with a reputation for ruggedness, reliability and fine finish. Ariel had also lived up to their other title, "The Modern Motorcycle", in offering some ground-breaking new designs. In particular, these had included the legendary Square Four, or "Squariel". Offered post-war in 1000cc form, from 1955 to 1959 this model became the Last British Thousand, until the Hesketh vee-twin over 20 years later. From 1958 there was also the all-enclosed Ariel Leader, a beam-framed 250 2-stroke twin, which ambitiously tried to combine the virtues of motorcycles and scooters.

The Ariel story had begun in the pioneer days. By 1925, under the leadership of Charles Sangster, they had hired their outstanding designer, Val Page, who quickly laid down the basis for a range of successful, reliable singles, as the marque's backbone. But in 1932, with the Depression biting hard, the company only survived after a buy-out by Charles' son, J.Y. "Jack" Sangster, a brilliant industrialist in his own right. It had been Jack Sangster who, late in the Twenties, had hired the young Edward Turner. Legend has it that Turner arrived with the engine design for what would become the Square Four sketched out on the back of a cigarette packet. Turner who, as any fule kno, went on to design the trend-setting Triumph Speed Twin, may have had his limitations in terms of detailed engineering, but there was no doubting the inspired nature of his conceptual design work. Before that time, four-cylinder motorcycle engines had been limited by having their pots arranged in-line along the frame (too long), or transversely across it (too wide).

Turner had arranged the cylinders in the shape of a cross, with one pair behind the other, coupled by geared flywheels (his Speed Twin would in fact be essentially half a Square Four). This layout gave built-in smoothness and compactness. The Square Four was always to be a luxury model, but Edward Turner had another touch of genius, and that was designing just the things which would appeal to riders so powerfully that they would buy, no matter what. Now he went to work on Val Page's singles, transforming these with deft touches, such as beautiful chrome-and-gold lined bright scarlet tanks, as well as by some tuning, into the sporting Red Hunter range. Ariel already had a formidable publicist in the inventive Vic Mole, the man who had come up with the Art Deco "Horse" motif. A thinly disguised Red Hunter had also featured as George Formby's TT mount in the pre-war comedy film, *No Limit*.

With a combination of this charisma and of all-round sporting achievement – the Hunters excelled in trials, scrambles, sprints and road racing – Ariel survived the Depression. The singles had been both refined and toughened throughout the Thirties. After Edward Turner had left for Triumph, which Jack Sangster had also acquired in 1936, the quiet, thoughtful Val Page and others developed the Square Four in ohv form to 600 and then 1,000cc versions. The latter in 1939 featured another first for a volume-produced British roadster: rear suspension, by the Anstey-Link plunger system. In good condition, for everyday riding it handled more than acceptably, as well as being a big improvement over the jarring ride of the rigid machines then available.

workplace. Another strong defender of the company, though he had come there from BSA, was their General Manager Ken Whistance. He was a forceful personality, as demonstrated by an incident after he had got wind of the fact that men doing the filthy, 'gutty' jobs in the polishing shop were stopping work from time to time to nip across the road to the pub. Whistance ordered this practice to cease, and when he then entered the pub and spotted a filthy group of men, he fired them forthwith. The men shuffled out sheepishly, and it was only later that Whistance discovered that they had been from another factory.

The Red Hunters' tradition of competition continued post-war, with trials and scrambles versions available over the counter; and an HT Trials 500 formed the basis for the most famous 4-stroke trials iron of all time, Sammy Miller's all-conquering GOV 132. But on the road, unlike their marginally better-handling, more powerful BSA Gold Star competitors, the Red Hunters were now unfussy, tractable and long-legged tourers, as well as being some 30lb lighter than their BSA and Matchless equivalents.

However, by the end of 1959 Ariel had turned over their entire production to the initially successful 2-stroke Leader and Arrow. Then abruptly, from 1960, came the dramatic home-market slump in motorcycle sales – and the US market was not interested in either 2-strokes, or enclosed bikes like the Leader. Triumph's Edward Turner was at the helm of the BSA Automotive Division and he tended to favour his own designs. There was no further development on the 2-strokes, and several promising Ariel projects were quashed. In 1963, with annual sales at around a dismal 2,000, Selly Oak was closed and Ariel moved in with BSA at Small Heath, where Ariel production ceased in 1965.

So, back to 2005, before *Short Way Up* had been thought of, I had located a 1954 Ariel NH 350 Red Hunter, at the UK old bike dealer I favour most, Andy Tiernan in Framlingham, Suffolk. Due to the Ariel's lack of MoT and matt-silver painted tank, Andy let me have it for £1,000. And here comes the bizarre stuff. To unbelievers, the concept of the Cosmic Exchange Co. is just a product of the acid-fried imaginations of failed hippies. But what are the odds that I and my Editor at *Real Classic* magazine, Frank Westworth, should both independently, and unknown to each other, elect to buy swinging-arm Ariel 350 singles, not models to which either of us had ever been previously inclined. And that we would do this within 24 hours of each other, with bikes found in the same area of England, *and to within £11 of the same price!*

Frank already owned a large collection of British bikes, many of them plucked from eBay, which is where he had found his '58 Ariel 350. To cut a long story short, my bike turned out to be a mixed bag, a good starter which ran well enough, but then shortly revealed a cracked frame. Despite the low purchase price, Andy Tiernan took it back without quibble and fixed it – there are good reasons why he is my favourite dealer – and I settled down to riding the Ariel through the summer of 2006. Though the 55-60mph cruising speed was equivalent to my old M21, and the Ariel provided a significantly more comfortable ride, the 350's acceleration through the gears was underwhelming, and by then it had become that bit too smart to be a winter bike. So I had sold it on.

In the autumn of 2007, after I had returned from the Isle of Man, things at home were no better. We were thinking the (for me) unthinkable, and getting ready to ask estate agents about putting our jointly-owned home, standing on the edge of a hamlet in the Vale of the White Horse, on the market. Meanwhile in the outside world, tectonic plates had shifted and the words 'Credit Crunch' first began to be heard.

That autumn, I drove down to Frank and his wife Rowena's bungalow in Cornwall and stayed the night. Frank had recently been diagnosed with diabetes, something I had suffered from, in the milder Type 2 form, for the previous dozen years. But in Frank's case he was told that it was life-threatening, and Rowena had him on a lettuce leaf and exercise bike regime, which would eventually lead him to a weight loss of over eight stone, and remission of the disease; they were both very determined characters. Happily that night they broke training, we ate out, and it was a convivial evening. We talked a little bit about our various problems, and I laid out my idea for one last proper ride in Africa, combined with charity fund-raising for the school. Initially they were dismissive, even derisive, as they said they had been approached too often by riders looking to fund their 'holidays' in foreign parts on charity money. But I made it clear that all the money raised would go directly into the existing UK-registered charitable trust for the school, and that I would be meeting all the expedition costs myself.

This turned out to be quite a live issue. In 2008, the Royal Princes William and Harry (along with their six Metropolitan Police protection officers) took part in a week-long "Enduro-Africa" charity ride – which for the participants was paid for out of the £4,995 sponsorship money each had raised, with just "a minimum of £1,500" from each being donated to their Lesotho charity for AIDS orphans. "When they ask for sponsorship," read *The Observer*'s headline, "tell them to get on their bikes."

Late that evening, Frank and I ended up in the Big Shed where most of his 30 or so motorcycles resided, suffering the slow ravages of Cornish sea air. Frank pointed to the 350 Ariel, the one he had bought at the same time as mine, and said that if I really did go to Africa, he would give me that bike to do the trip on.

I thought we'd better sleep on this, and see if the offer was still open the following morning. But it was, and Frank also suggested the name of the Ariel specialist he thought would be the best guy to go through the Red Hunter before we hit Africa; someone he had known a long time: John Budgen. I said I believed a 500 engine would have to be substituted for the 350, in view of the weight of stuff I would need to carry and the distances to be covered, but that should not be a problem as the two motors were interchangeable. John Budgen, as well as Frank and Rowena, would have a stall at an autojumble at Kempton Park that November.

So I went to Kempton and met him. John – a tall, well-built man in his 70s, but still side-car scrambling on a 1,000cc Wasp outfit – seemed sympathetic to my project. He said he would see if he had a suitable 500 engine. I said that ideally I would like to take delivery of the bike the following spring, 2008, so I could give it a really good shake-down run before the off, which would be May 2009. The departure and expedition dates were dictated by the weather: it would then be winter in Southern Africa, not summer's heat, and not the rainy season. John said he was too busy with existing orders, mainly building up versions of the famous Ariel HT and HS singles for classic trials and scrambles, to get anything finished sooner than August 2008. That still seemed to leave plenty of time, and by then our family house should have been sold as well. The estate agents had suggested a surprisingly elevated guide price. It was to go on the market in the spring, though my brother, who may be a bit shaky on the value of things but has always known their exact price, advised me in one sentence to sell immediately. I ignored him, of course.

Later, I drove across the Cotswolds and visited John Budgen at his home in the Gloucestershire village of Toddington. I met his delightful wife Pearl, and saw in his workshop an immaculate HT he was building up; took in the separate room full of well-organised Ariel spares, and had a good talk with John, who turned out to be an ex-copper, once based in Upper Street, Islington, close to where I had lived in the Seventies. We swapped family problems and I amplified on the charity side of the trip. John, an individual with a reassuringly steady manner, heard me out, and then committed entirely to the project. He also lent me a book titled *Mondo Enduro*, about an absolutely hilarious attempt at a shambolic but successful round-the-world trip by a bunch of ex-schoolmates on tired Japanese enduro bikes. It added one resonant word to my vocabulary, "blending", as in the traveller stealthily locking on to people along the way who could be useful to him. However, John did say that doing an engine-swap on a 350 would probably end up more labour-intensive and troublesome than building up a bike from scratch, out of the several engines and half-a-dozen frames he had cached. I said I was sure that Frank would not object to turning over this 350 to John for him to trade on, and knocking whatever he got for it off the cost of building up my own bike.

I was wrong about that. After a slightly inconclusive phone conversation on the matter with Frank, I got an e-mail from Rowena, tactfully letting me know that Frank was actually pretty fond of his 350, not least because of its originality and how he had come to own it; and that he would be distressed if he were to come on the bike at an autojumble, for sale at a large price, with an "As featured in *Real Classic*" sticker on it. So since they did want to support my run, Rowena proposed a compromise: handing over the £1,011 Frank had paid for the bike originally, towards the trip. This still seemed insanely generous to me and I accepted with alacrity, the money going straight to John Budgen. But it did illustrate the pitfalls of my increasingly single-minded pursuit of The Journey.

A start was made on the bike's 500 engine, in view of some emphatic e-mail advice from Gary Brown outside Durban. He said that the one thing I should make sure of was that the cylinder head was modified to take unleaded petrol or worse, as fuel quality in Southern Africa was highly variable. So once John had selected a cylinder head from his spares hoard, and valves to suit, I took them up to another key cog in the *Short Way Up* scheme of things, Bill Crosby at Reg Allen's, in Hanwell, West London, which is pretty much the last remaining Brit bike shop in the capital. A piratical, grey-bearded Londoner, who lost a leg from a bike crash in the Fifties, Bill had shown real determination in also founding and expanding The London Motorcycle Museum, nearby in Greenford. With our house move looming, I had done a deal with him to take a substantial proportion of my archive of bound and indexed classic bike magazines, period scrap books etc, as the museum was going to include a library, and that seemed the best place for my unfeasibly bulky collection. In return, Bill would provide parts and services relating to my trip. He was able to send cylinder heads direct to Sidi, the company that supplied the machinery to the rest of the country for inserting hardened valve seats into the heads.

Bill rang a few days later to check that the valves that John Budgen had supplied with the head were correct, as they had both been the same size and the guy at Sidi thought they should have been different. I checked with John, and he apologised for having sent two inlet valves, rather than an inlet and an exhaust. Sidi had caught it before they had started cutting the head. And anybody could make a mistake.

So with the bike build underway, what about a riding companion?

Chapter 3

SOMEONE TO RIDE
THE RIVER WITH

I immediately had one man in mind, but could hardly hope that he would consent. I had known Tony Page for several years, and he was emphatically the Real Deal. I had written up his trip to the Yukon by Vincent Rapide, his quarter of a million mile Norton Commando, and his half a million miles working as a courier on a Wankel rotary-engine Norton – he did not own a car. In the Brit bike community he was possibly best known as the organiser of the highly successful Beezumph race-track rallies for the Trident & Rocket 3 Owners Club, and could be seen tearing up the tarmac there, wearing a trademark undersized pink coat over his leathers.

It got better. Tony's background had been military; he was an ex-Royal Marine Commando. He downplayed the glamorous Commando image ("sitting under the hood of a Transit, wrapped in plastic and shitting into cling film"), but he had seen action in Northern Ireland, the Falklands, and a number of places in the Middle East and Africa which it would probably be unwise to specify, even if I knew them. He did say that he had done jungle training in one of our intended destinations, Botswana, and that while he was there one member of a stick of paratroopers had been trampled to death by a startled herd of elephants. I didn't know our Forces trained there, but then there was an awful lot I didn't know. Clearly here I was going to have to keep my hero-worshiping tendencies on a short leash, but that was not too hard. TP was mostly down-to-earth, typical Forces in being unassuming physically, wiry rather than brawny; and he was not short of self-knowledge, as in the following, which coincidentally began to partly explain why such an extraordinary individual earned his living as a motorcycle courier.

"I couldn't see there would be much call for my sort out in the world of nine-to-five. I mean, what was my CV going to say for a start? 'Qualified

Small Arms Instructor, very experienced in gun battles and handling paramilitary sources during counter-insurgency warfare, bad language and nightmares a speciality. Met the Queen.' ... and bingo, the job's mine?"

When you got to know him a little better, and always on his terms, Tony's stories would come. Like the night on the Falklands when he had dropped his lucky Mars Bar, and his platoon had voluntarily hung on under Argentine shell fire while he scrabbled around in the mud looking for it. Or the episode when he was with BRIXMIS, the outfit who, through a legal loophole, could gather intelligence in the GDR, East Germany, around Berlin (but would be badly beaten up if they were caught at it). The Russians were sending their wounded from Afghanistan for recuperation in East Germany, to conceal the extent of their casualties at home and, being as ever short of everything, they were recycling their paperwork orders from the campaign, in place of loo roll for the wounded. Tony and others had retrieved this potentially valuable source of Intel. Not the pleasantest work, but what Tony did enjoy, as he bagged up the soiled sheets, was the thought of the desk-bound spooks in Whitehall having to un-bag and work on them. My favourite tale was the reason why he drank very little. After one spectacular night on the lash with some mates, this ultra-macho man had woken up in a dumpster somewhere in Germany, with no recollection of the previous several hours, and now clad in just a mini-dress and a pair of plimsolls.

Tony was bursting, often angrily, with the big ideas that most of us pass by discreetly, but which his experience gave him the right to, and mainly concerning "Carpe Diem". There was one elephant in the room, the absence of a family or other emotional attachments for Tony, though in proper Forces' mode, no one was quite sure about that. But this he did believe: "Security is mostly superstition... avoiding danger is no safer in the long run than outright exposure. Life is either a daring adventure, or nothing." However not without balance: " ... always be careful that it does not turn into the story of a traveller whose adventure gets a bit too big and who just wants to go home."

True to his philosophy, when I asked Tony early in 2008 if he would come to Africa with me the following year, his response was simply, "Yes, of course". Before long he had got hold of an Ariel 500 of his own, and later in the year arranged for his boss at the courier firm to set us up with a *Short Way Up* website, complete with pop-up giraffes and perpetually putt-putting

Red Hunters, to help the charity end. My friend and colleague, the brilliant cartoon artist Nick Ward, sketched some ideas for a logo, and my pal Tom Carter developed this into its final form, which included the Ariel's "House of The Horse" head, as well as my personal totem, the 3,000-year-old Uffington White Horse, and an outline of our intended route in Africa. "That's maps taken care of," Tony dead-panned. He had once met an Australian outside Gus Kuhn's, with an R90S BMW outfit on which he and his pregnant wife were about to ride home, overland, using just a fold-out map of the world from Bridgestone Tyres. They had made it, too.

We kicked around a few things. Tony's main contribution about clothing was that we should each have a decent pair of shoes, giving me visions of Embassy 'blending'. In view of the incidence of violent crime in the region, I wondered if we should carry handguns? I really liked Tony's response: as a man more than proficient with firearms, all he said was, "If we ever had to use them, that would be the end of the trip." The journey was his top priority. Tony's connections meant that e-mails began to arrive headed "Spooks Say", with encouraging stuff like "... petty and violent crime (in Botswana) is increasing... if you are attacked, do not resist..."

Soon it was autumn 2008, the credit crunch had really bitten, and our house hadn't sold despite us changing estate agents and dropping the price. For me a couple of possible alternative relationships had bitten the dust. By now, however, stuff like that was ceasing to be a surprise. A friend in the trade (clinical psychology) had summed it up in essence as "... where a troubled mental state, originating from damage in childhood/early infancy, manifests its life and energy through ... attitudes and behaviours which basically act as defences against us facing the reality of our misery and inadequacy. The latter is unbearable in its power to destroy our very souls, so we contain it and avoid dangerous situations such as exposing ourselves to sharing and intimacy. Conditions which not only leave us open to the risk of the kind of hurt we experienced in the first place, but make us fearful and uneasy about the intimacy itself over any extended period of time. We need the intimacy desperately though, leading to tremendous ambivalence and tension." In my case the "attitudes and behaviours" had centred on the need for secrecy and maintaining a private part, often by means of adopting jokey, hyper-masculine or evasive masks. Years and muddled years had passed like that, and now just as I was getting an inkling of it, with libido on the wane (blame the diabetes?) and old age approaching, it was looking to be too late. The exception to it all, I hoped, had been my love for Rosie, my only child. I had done the best I could there, but still things were falling apart.

The trip helped to keep my mind off this stuff. By the end of September 2008 the pace was picking up, though my bike had not materialised in August despite several more visits to John Budgen. When pressed, he said that he had thought the August date had just been an approximate one, though he did now know that our departure date was coming up on 1 May 2009, and that it was inflexible. John had not been idle, however, and the bike was now in large lumps; rebuilt wheels with tyres (Czech-made Mitos items, an economical on/off road compromise recommended and sold by the VMCC), front forks, frame from a 1954 Ariel twin (virtually identical to the single's), and a '54 VH500 engine with bottom end now re-built.

In the meantime, progress often seemed to be impeded by bright ideas supplied by yours truly. Tony Page was fitting a traditional Craven rack and panniers to his bike, but I had sold mine a few years previously – don't do this with proven kit, you never know what's coming down the pike. So for luggage advice I had gone to Jeff Venning, a man who had done mighty journeys, including a trip to Moscow/St Petersburg and back, on a humble Francis-Barnett two-stroke twin. Jeff took the Ariel's measurements, then came to John's with me to provide us, for nothing, with a version of his own light, strong and well-tested design of pannier-racks, but in kit form, ie steel plates and lengths of tubing which he had cut and bent to the required dimensions.

The racks would take a set of light and relatively narrow modern Givi panniers from Italy. These would prove to be durable and to work well, the only defect being that, despite claims to the contrary, to remove them from the bike you first had to open them. But for John, the frames did prove a headache to adapt to the Ariel's rear end; and I hadn't realised that Jeff's arrangement did not include a top rack to take the main luggage sack etc; that had to be purchased separately from Hitchcocks, a really useful resource, and the premier supplier of spares for Royal Enfields, including the traditional Bullet singles still being manufactured in India.

But the top rack then had to be fitted in with the pannier arrangement, all time-consuming stuff for John. And he had no welding facilities, so the pannier rack had been brazed up, a less strong procedure than welding.

John did his best and ended up with a strong enough arrangement, but one which he was afraid was going to make removing the rear wheel in the event of a puncture a complicated business. Later, at the height of the pre-launch problems, I would literally wake up in the middle of the night and instantly fret about that scenario.

Other input from me which would cause problems included the desire for an easier-to-operate two-stage petrol tap than the stiff one that the tank had come with. I had chosen the '54/'55 design tank from a selection offered by John, despite its chrome strips and flutes being rusty and the paint scuffed and dull. That would cause some mockery in Africa but I liked the look of it, and my reasoning was also that a well-used – all right, a scruffy – appearance, might help deter unwelcome attention from the bike. Another thing I wanted was nylon-lined cables, which would need none of the regular application of lubricating oil that dust would then rapidly turn to grinding paste. Tony Page and all his companions on the Yukon trip had found out that dust in un-sealed cables or suspension units could very quickly wreck them. To that end, I also wanted to fit a modern K and N-type air filter on the carburettor. And a metal bash-plate to protect the engine's underside from rocks. All would prove troublesome.

So, Christmas 2008 came and went, but still no bike. We had plenty to do, however. There were the travel arrangements – we planned to fly the bikes out for an uncomplicated start, and to ship them back – and both these required an agent in Cape Town to smooth the way. There were medical preparations (a number of jabs which had to be paid for, plus three months' worth of my diabetes tablets and hearing-aid batteries, and Malarone, the anti-malarial tablets we had used in 2007, expensive but with no side-effects, though the medics did say that two months was the maximum recommended period for taking them); the charity end; and the paperwork. Though our intended route (South Africa/Botswana/Zambia/Namibia) was all in the same customs area and required no complicated visas, for the vehicles we did have to arrange the famous *carnet de passage* from the RAC. The *carnet*, designed to prevent unauthorised sales of vehicles abroad, required a percentage of the bike's value to be deposited, in return for a yellow, multi-leaf document, which had – without fail – to be stamped by the customs officials on entering and leaving each country, or the deposit would be lost. The upside was that it exempted you from all import and export duties. Tony Page knew the ropes from his travels, down to the actual guy to deal with at the RAC, Paul Gowen, who would prove extremely friendly and helpful.

I was also in touch with anyone I could contact who had relevant experience. Among them was Gordon May, who had published the Royal Enfield section of my six-volume classic British bike book as a stand-alone paperback, and was himself just off to ride a Fifties' Bullet overland to India. And Richard Miller, who had ridden a '55 Bullet from the UK to South Africa, and spent time down there before riding back a different way. Richard, an extremely self-effacing guy, had a lot of helpful advice. I had read his blog on the Horizons Unlimited website, which was dedicated to motorcycle travel, and that was where I located the air freight outfit which we ended up using, James Cargo, and the Cape Town agent they recommended, the highly capable Adrian Schultz of Econofreight.

Both organisations had handled freighting of the *Long Way Down* bikes for Ewan McGregor and Charley Boorman when they rode from John o' Groats, in Scotland, to Cape Town in 2007. The celebrities on their BMWs had taken on many more miles and much bigger mouthfuls of off-road dust than we were liable to do, and more power to them. But I intended our 6–8,000-mile effort to be the antithesis of theirs, with none of the killer deadlines the dynamic duo had to meet which, as they said themselves, had over-stretched them and left too little time to relish Africa. As our *Short Way Up* name implied, this was intended to be a contrast: the two-wheeled equivalent of Slow Food, with leisurely daily mileages and plenty of diversions. As I put it on the website: "Because there will be no film crew. No 'fixers' for the borders. No four-wheel-drive back-up. No back-up at all… for two 50-year-old, simple, rugged British single cylinder motorbikes. And their even older and arguably simpler riders…"

It was Ewan and Charley on the TV who had brought public focus on adventure motorcycling, but of course the story went back a lot further than that. The best-known figure had been Ted Simon, who from 1974–1977 had ridden a 500 Triumph twin 64,000 miles round the world, and then more recently, in 2001 at the age of 69, had set out to repeat the feat on a modified BMW twin. That time he broke a leg in Kenya, and survived a really bad bingle in South America, but still completed his journey. As impressive as his fortitude was his modesty, which shone from every page he wrote. I had met him at a Covent Garden bookshop when he signed my copy of his best-selling book about the first trip, *Jupiter's Travels*. After I had identified myself as a classic bike journalist, he had eagerly asked my advice on reliable Triumph spares suppliers, as friends in the States were always consulting him on that topic, and he said he hadn't a clue; he was a traveller on a motorbike rather than a motorcycle enthusiast, and he didn't care who knew it.

Ted's original trip on the Triumph had been a pinnacle of the British heritage. Today, much more suitable purpose-built adventure motorcycling machines abounded but, as mentioned, I had always been fixated on the ancient Brits. And the experience of many long trips on them in Europe and Morocco had taught me that virtually the only things that would bring them to an unfixable halt were the alternator electrical systems first adopted by Triumph in the Fifties, which had spread to the rest of the industry's big bikes by the mid-Sixties. Find a post-war machine built before then, with a reliable magneto to take care of ignition, whatever the state of the battery, and your British bike should be the equivalent of Samuel Colt's .45 revolver, beloved of frontiersmen because even if you had to fire it by hitting the hammer with a rock, fire it would. That was the doctrine anyhow, and with a skilled build by John Budgen, and Tony Page's mechanical talents, I reckoned we were in with a chance.

It was my great good fortune that my Editorial Director at Haynes, Mark Hughes, by mid-2008 had been convinced by the *Short Way Up* vision, and commissioned this book. Despite having 20-plus titles to my name, as an author, once you pass the age of 50, unless you're Jordan or J.K. Rowling, the chances of getting published diminish incrementally in this bean-counting world. So I was, and remain, in Mark's debt. He also efficiently arranged for fund-raising at Haynes to swell the charity coffers, which were ably expedited and looked after by Kathy Archibald of the Kawaza School Charitable Trust, based at Hampton-in-Arden. The book commission made it all seem more real. Just as well, since trouble times were on the way.

Chapter 4

KITTING OUT

Before that, I got a lot of help from a variety of sources. The principal one was the Southern Africans, Ginty Melvill, Gary Brown, and the Cape Town Triumph Owners Club (TOC) people they put me in touch with: Jerry Day, Bruce Kirby and "Spider" Wilbraham. Early on, Ginty had sent me, on request, a detailed suggested route which he had put together, with alternatives where appropriate, covering six sheets of A4, "all tar roads but not motorways", and looping round to include one of the four major events in the South African old bike calendar, the Natal Classic at the end of May. I did not have to stick to this route in every detail but, working with maps, it gave me a vital, realistic framework with which to plan.

On the kit front, I was too disorganised to do systematic begging/ligging for every last available item, but did sporadically ask sources which had provided products for testing in the past, and none turned me down. Chief among these benefactors were Phoenix Distribution who handled Arai Helmets; they provided the SZ/f white open-face helmet I requested. White to repel heat, and open-face rather than full-face because that's what I've almost always used, trading off possible damage to chin and jaw against the lack of constriction, better ventilation and, above all, a non-alien appearance which, with the visor flipped up, instantly let you communicate with people. The SZ/f was comfortable, particularly well-ventilated and fitted me well from Day 1. The visor system kept out the dust, and at the end of three African months the inside didn't even smell too bad!

Other benefactors included Dave at Brickwood Wheel Builders, who did the Ariel's wheels for John, and also gave me a set of spoke keys which would prove extremely useful. Also, Paul Goff, for donating halogen headlamp and LED tail-light bulbs; and Burlen Fuel Systems, for providing pure lead leak-free batteries for our bikes; trick items which under normal circumstances held their charge for up to two years, and didn't have to be topped up. Tony Page approved; he knew of a Danish rider who had set out across the Sahara with a mate, both mounted on Norton Commandos. In the middle of the desert, the mate's battery had boiled and, being an alternator-equipped machine, and evidently without the Commando's optional capacitor, this meant that his bike was dead. The Dane had left the mate there, and his ultimate fate was unknown. What had been the moral of the tale for Tony? "Well, never travel with a Dane..."

For riding gear I went to Hood Jeans, a family firm who manufacture jeans, trousers and jackets with pockets for Knox body armour panels, and lined with Aramid (woven Kevlar). They look like regular garments, but due to the lining have greater abrasion-resistance than leather. May/June/July, when we would be riding, was Southern Africa's winter and mainly temperate – but at the end of May the previous year it had snowed at the Natal Classic, and the guide books talked of occasional winter rain, and of the chilly evenings I remembered from our safari. So I was after something not too hot for riding through the days, but warm and shower-proof if necessary, and with protection from the pretty-well inevitable tumbles we were likely to take, especially off-tarmac. I had worn a black pair of Hood jeans for the 3,000-mile run to the warmth of Provence on my 1100 Moto Guzzi the previous summer, and knew that the lining didn't carry too much of a heat penalty.

It was also important to feel comfortable, both physically and socially. People don't always react well to black leather, and I wanted something to match the casual "slow-food" approach of this long, leisurely trip on old bikes. Tony had advised that camouflage, which smacked of military uniform, was a definite no-no in some areas. And old bush hands said that the colour dark blue apparently attracted tsetse flies and their very unpleasant bite.

Luckily Hood did trousers cut and lined just like the jeans, but in notably lightweight poly-cotton, rather than the 14½oz ditch-digging denim found on the jeans. They got the material from the company that supplied the MOD, which explained why the camo version was night vision repellent! I opted for plain green, with armoured inserts, and the trousers served me well. Along with a pair of Rohan lightweight strides for off-bike, I would wear them and nothing but, continuously for three months. This would lead Ginty's garden boy to conclude that "bwana must be very poor, only having one pair of pants". Well, he got the poor bit right.

Chris and Julie, aka The Hoodies, also gave me a lined and armoured blue denim jacket (and damn the tsetse flies!), which I considered using as a sole riding jacket, but in the end rejected in view of the likely weather – it is a Biking Law of Sod that if you ride out unprepared for the sky to fall, then fall it will. So finally I opted for a well-used, longer Belstaff jacket, with the warm lining zipped out; it was armoured, and made in notionally waterproof Cordura. Boots were also from Belstaff, a pair of Italian-made, long black motocross type which I had blagged while messing about off-road on a BSA for a while, and again well-armoured. For I had found out long ago, on that maiden run to Greece in fact, that the first things to suffer in even a low-speed tumble on two wheels are your ankles and shins.

Other useful input came from the Ariel Owners Club, in the shape of Vice-President Len Ore, and the Editor of their excellent club magazine, *Cheval de Fer*, John Mitchell, a very likeable man. I met them at John's place on the edge of the Forest of Dean, and they had canvassed experienced members for advice on what spares I should take. A lot of it coincided with the list that I had compiled myself over the years of motorcycle travelling, plus stuff I had gleaned from reading, like spare top bolts for the rear suspension units, items which had failed on the Norton and Panther ridden from China to Holland in *The Last Hurrah*. But it was good to cross-reference with others' experience, as well as to find out about Ariel-specific items, like spare gaskets for their leak-prone rocker boxes, and lock-wire for the sump plate and the four petrol tank bolts, which could not be tightened down hard without the risk of puncturing the tank.

I also got to ride both John's late Ariel Huntmaster 650 twin, based on the export Cyclone version, one of which had been owned by Buddy Holly; and his magnificently ratty 500 VH single, the type of bike I would be taking to Africa. While its acceleration paled beside the twins', the handling was reassuring, and it proved far more controllable at low speed on the single-track, grass-in-the-middle-of-the-road lane that looped round to John's house. That encouraged me.

After that I drove on up to John Budgen and delivered the modern air filter I had got from Bill Crosby as part of the magazine archive-swap, and the *third* set of handlebars I offered up; the previous two high, wide scrambles-type braced bars hadn't felt right, so now I ended up bringing a low-level standard BSA bar which, as the testers used to say, "fell readily to hand". Foam grips to absorb vibration completed that particular package. At John's the Ariel chassis was complete and looking good, but still with the engine out, though the barrel had come back from being re-bored.

This should have set some alarm bells ringing, as by then it was September 2008. For the next months John struggled with the kit-form rack and the universal carrier, fabricating extra bracing tubes and spacers until it was really solid. Christmas passed, and in January 2009, with the front end assembled, John told me the cables he had been sent were all wrong for the brake on this particular model. He said this puzzled him, because in the past he had bought several of the same cables and sold them on, with no complaints from his customers. He took the fork and handlebars down to his cable man, to get it right.

John had troubles of his own. Despite having competed on the Wasp outfit recently, his hip had now gone bad on him, so that he could barely get a leg over a bike, and could not kickstart one. His part-time helper/mechanic Bruce, who was also a part-time fireman, had been away, and could now only come a couple of days a week. John did the wiring himself. Then in mid-February, with just over two months to go until the Ariel had to be ready to fly out, his wife Pearl's health began to deteriorate, and indeed shortly after their 50th wedding anniversary he would have to take her for a spell in hospital. Under the circumstances I didn't feel I could spit my dummy when there was more delay as he fitted all new chains, then couldn't find top gear and had to remove the gearbox to rectify this; and getting the box back on was a two-man job, and Bruce didn't come for a day or two. John promised the Ariel would be ready by the end of the month.

It took him a whole day to sort out the gearbox. If he had been charging me by the hour the bill by now would have been prohibitive. As it was, the expedition costs had risen, a) because that's what costs do and b) thanks to the weakness of the pound. That credit crunch; there was just no escaping it. With financial apocalypse all around, I had already cashed in my remaining inherited capital and ring-fenced that money to meet the £50-a-day I was allowing for the three months in Africa, plus all the household bills and the monthly payments to keep the home fires burning. So to raise some necessary extra financial wind, with Bill Crosby's help I sold my big-bore BSA 726cc A65 twin. All classic bike riders know that you should never sell a sorted bike. But needs must.

The financial margins were still going to be tight, and I was working hard to get ahead with the long articles I wrote monthly for a classic car magazine, in case I couldn't get stories from Africa. It had previously been two articles a month but now it was down to one, and for less money than previously – that credit crunch etc. I would also be sending tales about the trip back to *Real Classic*. In late February I had gone to the season-opening "Bristol" old bike show, which was actually at Shepton Mallet, where Frank and Rowena were manning the *Real Classic* stand. I helped with the public for a while; people came and went, many faces familiar and some wishing me well for the trip.

I also had the pleasure of meeting for the first time one of the other contributors, Jacqueline Bickerstaff, a fine, witty and technically superb writer who had carried out the extremely difficult task of writing in exemplary fashion a book, *Original Vincent*, about the legendary marque, very few of whose products had stayed original! Jacqueline, like the racer Michelle Duff, was a motorcyclist who had undergone a sex-change operation, but it didn't stop her travelling far and wide on her Vincent or her veteran Triumph. So we talked about my journey, and Jacky was candid in the extreme, asserting unprompted that most of every day she spent travelling on classic two-wheelers she did in dread, though you often forgot about it afterwards and only remembered the good feelings. "So the difficult bit is the day you start," she said. "Getting out of bed and walking through that door. After that, things take care of themselves." I would find this to be true.

As the quote stuck in front of my desk had it: "Cowboy Up, Cupcake". I endeavoured to do so, as the *carnet de passage* came back with the wrong engine number recorded on it, and my daughter Rosie asked pointed questions about the cost of the trip relative to the amount of charity money raised. March arrived with the bike still not delivered, and I struggled through half-comatose days, with the "For Sale" sign still flapping outside our home.

Then it got really bad.

In the early months of 2009, Tony Page had been increasingly taciturn in reply to the stream of chirpy e-mails I had been sending him about shipping arrangements, our bikes, and progress or the lack of it. At first I took it as standard gruff Royal Marine minimalism, but the pessimistic tone finally worried me, and I wrote him a "Houston, do we have a problem?" note.

The answer was affirmative, and the details came flooding out. Tony had been relying on his December-to-April earnings with the specialist courier firm to finance the trip. Instead, at the eleventh hour, he said, that bad old credit crunch had meant that work had fallen off so dramatically that the company itself was in serious trouble, and he wasn't even covering his outgoings. Compounding it all was the fact that the owner of the storage shed where he kept his bike collection had fallen ill, and his family had immediately sold the property off, so Tony now had to find somewhere else right away, with a probable increase in rent. And his Ariel's gearbox needed rebuilding, again. In sum, he had had it. His last word was "Sorry".

Knowing TP as I felt I did a little bit by then, I knew he wouldn't have passed on the trip unless he absolutely could not do it, and there were genuinely no hard feelings. Tony continued to help me, loaning a grown-up water purifying kit and, crucially, chasing the purveyors of nylon-lined cables located near him to make up a set for my Ariel from the patterns I had provided. It was obviously too late to find anyone else, and if I am honest, even though the first, most basic piece of advice about the trip ("Don't Do It Alone!") was being violated, I experienced a bat-squeak of relief. I had almost always travelled alone on two wheels, and although Tony's tales would have meant no lack of evening entertainment round the camp fire, our different riding styles (he fast, me slow) and approaches in general (he systematic/brisk, me slow/shambolic), would inevitably have thrown up the odd problem. And when you are on your own, there's no one there to see you foul up!

So I swallowed it, and got on with chasing possible motor insurance deals, with the help of the Cape Town folk. This was not to be; at the London end there was a specialist company, but the cost was prohibitive. This might have made sense with a £50,000 Range Rover, but for a £2,000 Ariel it did not. The South Africans believed that there was an automatic levy every time you bought petrol, which funded a third-party insurance set-up for foreign drivers, and that further north you bought insurance at the borders. Apprehensive about lengthy border crossings, I tried to do this in advance by chasing a "Yellow Card" via the South African AA, but with no luck. Late on in the trip I was told quite casually that the South African third-party levy had been scrapped three or four years earlier, so I had ridden several thousand miles there, where the annual road fatality rate was 15,000-plus and rising, totally uninsured.

Chapter 5

READY, STEADY, STOP

A week later, on 11 March, the Ariel was at last delivered locally for its MoT. There had been a final flurry of delays. The last thing had been the petrol tank that John had intended to fit, which was held up at the sprayer who *didn't have the paint.* By now, with less than six weeks to go, I was insisting on collecting the bike, whatever, to get the MoT and start clocking up the intended 1,000 shake-down miles. But John's hip was playing up so it was only Bruce who had "got it running once". John said he would take the Ariel in his van to our friendly local MoT garage, The Forge at Drayton, as by coincidence he used to live in that village. He said it was all sooner than he would have liked, and that the carburation needed finishing, which he hadn't been able to do as he couldn't start the bike, and everything was "very tight, being new", and that the tank still wasn't sprayed but that he had come up with another one for now. This would be the one already mentioned which I'd settle for, as, though its chrome flutes and stripes were rusty, it was sound and I liked the look of it.

My main worry concerned possible difficulties I might have kickstarting the big single. I got to the Forge Garage that morning, but John had been and gone already. The bike was there, in the back area, along with the shell of co-proprietor Alec Taylor's Isetta bubble car, and his Nimbus 4; both his brother Rob and Alec himself had been hard riders and sometime racers, and were now sympathetic to anything classic on two, three or four wheels. The Ariel was looking good. Everything but the deep claret tank had been re-sprayed black, and this was set off by the new chrome on the wheel rims, handlebar, rear units and exhaust system. The engine was clean, the luggage unobtrusive and the racks sturdy. The separate headlamp looked well, and the newly-covered short seat was firm but good. Inside I swelled.

The bike's number plate, dating from 1966 when the frame had been re-registered as part of a special, was KYL 938D. "KYL" had to be "The Killer", though that seemed a bit dark-side. But "The Killer" had been the tag of ace rocker Jerry Lee Lewis, and when this Ariel turned out to vibrate more than somewhat, the singer's immortal lines ("You Shake My Nerves and You Rattle My Brain!") suggested that the bike should be called Jerry. Jerry Lee was also of course a famously awkward and unpredictable character, sometimes lethally so…

I tried an exploratory kick, and there was that depressing lifeless grind, familiar from as far back as the first proper motorbike I ever rode, my mate Victor's sometimes temperamental Matchless "Jampot" G3 single. A couple more kicks and my leg had knocked off the new, protruding air filter; we would soon go with John's suggestion to use the original, cruder air-box. If the bike wouldn't start, it could not be MoT-tested, so the kicking continued.

Working out the Ariel's "piggy-back" advance-retard and exhaust valve lifter controls eluded me, as there was no indication which lever was which. Eventually Alec Taylor took the magneto's points cover cap off (something I had never done before in my life), and established that the shorter lever was for advance-retard. The piggy-back levers were pattern ones, and the exhaust valve lifter cable kept popping out of its lever and, as Rob found later, also from the cylinder head – I hadn't been able to locate where it operated, there under the tank – leaving the valve open so that there was then no compression. That had produced a brief phase when I could kick it over, provoking backfires, though to no avail. Both Alec and I bruised our legs on the oil tank (Ariel had altered its design the following year) with only a couple more backfires to show for it. The Taylors helped when they could, but were busy with a stream of MoTs. It all conjured scenes of helplessness in Africa.

The garage closed for lunch, so I walked to the pub nearby for coffee and a sandwich, sitting alone contemplating a not-too-clever future, with just a month to go and a shed-load of problems. When I returned, the drops of oil under the primary chaincase had joined up to form a puddle. The rear brake light stuck on, draining the battery, as the brake pedal was tight under the footrest. This became clear when Rob was standing on the footrests to have another kick, and the left-hand rest suddenly swung all the way down. I was going to have to stand on these things, off-road. Rob removed the rest and tightened it, with major effort. "Preparation leaves a lot to be desired," he said caustically. As the afternoon wore on, with Rob and Alec very busy with MoTs, I began to feel a bit resentful towards John Budgen. My exhaustion, and the soreness from the futile kicking which would last for two or three days, underlined my physical unfitness. When Alec got a moment he had another go at starting it, and the kickstart fell off. I rang John, who immediately agreed to collect the bike again, but couldn't do so until after the weekend.

The following week he delivered it back to The Forge. The problem had not been a slipping clutch, or the timing as I had guessed, but the fact that the cush-drive on the mainshaft had locked up. The bike now started well, with a robust noise, and passed the test – except for the absence of a petrol cap. John kicked himself for having forgotten to bring it; and Ariel caps were larger than normal circular items, with a double screw-down operation, so we couldn't substitute anything off another bike. But once the cap arrived, at home I started the bike myself, third kick, getting a surprise when it came to life in a way seemingly unrelated to the kick itself. Singles do that. I rode a couple of miles down the road and back, and we were on. The Ariel's power delivery felt ponderous and the front forks were a little out of alignment, but I could live with that, and there were no head bearing or steering problems, and plenty of "bottom". Thanks to the re-covered seat and new Ikon shock absorbers, it would prove to be an extremely comfortable ride. Slow, yes; so all I had to do now was to become an eater of slow food, become once more another rider, a long-haul merchant.

The following weeks were a roller-coaster. That first weekend I did 60-odd running-in miles, trying to keep to 40mph; and there were some problems. Riding downhill towards a steep-sided crossroads we call Dead Man's Gulch, I had not changed down soon enough to get the necessary engine braking, and the 7-inch single-sided front brake, not the greatest stopper anyway, proved itself spectacularly inadequate. I simply could not stop at the junction, and just had to whip glances left and right as I shot over the mercifully traffic-free road and up the other side.

Later, stopping for petrol, I forgot to switch off the (stiff and awkward) petrol tap, an absolute necessity with most singles, and certainly with this bike, even on brief stops. The flooded bike would not start. I push-started it on a lucky incline nearby, successfully; but for the rest of the ride the petrol tank was slopping out juice via that unique big Ariel petrol cap, whose circular cork seal was not seating properly. By the time I had got home, oil had blown back over the engine, and some as far as the rear tyre. The engine had been backfiring too, and the control levers were set wide enough to hurt the hands. The trip mileometer didn't work; if you wiggled the large plastic stalk underneath, the whole face of the dial moved. But the vital mileometer itself, the only way to work out fuel consumed and distances between stops, would never let me down, though the dial face did continue quaking like a Chihuahua for the whole trip.

Molly's eldest son Richard came visiting, and helped me fix the cork seal on the petrol cap. While tightening down all round, I noticed that a tiny nut was missing from the top of the triangle of the offside of the dynamo, so that grease was leaking out, and there was a gap between the end of the casing and the cylindrical dynamo itself. Then when I tried to start the bike to check for the source of the oil leak, it wouldn't. I thought it might be flooding, possibly due to a missing grub screw on the petrol tap letting the reserve position stay partially open (that one would come back and bite me). I left it for a bit, tried again and the shank, the sticking-out bit of the folding kickstart, came off, together with its dome-headed nut and two washers. We re-fitted it and tried to tighten the dome nut, but the thread had stripped. Once again the vision of something similar happening in Africa was raised, in front of a fresh audience; and one of the spares I insisted on taking was an extra kickstart. Coming on top of the previous day's troubles, this was a very low point. Even Molly seemed to sense it, and offered me the use of her horse trailer to transport the Ariel.

But when I rang John the next day, he came over with the van by midday, bringing a box full of the spares I had specified: very generously he was letting me have them on a use-or-return basis, so there was nothing to pay. Taking the long list I had made of the problems encountered, he departed with the Ariel in the van. The same day I had e-mailed Tony Page to ask about borrowing a spare magneto, and amazingly he came right back saying he was just down at the place near him which manufactured the nylon-lined cables I had asked him to chase, taking delivery of a full set of them, which had been made up using a set of regular cables from John as patterns. The nylon-lined ones weren't cheap, but it was heartening to be getting them.

That evening I lugged a heavy, rusty wheel and tyre that John had loaned me, over to my pal Mike Coombes for a free lesson in tyre-changing and puncture mending. Mike, until recently the guv'nor of Crowmarsh Classics in Didcot, was an ebullient old friend, Cockney, competitive, critical and humorous, who didn't mince words. We set to work on the hard 25-year-old tyre, and the dark cold evening had its ups and downs. Mike had to leave me to it while he drove off to fetch his wife; I struggled on with my BMW tyre levers ("they're too broad," Mike had said) and the ungiving old tyre, and did get it off on one side. But when Mike came back he found me trying to get the other tyre wall off the other side of the wheel as well, rather than pushing both walls off one side. I hadn't thought it through.

"I've got a bad feeling about this trip of yours," said an unimpressed Mike, but at least I wasn't going to do *that* ever again. I was clumsy, and really unfit; re-fitting the inner tube, it was physical, sexual even, struggling to get the valve through its hole, but I persevered and gave as good as I got, verbally, from Mike. Soon enough he was in good teacher mode, reinforcing the memorable points, like "Start and end at the valve", and "Small bites" for the distance between the levers. He also emphasised encouragingly, as I did it all a second time, how old and hard this tyre was, so that my new ones, together with new, un-pitted wheel rims, should be a lot easier to work with. On an old inner tube, I also learnt how to mend a puncture properly. Eating in the pub afterwards, the landlord heard us talking about the trip, and gave me a fiver for the charity. I ended up tired, with a cut right leg where Mike had accidentally dropped the wheel on me, but quietly not feeling too bad.

John returned the bike the next day, with a much improved front brake thanks to him having used the car-type adjuster for it; with the oil leak traced to an AWOL bolt missing from the exhaust rocker box; with the carb adjusted; and the exhaust valve lifter now working after he had packed down the cable at the valve end. John said he had started it, standing beside it; he showed me how his bad leg/hip prevented him getting astride a bike, and said he would probably be giving up sidecar scrambling on his Wasp outfit. When he had gone, I had a problem starting, aggravated by the exhaust valve lifter cable jumping out again despite John's latest efforts. Though I relocated it, I had to push-start before riding my local six-mile test circuit. The brake was indeed a bit better now, but four miles in, at the foot of a hill, the bike died.

It felt like a fuel problem. I opened the cap, and checked that there was some juice, checked the plug, waited for five minutes, bumped the bike downhill and it started. I rode home the way I had come, and at the gateway it conked again. Hmmm. I did not have a trailer, and I did not feel I could ask John to come for it again: his living 40 miles away was a problem. But when I phoned him for advice, he calmly said that it might be the petrol cap, now that its gasket was sealing well. The original Ariel caps had been drilled from the top through their central bolt, and then out sideways, for breathing; but the pattern ones he supplied had no breather. I drove straight to Swindon Classics, a more rough-and-ready outfit frequented by Harley people, where Martin Cox drilled a hole in the chromed cap (though he broke the drill-bit doing it, maintaining Jerry's growing reputation for trouble). And it worked. I rode a dozen miles locally, and hot-started the bike at the end of it too.

Over the following three weeks of April the weather was blessedly good and I piled on the miles, riding through the blossoming Oxfordshire countryside in spring sunshine. All the bike's teething troubles (and what rebuild doesn't throw them up?) did not mean that I lost sight of its strong points. The handling was really pleasing, even compared to other Ariels I had sampled, and the comfort was excellent. For both, a large factor was one of my few successful interventions, fitting period-look shrouded Ikon rear units with adjustable damping, tailored for length and supplied at cost by my friends at BSA specialists SRM in Aberystwyth.

The problems so far had all been superficial. This was not always encouraging, for what it implied about the way the bike had been put together, but as yet there had been no major mechanical or electrical troubles which would bring the machine to a terminal halt. The engine also seemed to run cool however far we went, with the oil tank cool to the touch. More worrying was the Ariel's lack of power. Even allowing for running-in, and the relatively ponderous nature of big singles, it did not feel right. But in my experience there were usually ways around most problems, and at this stage all I could do was keep on keeping on, riding the bike as much as possible and dealing with the problems as they arose. Which they surely did.

Starting was now first kick every time, and the Burman box's gearchange was notchy but always positive, with neutral accessible at rest. And a final vital piece of kit had turned up from Paul Whitfield, a local friend: a section of plank cut to shape, for fitting under the centre stand. This not only made things secure on uneven ground, it raised the rear wheel for working on, and allowed the front stand to raise the front wheel too. And it fitted nice and tight under the rack. Sorted.

Soon I rode to John's in Gloucestershire again; one reason was that the clutch had become progressively stiffer to pull. The only real downside to the ride across the Cotswolds was a lack of power; there was nothing there for even slight gradients. I told myself it was just running-in. The brakes were better but still not great, and the front one graunched alarmingly at low speeds. John, his usual calm self, was good company as ever. Up on the bench, he dismantled the clutch, adjusted the cable, filed the adjuster at the handlebar end and removed some burrs from the (Indian-sourced) clutch plates. Result: a very nice clutch action again. Oil leaks and weeps were still present, and we found a bolt on the timing-side crankcase cover half undone. With the time tight for both of us, I told him I could live with the brake graunch, and the Ariel climbed the half-mile of steep wooded hill outside John's village strongly and steadily in 3rd.

I rode home via the local market town of Faringdon, visiting the bank to arrange traveller's cheques (a bad call) and a banker's draft to the Cape Town agent (ditto). I also called at the friendly auto-factors to order some of the socket-heads we had worked out would be necessary to remove the rear wheel etc. Finally, at the supermarket I stocked up on gin and vodka; I was back on the hard stuff, partly so I could sleep. My mood in these weeks had been tired to the point of zombified. I heard myself talking to a friend on the phone about bike progress in a flat monotone. There were little spikes of satisfaction as I or other folk came up with solutions, but basically I was trudging along, expecting perhaps a lifting of the burden when the bike was irrevocably shipped out.

Chapter 6

D-DAY COMING

The comedies continued, however. I took the bike to Swindon Classics to collect and fit a petrol tap of the same type I had fitted on my M21, with a built-in reserve lever, with which I was hoping to replace the existing awkward push/pull tap. We were also to try the Triumph bash-plate sent by Bill Crosby at Reg Allen, along with the wire-mesh headlamp stone-guard which I had already put on; check the fit of the nylon-lined cables; fit an in-line fuel filter which I had, and also the halogen bulbs kindly supplied by Paul Goff. My bright ideas, one and all, and at least the lights were good.

Otherwise the new petrol tap's gauze filter turned out to be torn, so Martin had to replace it with a modern white plastic micro-filter. He also found that none of the expensive nylon-lined cables was the right length or had the right fitments. We could only think that the set provided as patterns had been wrong, which left me with no spare cables at all. My heart sank again. Martin cut the bash-plate to accommodate the Ariel's side stand, but with the hourly clock running, fitting was left until later. My fuel filter didn't fit either, so Mart sold me and fitted a bigger, business-like custom chromed one, which would prove to work a treat. All the work had required removing the four-bolt tank which had also been lock-wired in place, and when it was drained to fit the new tap the fuel was an ochre/orange colour; residue from the inside of the tank, plus another bright idea of mine, the Redex additive I had put into the fuel, even though it was no longer sold as upper cylinder lubricant.

With everything reassembled I rode off, the front brake re-adjusted again, but back to graunching, until a mile later the bike conked out. Two lads offered to push, but we had no joy; this felt as if it was a fuel problem. Martin, summoned by mobile, eventually thumped up on a Bullet, I cut a wine cork (never travel without one) as a crude bung, and we swapped the fuel taps back over at the roadside, with most of the petrol going down

Mart's sleeve. The new tap's fine filter had been completely blocked with crud, so now I was back with the old one.

The next couple of days I put more miles on the bike, reaching 450 and changing the oil, happy to find the (wired-on) sump plate filter completely clear of debris. Then, with only ten days to go, it was (allegedly) Good Friday. Mike Coombes had agreed to check out the Ariel before he went off yachting over Easter. Round at his home that evening, as he climbed on the bike I simply said "Front brake", and "Vibration", because the latter had now taken pole position as principal problem. On the over-run, the flesh of your cheeks and lips quavered about, your vision literally blurred and the vibes through the bars made the grips feel as big as the proverbial cocoa-tins. Mike rode into the dark, allowing me to savour the rare pleasure of the exhaust note from the outside. He returned unimpressed. "This is not a happy bike," he said, citing the flatness and telling me his 250 grass-tracker had more power. He reckoned the front brake drum was oval, and said the ammeter didn't seem to be working. I'd noticed that…

With the seat off, because the tank wouldn't come off otherwise, Mike grudgingly admired the seat's clever sub-frame mounting which John had devised. Swarming over the bike as I vainly tried to take everything in, he removed the dynamo to discover a pool of oil in the concave space in which it sat. Oil leaks again? "No, Ariels don't breathe," said Mike cheerfully. "People will tell you different, but it's true. That's why competition Ariels have dirty great breather pipes, if not they piss out oil through the mag and dyno." Right. Why hadn't John, with his experience of building competition models, fitted my bike with a big breather? It was a nightmare, really. I was barely taking things in, all the news seemed bad.

In the magneto, Mike found the contact-breaker a little loose on the keyway, and tightened the centre nut. Removing the tank had revealed the air cable squashed in the steering stock (presumably from when Martin had replaced it), which was why it hadn't been working. The exhaust valve was all but closed up, and Mike set its clearance wider. Getting into the reconditioned Monobloc carb, he raised the needle one notch, and discovered that the hollow bolt at the end was full of solidified, compacted crud, which he scraped out. None of the cables had been oiled (my job, I thought guiltily) and going at them with a can, he got the clutch in particular nice and smooth again.

I took the bike for a ride down the road, the lights reflecting off the stone-guard's mesh, and though the top end was noisier, after the valve and carb work it definitely felt livelier. Mike was clearly frustrated about having no more time to do things properly, and after slipping a piece of rubber tubing over the valve-lifter lever beneath the bars (John had replaced the piggy-back arrangement) to help prevent it puncturing my leg in a tumble, he gave me the name and number of Lee Peck in Abingdon, who he said was a top guy and would definitely help me. As I got ready to leave, Mike said he knew I was determined, but once again, that he had a bad feeling about the trip.

It was 11pm as I rode off, and less than two miles away, the lights dwindled to glow-worm mode. Had the dynamo been disturbed, should I go back? Within a mile they had gone altogether, and I started a ten-mile ride home in the dark. Thankfully there wasn't much traffic but most of it felt they had to flash me; the worst bit being when I was then blinded and prone to lurching sideways. But there were no cops about, and a bit of moon helped me negotiate the familiar Downs road.

Then Easter stopped play for three days, so it was D minus six when, thanks to magneto ignition, I was able to go back to John for the final time. I had told him of Mike's interventions, and he was momentarily tetchy about how tightly Coombsie had done things up ("there's such a thing as too tight, you can chew up screw heads" etc). After checking the fuse, he was sure the lights problem was down to the electronic regulator; he had complete faith in Tony Cooper's work on the dynamo and mag, while he had sourced the regulator at an autojumble and wasn't sure that type was even still being produced.

I had come to the same conclusion in view of the non-functioning ammeter, and had already contacted Boyer-Bransden about a replacement. I also had not been able to work out how to recharge the Burlen Fuels-donated long-life, no-spill battery, which lacked conventional terminals. John separated the two close-set leads with a piece of cardboard, and successfully charged it, in one-hour bursts as Burlen had recommended. When I had mentioned Lee Peck, cagily, since I didn't want to ruffle any feathers, as "an electrical specialist" to fit the Boyer, John looked surprised. It turned out Lee was his sidecar motocross passenger! Small world.

My other main concern was still vibration and its effects; one chaincase screw had shaken out, a tank badge had split and fallen off, and the toolbox fastener and battery strap bolt had also gone. John replaced them all; but being used to comp bikes and unable to ride Jerry, he said its shakes felt "about normal". His immediate agenda was to tighten the chains, and he was surprised to find that in 500 miles the primary chain was "so loose it's unbelievable! And that was a brand-new chain, and a good one". This too should have set alarm bells ringing, but it was too late for that. He removed two links and re-inserted one-and-a-half. He next tackled the oil leaks which, though oil was everywhere, centred around the top end. The connection to the rocker-feed oil pipes was loose, and the type John had used had been too big; he went to work on it. The transparent fuel filter showed that the fuel was running clear now.

I had noted the sizes of the extra, bigger socket heads needed to loosen off the gearbox bolts, as well as ones so that I could undo the air cleaner, and one for the rear wheel spindle. For the spindle I could probably have got away with the usual big adjustable spanner, but sockets made everything a lot easier. Later I went to a tool specialist in Oxford and got the necessary, as well as a small, heavy-duty mallet to "assist" with removing spindles etc.

In the afternoon light we walked together over a field and through a gate to a barn full of second-hand spares, where we searched, unsuccessfully, for a suitable larger sprocket to raise the gearing, which might have helped with the vibration. John told me how he was selling off a lot of stock to the Club and others, and I got the sense that he was running his business down. Back in the workshop his final job was to tape on parallel clutch and throttle cables, which would mean not having to remove the tank if one of them should break on the road. Then we said goodbye – that weekend they were celebrating the fiftieth anniversary of John's wedding to lovely Pearl, though her health was still giving problems. John had just worked for five to six hours, for £60. The bike chuffed steadily home.

Next day I rode to Abingdon, and Lee Peck. Space does not allow me to do justice to the work which 38-year-old Lee, qualified engineer and active competition rider on a Triumph twin and a Cheney-framed B25, would do on the Ariel over the following three days. Quick and cheerful, working from his garage at home, Lee was a tonic, a teacher and a very present help in trouble.

On that day he first fault-traced the lights and confirmed that the regulator was the problem. I put in my order to Boyers, who would get their version to us the next day. Lee then set about the persistent top end oil leak, shrinking on smaller diameter pipes and lock-wiring them. Using flux and quenching, he shortened the cables for the exhaust valve lifter and the air lever; and got them working properly, and in the case of the latter, permanently. With the carb dismantled for fitting the air cable, he got the slide working as it should. He decisively rejected the bash-plate which would be time-consuming to fit, and of marginal value on the mostly-tarmac trip I had planned.

He took the front wheel off and checked the brake linings, finding they had only been contacting the drum at one end, for about 20 per cent of their area. He measured the drum – "that's pretty round, that is" – then made up a little spigot from an old bit of aluminium, to slide the drum onto so that he could work on it in the lathe, skimming the shoes until they were nearly all green. "They would have bedded in," he told me, "but you haven't got time." He persevered with polishing the front spindle and reaming the fork leg holes until everything was perfectly smooth: "you don't need any roughness if the wheel has to come off for a puncture". Re-fitting it, he tightened both sides, then loosened the off-side so as not to pull the forks in – and the fork legs were now properly aligned. We also did a dummy run removing the rear wheel, and found that it only needed two pairs of bolts unfastening to get the rear half of the mudguard off, and slide out the wheel. It wasn't easy, but it represented the end of another nightmare.

On the second day he fitted the Boyer ("it's very simple"), using his own rubber-sleeved nuts passed through holes drilled in the back of the toolbox; a timely anti-vibration move for shakin' Jerry. We had lights again. The cylinder head rocker-feed oil leak was still present. Lee found that one of the feeds to the end of the T-piece there, soldered on, could be pulled off. He cleaned the old solder off with a file and went to work with a blow-torch, holding the circular piece in mole-grips, which in turn were held in a vice ("Dad taught me years ago, if you hold it directly in a vice, the vice takes away so much of the heat"), then dabbing on fresh solder ("it's silver solder, a bit harder than the normal electrical solder that was on there").

And so it went. I had been unhappy with the 500's restricted turning circle and Lee ground off some of the bump-stops, so now you could U-turn, feet up, in a narrow lane. I had bought along the nylon-lined cables. Lee unsoldered their nipples and cut and adapted the clutch, throttle, and front brake cables. Fitting them as main cables gave silky smooth control; he removed the others to keep as certified good-fitting spares, and for the two taped-on replacements, he heat-shrunk plastic covering onto their exposed ends.

Firing up for a test run, the throttle jammed wide open, three times. A little collar on the end of the nylon-lined cable, which should have attached to the cable casing, had come off. "I'll do it properly," said Lee; nipples snipped off, inner out, a new collar substituted. Lee also glued on the petrol cap's cork gasket with a two-pack glue he used on split tanks, ie one that was unaffected by petrol.

When I took the bike out for a run, it was so different. The front brake was finally effective, and working on the throttle cable and air slide seemed to have freed up the carburation. "It finally feels like a 500," we agreed. I don't think there is much that Lee Peck can't do with metal.

Talk about "just in time". That final Saturday was D minus one. Next morning I rode 70 miles up the old A40, through High Wycombe and on up to Bill Crosby's London Motor Cycle Museum. The following day, Bill's wife Pippa and son James would take the Ariel in their van to the air freight warehouse. At the museum, Bill told me that he had had a competition Red Hunter as a road bike in the early Fifties, after he suffered the accident which would eventually lead to the loss of his leg. He was riding hard and angry at the time, which the Ariel could take, though it would sometimes make an intermittent, unpredictable dinging noise, but with no ill effect. Eventually a trade friend had taken the motor down, and discovered that the flywheel had cracked right through; "but it never did any damage," laughed Bill. "I couldn't break it." That was reassuring!

Jerry the VH was still not the fastest kid on the block. I knew that it could probably do with being higher geared, but all concerned had done their best with the time available, and this had been my vision for the last 30 years, a big single thumping across foreign lands. The one intransigent thing was still the vibration; I had sat at lights in Wycombe quaking, to the quiet amusement of a father and son watching from the pavement. I had read by chance the following: "Does the engine actually belong in this frame? If not, it may be vibrating in a plane that is normally damped out." But Rob Taylor believed that usually produced periodic vibration, not the constant kind as on the VH; and Lee thought it would be more likely to have stemmed from the re-bore, and fitting a heavier piston maybe had thrown the balance factor out.

Whatever. I was coming, Cape Town, ready or not. How did I feel? To tell the truth I had been too busy to feel much excitement. But I believed that would come soon enough.

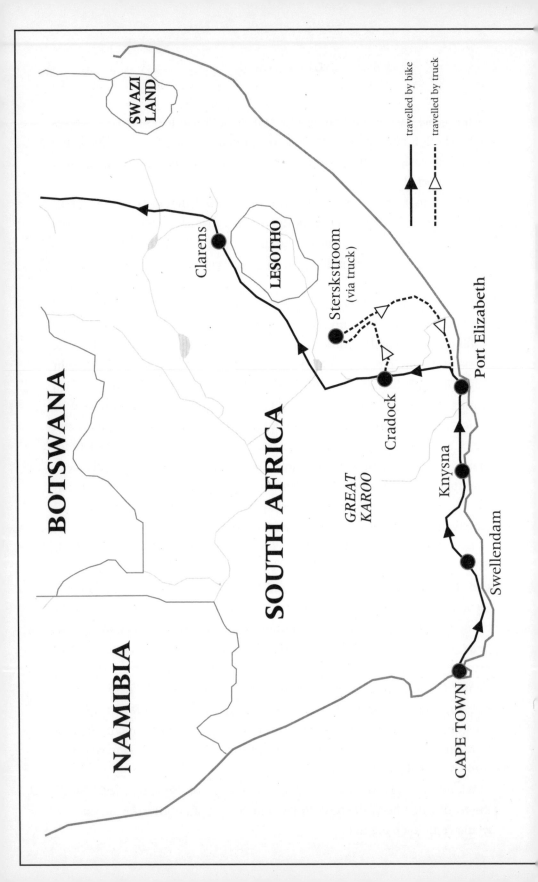

PART TWO

CAPE TOWN –
PORT ELIZABETH (TWICE)

"Writing and travel broaden your ass, if not your mind..."
Ernest Hemingway

Chapter 7

AIRSIDE AND CAPE TOWN

My departure day, 30 April 2009, had arrived. I awoke after four hours sleep to find much of the big bed still covered with things to pack, and half an article for the classic car magazine still to write; but the first half had gone well and was typed (I write long-hand and then laboriously put it on the PC with two fingers), so it felt do-able.

Molly was still being curt. I drove Rosie the six miles to the school bus, going over with her the lesson she had given me the previous evening on the new, small but robust digital camera I was taking, which had culminated in a remote picture of her and me together at the table. This was one of the few safe subjects: she still did not approve of my going. At the bus I told her I loved her and she said me too, and I got out and gave her a hug. Then she was on the bus as it pulled out; maybe turned away a little.

I went back to the dogs, Jess, the Border Terrier, and my girl Zoe, the 11-year-old black Labrador, and drove thoughtfully up White Horse Hill, to the same Uffington White Horse that featured on the SWU logo. The steep hillside, and the rippling slope above the valley of the Manger below, were a monolith's shrug, a wave that was taking tens of thousands of years to break. Some 3,000 years ago, men's minds had surfed the hill's flank and left a few elegantly minimal chalk lines, representing a horse, scribbled on its side. We walked up towards the chalk-filled trenches of the Horse itself, the dogs running free as there were no sheep up there that day. At the top I stood in the eye of the Horse, made my wishes (not about girls anymore, except Rosie) and turned round three times to seal them. It was a grey day but not cold. Except for the five token wind turbines to the west, the view of the Vale was the same as it had been on visits 50 years ago and more when I was young. Driving down, I asked the Horse's blessing on the road. It had never let me down so far.

At home the sewage had just been pumped from our biological (but currently non-functioning) septic tank, by a friendly guy. I took a last lot of magazine photos on disk down to Uffington Post Office, where there was a free Quality Street choc for everyone, to celebrate Dave and Rose's 12th anniversary running the place. Up on the notice board they had a cutting about the trip from the *Oxford Mail*, with a picture of me and the bike.

After that, the time just got away. I did spurts of packing, writing, checking e-mails (why was no one e-mailing me?) and got a miraculous last-minute call with a quote and contact details, from Damian at the shipping agency I was hoping to use to get the bike home, a last missing piece in the jigsaw of arrangements. Outside in the garden I could hear Molly and her son Richard. He was to drive me to the airport in my old black MGB GT, which he would use in return for looking after it while I was away. They were putting up a (hopefully) rabbit-proof fence around the raised vegetable patches, surrounded by old railway sleepers, which Molly had built.

I had hoped to leave at 2pm but didn't get the magazine piece signed off till 2.30, and we didn't get away till 4; packing was predictably fraught, although all the spares and tools had gone ahead in the panniers with the bike. I discarded things, a book, the Walkman and tapes. Meanwhile Molly, who told me later that she had just poked herself in the eye with a sharp fencing stake, had called up from downstairs and gone off without a face-to-face goodbye.

To summarise: I was setting out alone, thus violating the locals' Number 1 rule. I had missed a proper full shake-down run for the bike, was carrying way too much luggage, and my machine was, well, far from confidence-inspiring. So – everything about normal for a Wilson expedition. This was travel as stage-diving, jumping off in the faith that the world out there would catch you. There was no time to think that the house, our home for 15 years, might have been sold before I got back, so there would really be "no direction home", and that had some deep and disturbing echoes. The first time I had left the Vale had been in my eighteenth summer, when I had gone up to Oxford, leaving our home shut up and never to be returned to, as my mother was already in a London hospital with the cancer that would kill her two months later.

The two monster kit bags fitted in the MG's hatchback boot and, with Rich at the wheel, we were away. After five miles, at the top of Chain Hill, south of Wantage, I glanced over at the petrol gauge and it was nearly empty. Rich said, "The one thing…" and we went back into Wantage where he filled up. It was raining, but I trusted the MG and it didn't let us down. I experienced little stabs of panic. I had lost the directions to the Cape Town freight agent Adrian Schultz, but figured I could ring and get them again. But where had I packed this or that? It was slightly unreal as Rich started telling me that if Molly and I did split up, he hoped that he and I would still keep up, because Rosie was his little sis and as far as he was concerned I would always be her dad. It was welcome to hear.

Rich got us to Heathrow and dropped me off before 6pm. The bags were monstrous sausages on the trolley and at check-in, predictably, the Asian lady said that 20kg all-in was the weight limit for Economy passengers, and that the two permitted 50kg bags quoted by the online agency where I had booked the tickets only applied to Business Class. I played it guileless, pointing out that the agency had also mentioned exemptions for sports equipment, that a lot of the stuff was motorcycle related (true: jacket, boots, helmet etc), and that the motorcycle ride I was about to do was for charity. It didn't look good, but she finally cleared the bags, possibly to cheek her officious Asian supervisor who had come and given her a hard time about something else while we had been arguing the toss. She told me deadpan, "That is *cycling* equipment," as she and a pal conspiratorially let the bags on. The bigger one had to be physically shoved through, as it got stuck between the sides on the rollers, like I had been once in the tube of a Swedish water slide. This small success lifted my game.

Airside, I ate a burger and drank a last pint of Adnams at a concession pub called The Tin Duck, wary of the dip in mood from the alcohol. Inside the plane it was very warm at first but the atmosphere was good, South African cheerful, and before long it cooled, with visible dry ice stuff coming from the overhead vents. At 9.15pm the plane began to move. I was OK but still rather numb. Out in the world again, but as 69-year-old Ted Simon had noted in his book *Dreaming of Jupiter*, not getting the attention, not part of the travel attraction alert. But that was more than OK. The seat next to me was empty.

The following afternoon I was at my brother Julian's house in the posh Cape Town suburb of Tokai. The first possible dodgy moment, getting a reliable cab from the airport, had passed off easily when I walked out of the airport into the warmth, and a human chain of smiling and urgently gesturing blacks guided me across to a cab, which happened to be from the company that the *Rough Guide* had said were OK. The driver, an older man, was calm and friendly, and charged what my brother had said was right. The surprise, once we turned off the east/west freeway onto one of the motorways south, through beautiful wooded slopes and past the university, was just how far away from Cape Town proper Tokai was.

Once we were at No.10 ("<u>not</u> 10A", Julian's instructions had read), I found the keys and let myself in. Before long, our cousin, Mary Ann Dove, and her 13-year-old daughter Jenny, arrived. Mary Ann and her husband Andy – who worked for an upscale yachting organisation based at the Waterfront, but was away mountain-biking in Provence – had lived until recently in Johannesburg, and were renting the house from my brother, who only spent the first three months of each year here.

The cousin connection was as follows: my father's mother, Joy Jardine, had been the daughter of a Scots lay preacher. Family legend had it that Joy's brother Ivor, at the age of 15, had been caught by his father fishing on the Sabbath. The preacher had broken Ivor's rod over his knee and Ivor ran away to South Africa, allegedly arriving with just five shillings in his pocket. He had done well enough, however, to end up with a large farm in the Drakensburg mountains to the east, which was still (just) in the family. (The preacher had evidently been hard on his children, for my grandmother Joy had also run away, ending up in London on stage as a Gaiety Girl.)

My earliest memories of Ivor concerned the tins of chocolate biscuits, manufactured in Bourneville, outside Birmingham, exported to South Africa, and then sent back by Ivor to our grandmother Joy. She shared them with me and my friends, in those austerity years of rationing in the late Forties, on the double-decker bus through South Kensington, coming home in the dark, foggy afternoons from pre-prep school. The other thing, which I heard about later, was the violent exchange of views by post between Ivor, who had been an old-school white colonialist not afraid to use the N-word, and my father, the sports journalist Peter Wilson of the *Daily Mirror*, a socialist whose proudest endeavour had been his unswerving opposition to all forms of colour-bar and racial discrimination in sport. Ivor had lost three sons in aircraft crashes, two of them during the war. Mary Ann and her brothers were the generation after that.

Although this was our first meeting, I was slightly disappointed when Mary Ann made it clear that she and the kids had their own agenda and I would have to shop for my own food, but I had invited myself there and soon recognised Mary Ann as a nervously feisty lady with plenty on her plate. And walking the "brick road" for 15 minutes from the house to the Spar mini-market was good. This was South Africa's winter. Although it had stopped raining, the magnificent mountains behind to the west, which loured over the ephemeral suburb dismissively, were still shrouded in cloud. But it was warm as I walked, getting the feel of the place, checking out the California-style homes (not that posh, actually – all bungalows, for in South African lives there are no second storeys). All had the sliding automatic gates and "Armed Response" company signs in blue and yellow – was this security by Ikea? An older man in shorts walking two Jack Russells smiled and said hello. White, of course, like everyone else I saw, except the men tending the lawns, the girls serving groceries, and the bouncer in the bottle shop. My brother had announced to me that apartheid was still in place, but enforced economically now rather than by state laws. I hate it when he's right.

Back at the curiously cold house I supped Tall Horse Merlot with a giraffe on the label. It was excellent, especially with mild chilli biltong, in which I had happily found the core of the expedition diet. I went to sleep at the table and woke with a red face to the sounds of Mary Ann and the kids arriving back in their BMW 4x4. While Jenny was easy and outgoing, son Alistair was trickier. The first case of swine flu had just reached South Africa and, being unwell, Alistair believed he had contracted it and was dying. He proclaimed this noisily from his sick bed for the next couple of days, but I would get to know him later and he was a good kid.

Next morning I woke thinking of Rosie. There was a phone message from Bruce Kirby, my contact in the Cape Town Triumph Owners Club, about meeting that evening. Mary Ann and Jenny kindly took me down to a vast mall at Newlands, a suburb closer to Cape Town, where I tried to buy a SIM card for my cell phone. The assistant, a slick young Cape Coloured guy, was as wearily tolerant of my ignorance as any counterpart in Britain would have been. The card fitted but didn't work, so I had to buy a new identical phone plus R200 of credit, for around £35. This let me make local calls without them being routed back via the UK. I had always resented the being-on-a-leash aspect of cell phones, and until then had used mine very little. All that would change. Rosie, while explaining the camera, had also shown me where the phone card went. I next went to the South African AA office and spent nervous minutes hovering outside after my bag set off the alarm at the door, until a large white customer leaving told me pityingly to just come in. It turned out that the AA's computer system was down, so I couldn't join there and then, but they gave me a number to ring to do so.

In a taxi ordered at the information desk, friendly Peter drove me into Cape Town, on the way discussing the state of the nation. Jacob Zuma had recently been elected President, and, aside from the previous corruption charges relating to arms dealing, opinion was that he might have had to cut deals with extreme elements to win power. "We don't know, we hear stories," said Peter. At the traffic lights were ranks of hawkers who, he told me, were from other countries: Zimbabwe, Uganda, the Congo and Nigeria ("they do the drug business"). Soon the port was laid out below us. There were fine views of Signal Hill and the Lion Headed one, but when we got to our destination, the cable cars for Table Mountain, the summit was cloud-covered, "Table Mountain with the table-cloth on", so we drove down to Cape Town's showcase, the monster new Waterfront complex. On the way we passed a former prison that was now a hotel – some pretty extreme dreams awaited more sensitive guests? – and a building on fire, which turned out to be one of the city's many museums. There was thick smoke coming out of the upper windows, and three or four guys crossed the street ahead of us, loping towards it, laughing and grinning.

Back in Tokai, that evening Bruce Kirby from the Cape Town Triumph Owners Club (CTTOC) came for me. Big, bluff and good-humoured, we were easy right away. The son of a Rhodesian/Zambian police hero, Bruce told me that during his National Service he had gone into Angola in 1975 with the Cape Town Highlanders, one of five kilted South African Regiments. In fact he had carried the regimental colours in London for the Queen Mother's 100th birthday parade; that was despite a briefing by a 6ft 8in Guards Sergeant Major during which Bruce's cell phone had gone off in his sporran.

He drove us to the famous Forester's Arms pub. It was heaving because this was Saturday and there was a rugby match nearby, but it was pleasant sitting outside. We drank Windhoek lager, brewed in Namibia, as Bruce warned me off South African Breweries, who seemed to be the equivalent of Watneys in the UK back in the Seventies, producing a gassy brew from a company which had been ruthless in gobbling up smaller rivals. It was no surprise that Windhoek was a good drop. In my experience, as with Fix in Greece or the many excellent beers of Mexico, wherever in the world there had been a German/Austrian connection, as there had been notoriously in Namibia, you find good beer. We were joined by the club president Jerry Day, and Gavin Allison who was into vintage machinery.

We had good laughs there, and later at a Spur burger chain restaurant. Jerry was keen on inclusiveness in the club, both encouraging younger membership – the Holy Grail of all old vehicle organisations as the original fans of the marques die away – and on keeping the numbers he had. I heard about the four main South African old bike events: the Fairest Cape in mid-November, the DJ (Durban–Johannesburg) in March, the Magnum in August, and the Natal Classic from 28–31 May, which was my intended first destination. There were stories of one eccentric TOC member who, like the Fulton Mackay character in the film *Local Hero*, at club meetings would surreptitiously pack the free food about his person. After he walked off with a whole cake they had adapted a rucksack to take one, and presented this to him. Also the individual who went everywhere in shorts, whatever the weather: they gave him a pair of trouser bottoms. I didn't know it but I was soon to meet him, as Bruce was already arranging overnight stops for me along the road east, before handing me on to the Kickstart Club in Port Elizabeth. I was to be mightily in his debt.

The following day Bruce asked me over to his place nearby for a *braai*. I had been invited for a drink with my brother's neighbours, David and Fiona Price, an older couple whose property I accessed by climbing through a little low gate cut in the dividing hedge. They were interesting people, and we were chatting away in their well-appointed sitting room when Bruce, who had been looking for me next door, walked in wearing shorts, climbed over a sofa to say hallo, poured himself a glass of wine and joined the conversation. My English eyebrows were rising, but in fact the talk became even more interesting as Fiona had been a journalist locally and, though he had not met her before, Bruce had read her stuff regularly.

Back home, Bruce right away showed me into a workshop stuffed with racks of military Royal Enfield engines and, amongst much else, two complete maroon ex-South African Army BSA B31 swinging-arm 350 singles, one with less than 20,000 miles on it, which I immediately coveted.

Bruce had also just bought a smart runner for himself, a 1964 AJS Model 18 short-stroke 500 single. He had got it for £800, less than half of what he would have paid in the UK. That was how prices of pretty much everything, including fuel, food, drink and accommodation, proved to go in Southern Africa, and it would mean that, despite the weakness of the pound, which currently bought 12 to 13 rand, I would be able to do the trip on budget. Bruce had been riding the AJS that morning, though he claimed to be more at ease with spannerwork. This was modesty I think, as he regularly rode rallies on a friend's Indian vee-twin, a model whose unorthodox controls made it a particular challenge to ride.

I met Bruce's pretty, intelligent wife Heather, also ex-Rhodesian/Zimbabwean, and his two great boys Gareth and Ryan. Ryan had been born in a dire hospital, ironically not in Africa, where they said the healthcare ones were far superior, but in Dublin where Heather and Bruce had been stranded after his IT job there had collapsed. Bruce knew the Luangwa Valley, my destination in Zambia, from childhood. His family used to camp in a compound up by the border, where his father had to repel troublesome hippos in the night, quite a dangerous business. The *braai*, with chops and different sausages like *boerewurst*, was delicious, which would not always be the case elsewhere. Bruce offered to drive me into the mountains, but three beers in and full of barbie, we ended up just lying around on recliners, shooting the shit. As we lay there, a pair of wide-winged crane-like birds passed low overhead, making an appalling racket. "Hadida ibis," explained Bruce. "Because of the noise we call them Fear of Flying." Later we e-mailed Ginty Melvill in Lusaka.

When Bruce dropped me back in Tokai at 6.30pm I found that another cousin, Mary Ann's brother Roger, had already arrived for the evening with his partner Carol, a gynaecologist. Roger was known as "Dog"; their grandfather Ivor Jardine had handed out monosyllabic nicknames to each of them, and Dog's had stuck. He faintly resembled Mr Bean, and at first, from his slight slurring, I thought he was drunk, or even a drunk, but he soon told me that he was suffering from fairly recently diagnosed multiple sclerosis. He too had been based in Johannesburg, with a successful firm that supplied security fencing, a growth industry in Crime Central Jo'burg.

The fencing had not stopped him turning round in his chair at home one evening, little dog at his feet, to find himself looking down the barrel of a gun. The intruders cable-tied his wrists and threw him on the bed. Luckily, he said, he had a large amount of cash on him, and they left, satisfied with that. He said he felt OK about it.

Mary Ann had cooked chicken stew and couscous, and as we ate, with Carol's large earnest face turned tenderly towards him, Dog bemoaned to me, with his expression reflecting a weary knowledge of what I as a gliberal might think, how Zuma had announced that in five years time he would set up a National Health Service. "Better for them down there," said Dog, "less good for privileged people like us." The President was simultaneously going to ban all private practice, so that the excellent existing private healthcare facilities would go, and the white doctors mostly take what was known as a "passage to Perth", ie a one-way ticket to Australia. Later I recited the tales of their grandfather Ivor and the broken fishing rod, but to barely polite interest. Afterwards Mary Ann told me that Dog had done his National Service in the late 80s/early 90s, the final years of The Struggle. When going into the township riots he was, she said, never sure whether he could obey if given the order to open fire on the crowds with live rounds. She said the experience had changed him.

Next morning, after several nervous sleepless hours, it was time to pick up the bike. I rang Adrian Schultz, the agent, who gave me directions (again) on how to get to him, and Mary Ann, with Jenny, kindly gave me a lift there. We proceeded up to Cape Town, to a motorway network full of roadworks, updating the system for the following year's football World Cup. I tried to memorise the route prior to doing it in reverse. We ended up on the long commercial roads of Parden Eiland, a block or two from the docks, but salubrious enough. Mary Ann dropped me off, complete with helmet and jacket, at Econofreight, but did not linger.

Summoned by a fierce receptionist, Adrian Schultz was a small, very sharp man. I guessed he was Cape Coloured, ie mixed race, who make up over half of Cape Town's population. You couldn't ask if he was that or Indian, but he certainly fitted the Coloured's rep as the smartest bunch, with unbeatable Cockney-like repartee. Adrian was more business-like, and his operation had been faultless. All Customs clearances were taken care of and there, up on a loading bay, was my Ariel, Jerry. The contents of the panniers, as I discovered later, were just as they had been on departure, despite my having had to leave the prominent red key in their lock for Customs. I would recommend Econofreight to anyone: they charged only what they said they would, and performed as promised. This was in contrast to the Port Elizabeth lot I later used to sea-freight the bike home, who were vague about the clearing charges at the far end, which turned out to be a whopping £240, almost as much as the shipping charge for freighting. And the bike would end up with a smashed rear light housing.

Watched by a couple of black workers, I pushed the bike out, feeling a slight frisson to have its wheels touch African tarmac for the first time, and Adrian took a picture for me. We still had some business. Because it had already been booked, and I was reluctant to hand over my credit card details to an unknown quantity, I had sent off a banker's draft to him in payment, despatched by recorded post as no courier firm would handle drafts or cash. Adrian would have preferred fuss-free payment by card, and here was one reason why: the draft had not arrived yet. Well, it had been a public holiday on Friday here and on Monday there, but now I had to fill in the credit card form and, after meeting Adrian, had no qualms about doing so. He agreed to hold off charging the card until Wednesday, in case the draft turned up. I gave him my new cell phone number, and then kitted up, turned on the petrol (the airline had allowed half a gallon of fuel to remain in the tank), adjusted the choke and advance/retard and, with Adrian and the guys watching, kicked it over. Jerry caught third kick, nice and noisy, and we were off.

Colonial history meant that we would be driving on the left, as in Britain, all the way, and traffic was light. Only partially laden with the panniers, the Ariel moved along OK, though the brakes, while improved, still needed anticipation. I had spotted a gas station two or three blocks away. Here was a point of etiquette. The Rough Guide said that you should tip whichever of the many attendants filled you up/wiped the windscreen/checked the oil, for full-Fifties-style service was still in place in this labour-intensive set-up. With the bike, you just got the fill-up. The fine big unsmiling lady in overalls did that – petrol, like most things, was about half the price it had reached in the UK – but brought the change and didn't seem to expect anything. Oh dear.

I rode back the way we had come. The traffic was sometimes choked because of the road works, but in general much lighter than in any equivalent European city, and I felt comfortable back on the Ariel, so comfortable that I turned off south too early and found myself on a dual carriageway running parallel with the one I wanted. There didn't seem to be any likely-looking turns that would take me off to the right, so after 15 miles, when the dual carriageway ended, I turned right into a town called Retreat, which seemed like pretty much all-black. After a while I stopped at a petrol station and, with the motor still running, asked for directions. The guys' expressions asked that I killed the engine. I still barely understood them, but gathered that getting across the railway was the problem, and they were telling me how to reach a bridge over the line. Then I got off the bike, pulled it on to its stand (mercifully easy to do – well done Ariel), re-mounted, turned the fuel back on, kick-started it and rode on. That was the drill, every time. I found the bridge, crossed it and saw a sign to Tokai, poked about and ended up on the motorway going north. Got off on the exit north of the Tokai one, cruised south past a winery and finally saw the Spar where I had shopped, and rode back down the brick road and home. A small drama, but it helped build confidence.

The next problem was packing the big bag. I discarded more stuff – the air mattress, the smart shoes which Tony had advised, the little photo album with pictures of Moll and Rosie – but the black bag was still monstrously big and heavy. I have pondered why this should have been. Some of it was uncertainty as to how things would pan out. When Tony was on board we had planned to camp in the bush, so I had a light sleeping bag/mat/cooking tins and knife, fork, spoon etc. OK, I was carrying stuff for a three-month trip, but I have travelled a fair bit and know ways to keep the weight down. In addition to the riding gear and motocross boots I was wearing, I only had one major change of clothes and one pair of walking trainers. My Luddite dependency on the printed word did not help. The exercise book of notes and information, the travel journal, two Ariel handbooks, the *Rough Guide* – all these could have been transferred to, or accessed from, a hand-held electronic device.

And now you could even download novels. I had brought two books. On one disastrous solo trip to Turkey I had ended up stuck out in the east, where no other English reading matter had been available, with only a Booker Prize-winning novel from New Zealand, *The Bone People*, which had proved a torment to read. Harold Brodkey had blighted part of another BSA trip to Provence. So I had chosen carefully: *Thirteen Moons* by Charles

Frazier, a picaresque, complex tale of the 19th century America frontier from the author of the excellent Civil War novel *Cold Mountain* (shame about the movie); and *The Road Home* by Rose Tremain, who I had rated mightily since reading *Restoration*. I would sip at these works sparingly, reading slowly and carefully in the evenings, and they both repaid the attention one thousand per cent.

On the subject of books, preliminary reading back home, in addition to the excellent Bradt travel guides, had been Alexandra Fuller's *Scribbling the Cat*, a highly-strung but powerful account of a white Rhodesian veteran; *When a Crocodile Ate the Sun*, Peter Godwin's very moving story of his parents staying on in Zimbabwe; and perhaps the most enlightening of all about Africa in general, *The Cobra's Heart*, by the journalist and writer Ryszard Kapuściński.

Security considerations for documents and money had also loomed large. So, in addition to my regular cotton body-belt, and a Velcro-fastened wallet that went round the ankle, I had been seduced by yet another that slung around your neck, and a fourth, an external body-belt where you could access documents easily at frontiers. I had also liked the idea of the Pacsafe, a range of lockable steel wire webbing cages into which you put your bag and used the final loop of wire to lock it to something solid, which in my case would be the Ariel. This meant that you could theoretically leave the bike and luggage safely for a while. Later that day the first dry run at fitting the monster bag inside the Pacsafe proved that it was a swine of a job, taking ten minutes or more – and on the day of the off, with the bag really full, only three-quarters of it would fit inside the mesh. Still, the mesh web did compress the bag, and on two or three future occasions I would be glad of everything being locked to the bike. As the trip wore on I got lazier about struggling with the Pacsafe every morning but, whether in use or not, it still added several extra pounds to our load.

Chapter 8

INTO THE BLUE

On Tuesday, 5 July, I was really off. The first leg would involve a bit of oceanside running, then swinging inland and up to Swellendam, where Bruce had fixed me up to stay with an outlying TOC member. There was a nice blue sky visible through the windows of the cold house, and the garden boy was watering the lawn, wearing just one Wellington boot (I later found out that this not uncommon sight was due to the local dogs' habit of tearing at their heels). Soon after, a neighbourhood 'feral' peacock would appear in the garden. After breakfast I loaded the bike. The panniers held the tools and spares, the big bag was for personal stuff, and the magnetic tank bag had a puncture kit, tyre inflator aerosol, hand-cleaner and rags, spare links, plus a lot of other useful stuff I had learned to carry over the years, things you might need immediately without having to unpack the panniers. The tank bag top was a transparent pouch into which I could put the day's route or a map. Finally there was a black vinyl helmet bag with a steel mesh inner, which I had bungeed to the top of the big bag and used to carry top-up oil, as well as the shackle lock for the Ariel's front wheel.

It was time to go. I wheeled the laden bike out of the big garage and handed over the garage door remote to Mary Ann, who closed it. As it shut, I had now definitively left that particular sanctuary, because Mary Ann was leaving the house for a couple of days to take Jenny off to boarding school. I got her to take a photo, awkwardly gave her money for the maid, and said goodbye and thanks before they drove off. Then I went back to struggling with the lock of the offside pannier which temporarily wouldn't close. These Givis, irritatingly, had to be opened so that you could work the lock mechanism inside and detach them from the bike. For the first couple of days also, I lashed the handles together, mindful of the Krauser pannier on a hired BMW in Australia which had detached itself at speed and exploded like a depth charge behind the bike. But the Givis stayed put and, when re-fitted later to my Moto Guzzi, could be taken off still closed and locked, as they should. Just one of those things.

So off I went. The front end immediately felt light so I stopped and tightened down the Bakelite knob of the steering damper a bit. I knew the bike was over-laden, but I also knew that British bikes would take abuse in that department. A two-up trip in Morocco with too much gear on a Norton 650SS came to mind. If I kept an eye on the tyre pressures and watched out for loose spokes, I figured we would get away with it. The bike rode just as it had in England. Easy starting and reliable handling were off-set by noticeable vibration and a lack of real power. Cruising speed was 43mph and the vibes prevented us from topping 50mph. Within those limits, it stuttered along.

I rode steadily up the M3, but then at the top was unsure of my turns, since the one I thought I wanted, the N2, indicated the airport and Somerset *West*, when I was heading *East*. But the looping turn looked familiar from the day before, with a black guy slowly flapping a red warning flag at the roadworks. I wasn't sure though and, a little further on, pulled off onto a cross-bridge (*radical* front-end wobble as I slowed down) to check the map. Somerset West was to the East, so we were OK. Back on the motorway at an indicated 50mph tops, the traffic, mainly trucks, intermittently sliced in ahead of me or filled the blurred bar-end mirror completely, but mostly it was OK.

The weather ahead looked misty and cold, but that would pass. The section of road with rain grooves was not too amusing. I had worked out that it was about 20 miles to my turn off, the R44 down to the coast, and at about that distance, signs for the M44 came up. But I could still see the townships of the Eastern Flats on either side, so I passed on that, but pulled off later at a ramp where I could see no guys hanging about at the top. Checked the map again and found out that I had been in error and that my turning was 10km further on. The road signs were all in kilometres so it was back to the traditional brain gym on European trips, dividing the distance by eight and multiplying it by five, to get the figure in miles.

The R44 took me to Strand, a depressingly suburban, developed town with lots of stop/starting at a great many traffic-lights – sorry, robots, as they were called out there. But everyone seemed cool on a nice sunny day, as I watched out for dogs and got the hang of four-way stops (intersections where the last to arrive is supposed to be the last to leave). They worked pretty well – it was just that you had to notice them in the first place.

Gordon's Bay, shortly after, was the real deal: a pretty seaside resort where you could smell the ozone. There were traffic calming humps which we negotiated in 2nd or 3rd. The bike was OK unless you braked hard at the last minute, which would set off a front end wobble. On a hillside beyond the town I saw my first DO NOT FEED THE BABOONS sign, and then we were into the most amazing coastal road. Excellently surfaced, winding up and down (but never too steeply) beside the sparkling ocean below on the right, and for about ten miles there were no cars behind me.

The laden bike was fine as I remembered to relax, grasp the bars only lightly, anticipate to avoid braking, and take the bends in slow swooping curves, with great, attentive pleasure. I thought the vibes were not so bad, but they were there, as my right hand eventually began to get sore. We passed a couple of seaside places, but there were no roadside halts, you had to drive into the little towns with their pastel-shaded houses and seek them out, wasting time. Then we cut away from the sea. I had told myself to stop every 50 miles and we had done more than that already, with the bike perhaps feeling a little unhappy on the long straights. I certainly was. On those straights I began getting a first inkling of the scale of the journey, and started to wonder if I could do this. All right, it was after 1 o'clock, I needed food and my diabetic pills – but was I or the bike going to be robust enough? That morning was truly a roller-coaster ride, from the anxiety of getting out of Cape Town, to the exhilaration of the switch-back coast road, to the first daunting insights after that.

Then Betty's Bay hove into view, with a BP station and a café next door, right there on the roadside. I topped up with fuel, then parked up, worrying that the bike was partially out of my sight, and went into the empty café, where signs announced "FREE BEER – TOMORROW" and "BE NICE OR GO HOME". I ordered and went back to sit outside, where an ornamental water-spout trickled pleasantly in the corner. The food and coffee were good, and I sat listening to the different voices as a few people arrived, including a couple of Harley riders; and re-grouped, writing the journal and resolving to really sort out the kit that night, and leave the excess for my host to take back to Bruce.

The break was restorative. I rode on, the sea somewhere off to the right, under steep falling mountains, almost Scottish, then through marshes, woods and coastal hamlets, Kleinmond and Hermanus. By mid-afternoon I turned inland and up towards Swellendam; with 50 miles or so to go, a mile out of Bredasdorp I stopped by the side of the rising road. Further on up the empty highway an official car of some kind parked – to keep an eye on me? To the left a swooping field fell away with, far down in the dip, some newly-built traditionally styled houses and, beyond them, rocky, boulder-strewn mountain outcrops bulking behind. I walked around the bike, stretching, then sipped water from the tube of my Camelbak pack, and ate a ginger nut biscuit. I noticed four or five antelope in the field in front of me, and the silhouette of ostriches on the skyline which I would be climbing towards, before the pass ahead. The fact hit me: I was really back in Africa, on my own.

The pass turned out to be not too fierce, though the bike seemed to be getting better at climbing without running out of puff – maybe the "it will sort itself when it's properly run in" scenario would come to pass. Meanwhile, I also experimented with the advance/retard lever on the steeper climbs. The roads were mostly empty. Once, a big wide truck approached from the opposite direction, carrying a bulldozer with a massive shining blade, and a sign that said "ABNORMAL". The roads had a yellow line "crawler" inside lane and I would usually pull over for things coming up behind in my vibe-blurred mirror, and sometimes get a flasher-wink of thanks when they passed. As Swellendam approached slowly, kilometre by signposted kilometre, I got stiff, with clawed hands and a sore rear end. My spirits lifted at the sight of the half moon hanging in the daylight sky over distant farmsteads, with the red dirt side-roads peeling off towards them, snaking away, undulating, into the vast country.

Dark clouds were looming over the mountains above Swellendam, but luckily the rain held off, as it took half-an-hour's tooling back and forwards through the town and following incomprehensible misdirections, to get to the house of my host, Graham "Corkie" Corke. It was opposite a hospital, which should have been easy, but the hospital was down a sidestreet at one end of the town with just a single tiny sign to tell you the turn. So Jerry and I were hot and bothered when we finally parked outside. We had covered over 200 miles that day.

Corkie was from Derbyshire, though in a typical confusion, initially I thought his accent was Brummie. There was another guy, bespectacled Robin, sitting at the table, who smiled at me and then went on working away at a laptop; he was also staying. Given the absence of women, I briefly wondered if I had wandered into a gay set up, until gradually it dawned that a) Robin was Corkie's accountant and b) Corkie's girlfriend was simply away in England.

Corkie was a larger-than-life figure, a self-made businessman who had worked as a deer-stalker in Scotland (there were animal heads mounted on his walls) before starting a chain of eight care homes in the north. He had left Britain out of frustration with its regulations and, once established in South Africa, his (second) wife had left him. Clad in shorts – he was indeed that permanent shorts-wearer of the TOC – Corkie was keen to show me his toys. "Speed's my thing, Steve," he proclaimed, unimpressed by my choice of the Ariel for this trip, though it later emerged that when his wife left him he had ridden from India to China on a 500 Royal Enfield Bullet single, not with a tour but on his own.

Corkie's garage was down in his basement. It would have needed some trials-type riding to get the Ariel down there through the garden from street level, so it stayed parked on the street. That worried me a little, though it seemed like a quiet enough road. A local mechanic was down below, working on the ignition of Corkie's modern Buell vee-twin. But his pride and joy was a balls-out 650 Triumph twin, based on a 1957 T110 – "but it's evolved" – with Norton forks, a Morgo rotary oil pump, Boyer Bransden electronic ignition, alloy barrels and an 8-valve cylinder head from a 1960 Weslake, and strengthened Puma crankcases, plus a US export gas tank modified to carry the oil as well as two gallons of fuel. Stock Triumph 650s had ended up good for just over 115mph, but Corkie claimed this track bike would do 150, and I had no reason to doubt him. He had also just restored one of the smoothest Triumphs of all, a '55 6T Thunderbird, for riding around locally. It stood next to an absolutely mint 1959 T120 Bonneville, the famous first year of that legendary model, in correct blue and tangerine paint. I later found out that this one had been restored by Jerry Day, the TOC President back in Cape Town. I told Corkie I had written a book about Bonnevilles, but he was unimpressed.

Corkie, of course, had the wherewithal to indulge his hobby. He had cracked the cylinder head on his rare Velocette KSS Mk II overhead cam roadster, and having it repaired by specialist Don Goodall in the UK had set him back £5,000. But he was no stranger to the spanners himself and had done a full restoration on a Morgan 3-wheeler. The final toy he had to show me was a black powder replica "hogleg" Colt revolver in a Western holster. Current South African laws made it a difficult business to own firearms legally, and many people, like cousin Mary Ann, did not want guns in their houses. But the black-powder historic aspect provided a loop-hole, so Corkie's home was his castle.

There were also real blunderbusses hanging on the living room walls, together with models of what would soon emerge were Corkie's own planes. He had two 1940s Piper Clippers, a relatively rare variant on the Cub – "they do everything, but nothing outstandingly, they can carry weight though" – and a 1934 De Havilland Moth bi-plane. There had always been a strong connection between Southern Africa and flying, not just as a logical way to deal with the vast distances, but because the bankable good weather had made it a favourite place to train RAF pilots in safety during World War 2. Training took far less time there than in Britain, with its unpredictable weather. Many pilots then returned after the war to make their homes in the region. Even today, it is less than half as costly to learn to fly in South Africa as it is in the UK.

Corkie and I walked off down the hill for dinner, on me, and some very welcome beer. But none for Corkie. Back in England, two years previously, he had been sat stationary on another Triumph twin when he was hit hard from behind by a white van, which had left him with a broken back and eight fractured vertebrae. So he took no alcohol, because he was still on powerful painkillers, "but if it's wet, you still feel it, boy you do". The pregnant black lady serving us then spilled a beer into my lap, so at least now I smelled completely like a biker. It had been quite a day.

Chapter 9

THE SEX SHOP
AND THE SMALL TOWN

The next morning, early mist was burning away as Robin departed and Corkie cooked me breakfast, very kindly saying that if I had time to kill before the Natal rally I could come back and stay with him over the next fortnight if I wanted. He also suggested that I didn't push on to Knysna and the next hosts as planned, but stop on the way at his girlfriend's guest house in Ladismith. Since Knysna was well over 200 miles away, I was not unwilling, so phoned the Knysna folk and arranged it. As I did a nuts/bolts/tyre check on the bike, a young black couple arrived at Corkie's to work, and he spoke to them forcefully about mislaying some cleaning kit, and how it would not do if they were to be left in charge when he was away in two weeks time. They cast their eyes down, I cringed, but before long they came up with the cleaning stuff and Corkie was cooking them breakfast too.

I had told him I would shortly need some straight SAE 50 oil, and he now said he thought he knew where there was some. With no further explanation, we hopped in his Connaught Green Land Rover, drove out of that end of town and were soon bumping up a track and through a gate to the local air-strip. It was deserted, just a control tower, a clubhouse and a couple of hangars. Corkie showed me the clubhouse, gave me a litre of the oil, which was as used in their planes, and then disappeared into a hangar, pushing its rolling door back and emerging pulling out one of the blue and white Pipers. He told me how he would fly down to the beach with his girlfriend and land on the sand for a picnic. There was ground mist lingering, but soon Corkie judged it clear enough and before I knew it I was climbing carefully into the cramped cockpit beside him. People must have been smaller in the Forties, because there was very little room for two fat laddies. I had no fear of flying or heights, the parachuting had seen to that, but the speed and simplicity of this process did take me by surprise. It seemed no more complicated than hopping on a motorbike.

Corkie taxied bumpily onto the long runway, spoke to air traffic control somewhere, then revved up and we were bumping down the now not-so-long runway, and finally airborne, up through the lingering mist. We gained height, banking over the rows of toy coloured bricks that were the township huts, climbing further until we were level with the tops of the mountains towering over Swellendam, up with the little fluffy clouds, banking again to turn back over the town itself. "There's the 'ouse," came Corkie's voice, "there's yer bike." The sun glittered through the warm Perspex bubble, with the spar supporting the wing above us pressing in on my left as the earth wheeled slowly beneath. It was a hell of a way to start the day.

I didn't get on the road again until lunchtime, but Ladismith was only about 70 miles away. I gassed up outside town, explaining/bragging to the African attendant how far I was going and for how long. "Three months," he said thoughtfully. "That's a lot of meals, a lot of food." It was a different perspective. I turned left up the Tradouws Pass, where the gradients emphasised our lack of power and Jerry struggled a couple of times so that we had to drop down to 2nd gear. Then we got onto the R62, a well-known road, already recommended to me in the UK by Richard the Bullet traveller. Just beyond a famous isolated shop/bar with "Ronnie's Sex Shop" painted on its wall, the mileometer passed 1,000. It was a hot day, with the road unreeling in long undulating straights. I was flashed by an oncoming truck and knew from the *Rough Guide* that this meant a speed trap ahead. And sure enough there was a cop car in the next dip, though at our speeds we had nothing to fear.

The sun, the barren sandy land, and the long straight up-and-down roads were enervating. Still coming to terms with them, all I could think of were the deserts of the American South-West, Arizona, New Mexico, which I had seen from a Greyhound bus and about a thousand Westerns and road movies. Around half-way, I stopped at a roadside "shade" area with concrete seats and round thatched sunshades. As I unlimbered, a guy on a BMW 1200 pulled in, complained about its blandness and, like everyone I had met so far, wished me a good trip. Black truck-drivers sometimes acknowledged with a wave too, and one of them passing tooted. I was often to be warned about stopping at the roadside alone, but I really didn't have any selection.

In those conditions this bike, and arguably its rider, needed to stop every 50 miles or so, and if there wasn't a town then it had to be the roadside. I was lucky, I guess, though always mindful of Harvey Keitel's words in *Thelma and Louise*: "Luck'll only take you so far."

Another two BMWs pulled in. The Bavarian machines were definitely the weapon of choice hereabouts. The second most frequent question I would be asked was, "Why aren't you doing it on a BMW?" The superficial riposte was to point out that Ewan and Charley's BMW sub-frames had fractured both on their West-East trip and on the first day off-road in Africa. The real reason, the path of righteousness, was harder to explain, even to myself, though I had once owned a BMW R100CS airhead twin, but couldn't get on with its handling. These BMW arrivals were a pleasant couple on a twin, and a bulky bald Boer on an F650 single, friendly but uncommunicative as Afrikaans was his main language. They were from Pretoria, and gave me their card, asking me to stay on my way north.

I carried on for the remaining 30 or so miles, plonking along the undulating straights in the afternoon heat, trying to muster the build-up of speed on the downs so that I could stay in top gear for the ups. I obviously overdid it, as on one long hill the Ariel gave an almighty backfire, and seemed to lose power. I changed down and feathered it along, being disinclined to stop in the emptiness, and gently carried on, willing the bike to keep going. Which it did, though it was hot and rattly at the top end when I pulled up at the Hatari Guest House in the little crossroads town of Ladismith. But it hot-started OK after I had gone in and registered, before riding round to the garage at the side.

With that backfire I had experienced my first real dread. It was not strong yet but it was there. I knew I would have to use the two-and-a-half weeks before the rally to get the Ariel sorted and up to better power and speed. I just hoped that someone would know someone.

Hatari was nicely done, an old colonial house with tall ceilings and no locks on the doors, my room imaginatively furnished and with an en-suite shower, which I used. The caretaker landlady was a large Boer, friendly enough, with a wan young blonde girl assisting her, and the only other resident was a fat Afrikaans-speaker who wandered into the kitchen/dining area in shorts and an under-vest, cheerfully lowering the tone. Before supper, I went for a walk around Ladismith in the twilight. It was a very small town and when you got to the edges, there was immediately the desolation and emptiness of the barren land. I found a bank to change money the next day; otherwise there was only a black bar, but plenty of churches. Again I thought of the USA. I hardly knew the middle of that country, but felt that I was experiencing the sense of isolation and loneliness, reflected in so many books and films, underlying small-town America.

That night I dreamed: I was going for karate lessons, and the spiral stairs I was climbing were attached only to the inside of a circular wall, becoming narrower as they led you up to a high place where they stopped. In front lay the Void; on the wall were polite printed instructions to go back, and not to disturb the lessons in progress as you did so. Climbing back down, I looked in on one room of hyper-fit sumo-type warrior trainees; and even the sight of another less advanced class did not dissuade me from leaving.

In the breakfast room the next morning the TV indicated a 40 per cent chance of rain. It was certainly cooler, which I hoped would be good for the bike. The cooked breakfast was good, though warm milk with tea, and spiced chicken livers as part of an "English" breakfast, took some getting used to. I then spent an hour and a half in the bank trying, ultimately successfully, to change my traveller's cheques. These had always been a secure way to carry money, refundable if they were stolen or lost, and had served me well on previous journeys, but it now appeared they were yesterday's men, and from then on I would encounter extraordinary difficulties in cashing them. Plastic was the thing, though I later met a round-the-world traveller in an MG Midget who told me how all through Pakistan his travel money card had been rejected, and when he reached India the same thing happened. He had asked at the bank who said the card was being blocked because "someone had been trying to use it all over Pakistan..."

As I loaded up the bike and got ready to leave, the wan serving girl watched silently, and finally said: "It is a Harley-Davidson?"

A few miles later I was wishing it was, as the poor old bike was still slogging up a long gradient and I was depressed with it, until I realised that this was the 600-metre-plus Huisrivier Pass, a genuine challenge. Soon we were waltzing down the other side through some fine downhill curves, the R62 finally indicating why it was cherished tarmac. We rode on, through Oudtshoorn, the ostrich capital of South Africa. The landlady had been unable to believe that I would not be stopping and taking the opportunity for a spot of ostrich-riding but, more shamefully, I didn't even stop for any of the numerous photo opportunities with the ostriches fenced in by the roadside.

In a shade lay-by just beyond, I stopped for a rest, and answered a missed call on the cell phone from Adrian Schultz at Econofreight. He still had not received my banker's draft, but very graciously agreed to hold off charging my card for another couple of days. I took my pills, washed down with water from the Camelbak, which by now felt like a second skin, and where I also kept biltong and biscuits. I was snacking when a Henry-Fonda-In-Golden-Pond-Era American pulled up, skipped out of his rented Kia with a half-eaten sandwich in his hand and said chirpily, "Share?" He was an intrepid old solo traveller, full of tales of accumulating air miles, of how his daughter had subbed him to visit Vic Falls, and how he stayed in R100-a-night backpacker places, but after a while his one-note narrative became tedious.

The roads soon began to descend and we reached the spectacular Outeniqua Pass, running down the mountain to the comically-named but large seaside town of George. Beautifully surfaced and cambered, with passing lanes where they were needed, and great views down to the sea, Outeniqua was on a par with anything the Mediterranean corniches had to offer. Going downhill, the Ariel was not disadvantaged and, concentrating hard, using engine braking to conserve the actual 7-inch stoppers, we enjoyed an exhilarating waltz all the way to the bottom, where the engine seemed to perform a little better at the lower altitude. More good riding followed, eastward along the famous Garden Route, with the sea sometimes in view to the right. Of the seaside places, Dolphin's Bay and Wilderness were the prettiest.

In the afternoon, in a small town further on I stopped for a bite and a drink, partly so as not to turn up at that night's digs too early. That day's mileage would be only around 160, though it felt like enough. I parked the laden bike where I could see it, and was fanging down on a burger served by a friendly but watchful young Coloured lady, when a black guy with a backpack and a dirty shirt came in tentatively and hung around until the proprietor, a large Coloured gent, came out and told his daughter to give the man a Fanta, which she did, though asking him to step outside when he lit up a cigarette. Two black police arrived, a mixture of bored, knowing and dominant, like cops everywhere. The owner said there had been a break-in the previous night, and the backpack guy had seen who did it. The cops were very savvy, and knew the suspect was someone who had worked there. They were loud but fundamentally polite. As I rode away, I saw a little way further on a classic car dealer with a Morris Minor in the line-up along with Fifties' American Iron.

After mild difficulties, I found Tony and Lorna Lyons-Lewis' place beyond some flat estuary-type country in the seaside resort of Knysna, which was probably the nicest of the lot. Tony was a mildly strange man with a manner slightly unctious, slightly manic, but never less than friendly. We got the Ariel into his garage, alongside three beautifully restored silver Nortons, two of them vintage. Tony had made many of the parts for these himself; he was top class, totally meticulous. Also present was an equally immaculate 1964 Mini Cooper S; the only imperfection on it, he told me, was the marginally non-standard bucket seats. Minis had been sent out from England in CKD (Completely Knocked Down) form, and South Africa had imposed a local content requirement which was judged by weight; hence the slightly different, heavier seats. The bare bones of an MG TC Roadster were also there awaiting the treatment.

While there was still some light, Tony whisked me off in a daze of tiredness up to the inaccessible Points, high bluffs overlooking Knysna's lagoon, with ultra high-end houses taken to ridiculous levels of opulence by Russian oligarch owners. As we parked, a black boy materialised to "look after" Tony's BMW. "Are you happy?" he asked cheerfully. "I'm always happy," Tony laughed curtly, using the no-nonsense tone I would become familiar with elsewhere. I was not sure if the kid had a screw loose, and didn't quite like the tone, but colluded by avoiding eye contact. We walked up to look down the steep cliffs onto the lagoon with its tourist paddle-steamer and its tricky entrance. Tony mentioned that it was a favourite spot for scuba divers, and I told him how I had once, aged 11, been the youngest qualified skin-diver in England, training not with the official organisation but with an extraordinary man, an ex-test pilot and solo yachtsman, out in Dartmouth Harbour.

"Trevor Hampton," said Tony, electrifyingly. This was beyond coincidence: we were in Cosmic Exchange Co. territory. Tony had been restoring a pre-war OK Supreme racer and, wishing to verify that it was a real works race bike and not a modified roadster, had been put in touch with Captain Hampton who before the war had raced for OK Supreme. I had not been in touch with the man since the mid-Sixties and he must now have been in his 80s at least, but Tony said he had replied to the enquiry with pin-sharp accuracy, providing the necessary details of the works' engines to confirm that Tony's had been one.

We went back to the car and drove away downhill, giving the kid nothing, but then Tony braked hard after a curve, whistled and yelled something in Afrikaans (he was bi-lingual) and, when the kid leapt down the hillside, tossed him a coin. We drove by the nice waterfront area, then back for a beer, though there were no seconds, and they said grace before nervous but nice Lorna served a delicious supper.

After that we had a long session with the maps, plotting my next moves. Beyond Port Elizabeth, the coastal strip through Transkei to Durban had been described as "very dark" in Ginty's itinerary, and Bruce had just had his hub-caps stolen passing through there. Probably no place for a solo biker, so we decided I could head north after Port Elizabeth, and then loop around the top of Lesotho. I had been idly thinking of visiting that mountain kingdom, but almost all the roads were dirt and it was not advised; the famously long, steep, zig-zag Sani Pass road which I had been thinking of trying to ride, cousin Mary Ann had been proud of getting down in their BMW 4x4 while Land Rovers and others fell by the wayside. Looping round would mean I could then hit the reputedly beautiful Drakensberg from the north, and work my way down to the Natal Rally.

We also plotted out the route that Ginty had suggested for getting from the rally to the Botswana border. However, while undoubtedly fine riding country, this turned out to be way east, in tropical territory bordering Mozambique. We concluded it would be too much effort for the bike, but I did have three weeks to fill. I had been very taken with Knysna, and to that end began to think about staying there for a week. Before we turned in, Lorna volunteered to put my washing in the machine and dryer. I was encountering such kindness.

I woke up the next morning having slept for eight unbroken hours – a complete blessing, five to six had been my norm for as far back as I could remember. I had a bath and, with Lorna out, Tony cooked us breakfast. When I raised the subject of a week at a B&B in Knysna, he offered to put me up. Afterwards, at my request, he took the Ariel out to assess it. He donned a full-face helmet, after a cautionary tale about a friend who had died while riding a big vee-twin wearing just a minimal cruiser-type lid. Yet Tony was riding in shorts and sandals! Well, hey, this was Africa. He came back reckoning the Ariel was good, but might need its timing advanced for the mountains to come.

I rode off at midday for Port Elizabeth, well refreshed, thinking I might come back there soon. There were some long, long climbs on the coastal road, and on one of them the bike hiccupped in 3rd, just to keep me on my toes. The road ran though forests, over bridges, across a series of ravines and onto a bit of toll road, where the charge was the same for a bike as it was for a car. I stopped at a petrol/eatery complex by Storm River, gassed up, then sat down outside for a burger, watching the bike as parties of VERY LOUD Boer men clustered around it, many laughing raucously.

After an off-road section where the highway was under repair, I settled down for the rest of the 200-mile slog to Port Elizabeth, ducking in and out of the yellow-lined crawler lane to let traffic through. Somewhere I realised that I wouldn't be going back to Knysna. I was the Great White Shark of the highways: I had to keep moving on.

Chapter 10

PORT ELIZABETH

Luckily, Tony and Verna Barlow lived in the nearest, western end of the major city of Port Elizabeth in the Eastern Cape province, and there was a handy tall water tower to mark the turn-off. I arrived as darkness was coming on and, thanks to clear directions, rode pretty well straight to their house. Tony emerged from a pink keyhole door in the brick side-wall and gestured me round to the double-garage entrance at the front. The garage space held half-a-dozen or more of his smart classic bikes, mainly Nortons, as well as a Porsche 911 under wraps. But there was still room to park up the travel-stained Ariel, with a sheet of cardboard underneath to catch the oil leaks.

As I stood there, slightly road-dazed, ears ringing and blinking like an owl, up rode another, much smarter Ariel, a 600 VB side-valve single with a matching sidecar. From the thickness of the pebbled glasses which its bearded rider wore, I guessed this was Myopic Mike, who I had heard about in Cape Town and Knysna. I had been told that Kickstart Club member Mike Wood, despite marginal eyesight, rode like a good 'un and provided the clubs with much amusement, via incidents like the time his o.i.f. BSA A65 twin, "Spock", had caught fire on a run to Knysna, and then he had started a minor bush fire by ripping the burning fuel tank off and hurling it away into the veldt. A tall, upright, broad-chested man, I warmed to Mike immediately.

Two other Kickstart members and their wives were already there, as the Barlows had kindly organised a *braai* to welcome me. Energetic Verna showed me to my room. There I called Tony Lyons-Lewis on the cell phone to let him know that I had arrived safely, though I could hardly make myself heard over the violent barking of the guard dog from the property next door. Tony Barlow was all for it. The Barlows' house featured a lot of security against the rising tide of break-ins, including white lattice lockable gates at all the exits, as they got money off the insurance for fitting them. Tony told me that intruders, and there were usually at least five of them as things had become more sophisticated, if they got in would make you tell them your PIN number, then hold you while one of them went down to the bank to check it was correct. When the Barlows came back to the house, they always looked first from outside to see that the alarm had not been disabled. And so it went.

Now it was time for beer and *braai* with Tony, an ex-General Motors executive – Port Elizabeth was South Africa's Motor Town, where they still made VW Golfs in the old Mk 1 shape. Tony was powerfully built, a bit like a shorter version of Tony Soprano though, as framed newspaper clippings on the wall revealed, he had been a successful marathon runner until a medical condition had intervened. Unfailingly courteous and relaxed, he nevertheless didn't miss a trick and, as captain of the Kickstart Club, had the necessary air of quiet authority.

Also present were Alec Ould and Darryll Moresby-White, with their wives. They and Tony brought me copies of some of my motorcycle books to sign; it was strange to see the books again, such a very long way from where they had been written and printed, but nice to be made a fuss of. Darryll, a skilled motorcycle engineer, took me to task for having commented in a Norton introduction on the relative harshness of the ES2 single; he owned one and assured me that his wasn't like that. Darryll was humorous; when I asked if I could take his photo, he said, "What, this is the whole police file?" With the accent and phrasing, South African people's diction often seemed to me to sound Jewish, but there was plenty of room for confusion all round. When I asked them why the Afrikaners, like the crowd at Storm River that afternoon, talked so loudly, Darryll explained that you talk loud because, if not, others might think that you were whispering about them behind their back. But in fact, he had thought I was asking about black Africans.

It was a good convivial evening. Mike Wood left early as he had to go to Johannesburg the next morning, but he gave me his phone number in case I came back that way. Tony and Verna proved excellent hosts. Out in the garden next day, Verna showed me their big tortoise eating scarlet bougainvillea flower petals; she called sparrows "quickies", and fed a little one-legged bird with grated cheese. She eulogised her 10-year-old grandson, who she claimed was psychic like her, and showed me photos of him during and after his first supervised kill of a wild boar at a game park. He had been blooded, as the English used to do to horse riders with a fox's brush after their first hunt. Verna was also proud of her Boer heritage, telling how her grandmother had always had a batch of *boerebeskuits* – hard, rusk-like biscuits – ready baked, as she never knew when the men on the farm might need them instantly when they were called out to "go commando" on horseback against the British or the natives, potentially for months at a time.

I had arranged to interview, for an article in the classic car magazine, two of the guys who, for the Morris Minor's 60th anniversary, had successfully driven three early side-valve engine Moggies up from Cape Town through Africa to Cairo and then through Europe, to the UK celebrations at Stanford Hall. Their journey kind of put my little expedition in perspective. One of them turned up at Tony's on Sunday morning, in a Model T Ford. The Barlows had kindly agreed that I could stay another night so that, after seeing the drivers, I could write up the 3,000-word story. Verna generously offered to take dictation, type this into their computer and send it for me, though she made it clear that she didn't approve of my colloquial style of writing. I asked Tony if she did similar work for him and he replied that she used to, but it always got him too cross!

Verna also insisted that I call home on their land-line: that day was Mothering Sunday. As with other hosts in South Africa, I had instinctively not gone into detail about the state of my marriage, since in a culture where it was still normal to say grace before meals, and where as far as I could see divorce was a marked rarity, it probably would not have aided the "blending" process. I was beginning to see why things were that way. In the white tribe's beleaguered minority position, strong families were essential for survival, in the same way that the vast, harsh environment cried out for a religion, a spiritual dimension to make sense of it.

I was glad that I was able to call, however, as while the wife remained cold and distant, Rosie was still high about a trip to Paris with her half-brother Tom, and then casually mentioned that the weekend before, at a Pony Club rally, she had fallen off her good horse Rocky twice, the second time catching a kick in the head and concussion. She had vomited, and the ambulance men kept her there, as did the local A&E department. But she had been judged well enough to go to school the following morning, and seemed OK. While this news and the fact that I hadn't been told about it was disturbing, at least I was in the loop now.

The day before, on Saturday morning, Tony got out his Cadillac, which proved infinitely superior to a friend's one, a wallowing barge I had driven in LA; this one was mainly a re-badged Saab, from another part of the GM empire. Under blue skies we drove into the city of Port Elizabeth, where everywhere the Barlows pointed out evidence of incompetence and corruption. We came in through part of the old centre, which once housed spacious colonial homes but had been allowed to be turned into a strip of dealerships. The main thoroughfare leading to the 19th-century town hall was now all black, with plenty of hawkers and street traders, and a burnt-out building which had stayed that way for a couple of years (though its owner, the area's principal property magnate, was in fact Irish). Verna told me how the now-pedestrianised square in front of the town hall was where, in the Forties and Fifties, she and her friends used to go cruising in cars on a Saturday night. Like Bruce Springsteen's *My Hometown*, it must have been a tough transformation to witness if you had grown up there. They were, however, both admirers of the achievements of Nelson Mandela.

There was a rapid transport system under construction down the centre of the main drag, but this remained unfinished and Tony said the government had not yet bought the rail buses required. The start of the World Cup was less than a year off, and the system led to the new sports stadium under construction for that event, an impressive structure with a segmented roof, like an opened tangerine. But although the stadium's first game (a rugby match v the British Lions) was just six weeks away, some of the roof segments were not in place, the steps into the stadium were not built, there was apparently little or no provision for parking, and the whole surrounding area was still, well, a building site, with everyone hard at work, although it was the weekend. But hey, this was Africa…

Cruising along the freeways by the industrial area parallel to the sea's edge, we ran beside the increasingly derelict railway system. In Knysna, Tony L-L had already told me how the tourist narrow-gauge coastal steam line had been washed out by floods a few years previously and never reconstructed by the government, and here I saw its derelict little steam engines. There were a few luxury trains, which were expensive but safe, but the Barlows said that the rest, when they were running, were unreliable and dangerous to travel on.

From the back seat, Verna asked if I had heard the black US preacher's speech before Barack Obama's recent presidential victory, about Obama not really being black, and how blacks had never built brick houses or generally ever achieved anything for themselves. "I have it on tape, the whole *tootie*," she offered eagerly. I riposted as best I could that it was surely enforced poverty and lack of education, not the fact of being black, which had caused those kinds of disparity. I sensed Tony was embarrassed by both of us.

Later, back at the house, Verna would print out and present me with a diatribe off the internet, triggered by a newspaper article suggesting that it was not too late for the "previously advantaged" to apologise for apartheid. The response began: "We are sorry that our ancestors were intelligent, advanced and daring enough to explore the wild oceans to discover new countries and develop them. We are sorry that those who came before us took you out of the bush and taught you that there was more to life than beating drums, killing each other and chasing animals with sticks and stones…"

And so on. I had already seen that there was certainly much to regret and fear, now that the racial boot was more or less on the other foot, but this kind of white supremacist rubbish was still dangerous, and it had some very nasty roots. Some of the prime movers of apartheid in the pre-war *Broederbond*, such as future South African finance minister Nico Diederichs, future controller of state broadcasting Piet Meyer, and above all future Prime Minister Hendrik Verwoerd, had all espoused European fascism and spent time in Nazi Germany in the 1930s. So the link was direct between apartheid and the loathsome anti-life beliefs (which my uncle had died in the Libyan desert fighting against, as had thousands of white South Africans, and my father had given up six years of his life to combat as an army journalist, including the first four years of mine). And yet circumstances, and my own fallibilities, would mean that I would find myself relying on people who believed, in greater or lesser measure, in white superiority, but would be untiringly, unstintingly generous to one of their own: me. This was not simple stuff.

Back in the car, further west along the shore at Marine Drive came a bright new tourist strip of holiday apartments and a casino. *The Rough Guide* mentioned B&Bs, so I could stay there if I needed to stick around and get the bike sorted out. It looked good, the weather was lovely and the sandy beaches were clean, despite proximity to the industrial area. "You can have a nice walk along here," said Tony. "But not alone."

Just inland, we drove around the campus of the smart new university, with good new buildings, and all black students, no exceptions visible. Tony went out of his way to thank a black guard who opened a gate to let us off the campus. In the same way that Verna talked easily to the young black waitress, a student working her way through uni, in the steakhouse where I took them out that evening. There was an all-white clientele, bar a couple of light-shaded Coloureds. Voluntary segregation seemed to be the order of the day.

Before that, in the afternoon, I had fired up the Ariel, and followed Tony's Cadillac, driving a bit too fast for our comfort, the eight or nine miles to Darryll Moresby-White's home. After I had aired my worries about the bike, Darryll had been volunteered to check it over and, before I got into the hills, maybe advance the ignition timing, as recommended by Tony in Knysna. While the Ariel's engine cooled, we checked out Darryll's half-a-dozen machines, including a magnificent and rare black and gold Velocette KTT racer, up on a bench after a complete rebuild. Port Elizabeth had a strong tradition of motor sport, and this bike had killed its initial owner, a car dealer, the first time he had taken it out in a practice before racing. It had been little used since. A potential buyer had flown out from England the previous week just to check it out, and Tony had said that Darryll was not about to tell us whether negotiations had been successful, as the bike was potentially worth £25,000.

Darryll was in his 70s but enviably limber. He was funny and precise while working on the Ariel, rehearsing and explaining the ½-inch BTDC measurement, and getting consensus from us before taking each step. He established that the ignition timing was very near spot on, and did not advance it. The spark plug, however, was very black, meaning over-rich running. He dropped the carburettor needle back, reversing Mike Coombes' input, and recommended the Champion N9 plugs he used on his Norton 500 ES2, which (illogically) in hardness were between the N3 and the N5 which I was using.

My heart sank when I kick-started the bike and the throttle jammed wide open a couple of times, but it was only that the cable had got disturbed and jammed tight under the tank when we re-fitted it. Things soon settled down and Jerry was still starting really well, despite the discovery of a severely slack magneto chain. So, no magic bullet, but the bike was no worse, and running leaner might be better. During a slightly hairy run back – night had come down fast and one of the iron rules on two wheels in Africa was "NO NIGHT RIDING" – we stopped for petrol, and I was chuffed to find that a) the straight SAE 40 or 50 oil, which I used and which in Europe was now an expensive specialism, was available on the Shell forecourt, as Ginty in Zambia had said it would be, and b) that the Ariel appeared to be returning 90 miles to the gallon!

Chapter 11

HAD A BAD DAY

I packed the bike on Monday morning. Checking the oil tank drain plug for tightness, I discovered that one of the tank mountings had fractured. Tony Barlow cut me strips of old inner tube to fold up and wedge in between the tank and frame, and then taped them up to hold the tank so that it didn't shake. Verna gave me an apple, and I set off on my own again for 30 miles along the wind-swept coast highway, then turned left, heading inland along endless, progressively rising roads. The morning was hot despite the breeze and the bike seemed to be a little better for the leaner mix and new plug, cruising at 50mph rather than 43. I got slowly up the first, well-graded Olifantskop Pass in top, but the climbs continued, through rolling, empty land towards fine hills ahead. These were excellently surfaced roads with just the odd truck for traffic – old bike heaven in that there was no constant hassle from faster vehicles coming up behind. Monotony battled with contentment – I was rolling! – and with bike- and trip-anxiety.

For lunch, after nearly 100 miles, I stopped at Cookhouse. A long row of guys were sitting on the side of the road opposite the petrol station, which featured a "traditionally built" lady attendant like you wouldn't believe, her figure emphasised by the uniform with trousers. There was a clean, nice diner/general store, run by Boers, though it was a gaunt but friendly old black woman who served me with an excellent pot of tea and a chicken and mayo sandwich, crusts cut off, on a plate sprinkled with herbs. The bike was parked where I could see it, and a sad, tattered bum vagued about nearby; an anxious woman with slung child came in with her mother, I thought to beg, but in fact to collect a sack of meal.

After lunch was less good. There were 80-odd miles more of hard climbing and the bike vibrated badly, feeling less and less happy. I tried to tell myself it was the altitude, for by the time we reached Cradock we had gone from sea-level to 6,000ft. Before the town itself, which lay on the eastern edge of the Great Karoo wilderness, was the township, with the roads around it lined by Xhosa men and boys selling from massed collections of their speciality, wire models of the metal windmills found on the local sheep farms. But by then, Jerry was not a happy bike. I could hear a deep noise coming from the exhaust, and when I stopped in the town itself, oil was spattered everywhere and oozing from the screws and from the timing side crankcase; later it would take a litre of oil to top up. The climb had asked too much of the Ariel.

 I parked up and walked into the famous Victoria Manor Hotel, on a wide side thoroughfare, Market Street – wide enough to turn an ox-drawn wagon, at a guess. The interior was gracious and the desk folk likewise, with a We-are-the-keepers-of-Heritage subtext. The place was full, but they could rent me one of the pastel-coloured *Teishuise* single-storey Victorian houses that made up the street. These were furnished with period furniture and crockery, and in my case included, somewhat bizarrely, a section of wrought iron railings propped against the wall of the bedroom. It was expensive at R420, but not really, because that was only about £30 and it included an outstanding breakfast buffet in the hotel. The bike stayed in the yard behind the hotel, guarded by a rota of friendly watchmen, identified by their broad-brimmed zebra skin hats.

With night fallen, in a dull maze of tiredness I walked up the main drag, Voortrekker Street, to a steakhouse by a Total station. I was the only customer there, drinking a glass of wine and eating ribs and too much ice-cream and coffee, sitting in the lit glass wall window as figures passed behind me in the dark outside. I watched TV in Afrikaans with English subtitles, wildlife and a soap. Later I felt quite intimidated, in a dull sort of way, walking back alone in the dark, after all Tony Barlow's warnings that morning about not stopping on the side of the road, including the "shade" lay-bys – "they will take all of your things". In the dark where some scaffolding covered the sidewalk, I did get hassled by a couple of young sellers of windmills, but there was not even an undertone of menace when I told them I was on a motorbike and didn't have space for a windmill, and walked on.

It was only 7pm when I got back, lay down and almost immediately crashed out for three-and-a-half hours, waking to mental turmoil but managing to maintain some balance. The bike's condition after today did not bode well for the trip. I still felt that I could not back out, and the problem as I saw it was that even if I did find a friendly master mechanic to help with the lack of power, they would be unlikely to find a cure for the vibration (which I still thought probably came from marrying the single engine with the twin's frame), and that would make for more trouble later. But I hung on to the mantra of thinking positive, eventually slept OK, and next morning, after an outstanding breakfast in a dining room where black and white business people ate together, felt much better.

I was headed for an outlying member of the Kickstart Club, Melville Price, whose farm outside Sterkstroom was only about 120 miles north-east of Cradock. I had spoken to Melville on the phone, and he had an acquaintance in town, Darney Gerber (pronounced Danni Herber), with a collection of old vehicles including a 1920s 250 BSA single. So I walked through the town. Cradock was a busy junction on the Great Fish River 500 miles east of Cape Town, which I knew from reading Peter Godwin was the start of "the real Africa, Black Africa … [that] is where the climate changes from a tropical one, with dry winters and wet summers, into a Mediterranean one [on the Cape] with wet winters and dry summers. And the crops the Bantu people could grow in the tropical north – millet and sorghum – didn't work down there". So in the absence of the Bantu/Xhosa, the Dutch had been able to establish themselves on the Cape.

At the big tyre place Darney managed, though he was away in Port Elizabeth, I was driven to his home and had a quick look at his two vast commercial-size garages, full of trucks and cars, sitting behind the wheel of an early Fifties straight-6 Hudson saloon; it had been a Hudson Hornet that Jack Kerouac's buddy Neal Cassady had sold his soul for. I remembered that Tony Barlow had been disparaging about classic US cars since riding long distances in the back of them as a middle child had regularly made him sick.

Then it was back to the bike, wipe the oil off and top up, check round the nuts and bolts, load up and chug off eastwards into the empty bush on R61, the weather still bright, though clouds were building to the north. The bike felt OK following its night's rest. But after 22 miles of not-too-hilly Texan landscape, at around 11 o'clock, what felt like the inevitable happened, and we slowed abruptly as power fell off. I whipped the clutch in, but it was fuel – which was gushing out from where the rear, reserve plunger of that push-pull petrol tap had been missing the grub screw which retained it, and now had fallen out. I flapped around, staunching the flow of petrol with a thick paper napkin from last year's Provencal trip, taping it temporarily in place, while digging out a tube of epoxy stuff from the tank bag, moulding it onto the tap, some falling off but the flow staunched, moulding another lot on and taping that in place, not too effectually, so finally wiring the tape on, and it seemed to work. Then I looked around at the sparsely trafficked road stretching empty for miles in either direction. And checking the fuel, I realised that the reason the flow had stopped was because the tank was actually empty.

So I pulled out the cell phone and called out the AA. Hardly heroic self-reliance, but I had joined, so what the hell. Their controller asked endless irrelevant questions from his script as I fretted about the phone's credit running out. After that I rang Melville Price, got his wife and let her know the score; at that point I was still hoping that the AA, as in the UK, would get me and the vehicle on to my destination. Then I was left to sit and contemplate my situation. As the occasional bakkie (pick-up truck) and lorry drove by without pause, I discovered another Bad Bike Thing – the little nut on the dynamo cover had gone missing (again), so that grease from it had joined the oil/petrol symphony all over the engine. I ate biltong and biscuits, suffered a sore lip from some of the petrol etc still on my hands despite having deployed wet-wipes, drank water and read *The Rough Guide*. Then I stopped to turn my back and endure the arrival of the rain that had been threatening.

But it was not bad, despite the wind, and passed quickly. Then, miraculously, a skinny young biker called Ray, on a Honda VFR, stopped and turned out to be from Sterkstroom and, he said, to know Melville well (though later it would turn out that Melville didn't know him). This was heartening. Less so was a call after he had ridden on, from the lady at the recovery mob, who did not sound too friendly, either in general or to the proposition of taking me on to my destination. At around 1.30pm, the truck arrived, driven by a tall overweight Boer youth in shorts. I tried to get him to take me on, but he said the bakkie didn't have enough juice. I said I would pay for that, but he phoned the lady boss and she insisted on it coming back to Cradock. At that point, three mean-looking youths pulled up in a truck from Darney's tyre place; it later turned out that Melville had contacted them, and if Fat Boy hadn't been there, we might have worked something out, but as it was they just sneered at the bike, talked Afrikaans and drove off.

We loaded the Ariel and returned, unhappily, to Cradock, and into the compound of Custom Motor Services, on the black side of town. The Dragon Lady whose all-too-apt name, painted on the outside wall, turned out to be MOO D. KLONG, proved to be a short, nice-looking but utterly implacable Oriental. Despite the fact that I went in swinging about the AA's duty to get me to my destination, and although she admitted that my request to go to Sterkstroom was on the AA computer, she would not do so until the following day ("can not pull people off other jobs"), and on the phone to the AA, despite describing me as "very unhappy", she got her way. She then did some totting up and concluded that I owed her R250 (about £20) already. Understandably, in view of the country's vast distances, the South African AA is not like ours and they only pay the first R500 of any recovery cost (though they do dispatch an armed response team if you break down somewhere dangerous). Moo D then calculated that tomorrow's trip would cost me R2,500 (about £200).

I rang Melville Price again, and he offered to come and get me. And confirmed that he had a variety of the necessary petrol taps (modern ones, which I might have been able to source in Cradock, would not have fitted the tank's UK Plumber's Gauge thread). Mightily relieved, I insisted I would pay his diesel. It was 2.30 by then, so if he got here in two and a bit hours he would make it before Custom Motors closed at 5.30pm. Moo D. had at least said that I and the Ariel could stay there until then, and a very large and more sympathetic black assistant had helped me unload the bike. I went out to look for a drink and a bite, but though this was nominally Main Street, the part of town where I had been before seemed far away and this bit was very African. As I watched, across the street an angry black guy was lunging with a baseball bat into the back of a van full of screaming people until they drove away. I found myself an out-of-the-way spot, sitting on the yellow mudguard of a trailer, and wrote up my journal. In the background the radio played familiar phrases, Daniel Powter's *You had a bad day* and Coldplay's *I used to rule the world*, the same songs Rose enjoyed when she won the endless Radio 1 v Radio 4 struggle in the car on the way to the school bus.

At 5-ish, Melville turned up in a well-used bakkie, looking very English with his red face, his battered Rogue canvas hat, and a slightly quizzical expression. The big black guy helped us *lift* the Ariel into the back of the truck when Melville's plank proved insufficient.

Melville was very welcoming, though slightly country taciturn. We thrummed back over the 36km to the distance post where I had conked, and where I thought I had left the *Rough Guide*, though I later found this where it should have been, in the Camelbak pack. This believed-lost property paranoia had started out in Cape Town with my Maglite torch, and would continue. Night fell quickly as we talked briefly about the trip, and about his sheep farm of some 3,000 hectares/7,500 acres, which had been in the family for over 100 years. The home site in the 19th century had been a hotel for people going north in wagons up the steep Bushmanshoek Pass, which began just beyond his place. Melville told me that I had been lucky. A few miles further on from where I had broken down, there was no cell phone coverage. Later he said, gently, something that stuck: "There may not always be a Melville..."

The fact that there was this time was partly due to his wife Alison. The previous year, in what she would later say was a bit of a mid-life breakaway, with their two children having left home, Alison had gone to England for a course in Gloucestershire about caring for the elderly. Things had gone badly pear-shaped, and one evening she had been left high and dry in Putney, a stranger in a strange land and a bewildering city, with all her luggage and nowhere to stay that night. But when she had phoned one of their few English contacts, an old schoolmate of Melville, the guy had come and picked her up immediately (in his diminutive Smart Car, so her luggage had been a problem), driven her to Uxbridge, West London, moved out of his flat and given her exclusive use of it for the rest of her stay. So Melville was disposed to help an Englishman.

In full darkness we stopped at a really country, two-pumps-and-a-juke-joint petrol station with no one about, to check the truck's spare tyre pressure, and the skinny tie-down straps on the bike. Then we turned off the tarmac onto a dirt road short-cut, which saved 30km – that was how he had arrived so promptly – but was a rough ride. We rattled on over corrugated surfaces, checking the angle of the bike frequently. At 80kph it clearly required concentration. Melville had done the trip once already this afternoon, and I was very conscious of the generosity from a working farmer. He checked out lights in the bush – more new settlements, just African subsistence farming, he said. Melville told me that white farmers were leaving. When he and Alison had started out, 22 years ago, there had been a community of over 20 neighbours, but recently they had all seemed to go at once, which made it lonely, especially on the remaining wives.

In the distance I watched dry lightning illuminate the far hills. And then a white light flaring vividly to red, which Melville said was an overhead power line spur arcing, causing a real danger of disastrous bushfire. I later learned that Melville was a volunteer fireman, and that a few years previously a bushfire had got close enough to his home farm to destroy some buildings and vehicles. He tried to phone the farmer on whose land it was happening, but there was no signal. Then the only other car we would see came by from the other direction and Melville said, "That's him, in his pride and joy, his Mk 2 Cortina".

Getting closer to home, we drove along a boundary fence of an adjoining game farm owned by a wealthy absentee Scot, who maintained it just so he and his friends could fly in now and then for a weekend's shooting. Melville had never even met him. Melville said that he got a guy in to cull nuisance game on his own land. This included fallow deer – there were antlers in his garage – and lynx, which took sheep and had to be shot at night. But he said the main predators were the "two-legged kind". Stock theft was a big problem. Later I asked him whether his staff would stop a thief. With a pained expression he said, "I'm afraid it *is* my staff". Apparently they referred to poached sheep as "takeaway".

Chapter 12

ON THE FARM

Then we were bumping down Melville's drive and pulling up in the yard. We left the bike on the bakkie and brought the bags into the designated B&B room, a very large, high-ceilinged area which had been Melville's workshop. The B&B was a new venture for Alison after the caring course had not worked out, and the big room had two beds, an en-suite bathroom, TV, tea-making stuff etc. Through in the house, Alison was rugged up against the cold and extravagantly coiffed (she did hairdressing locally). She had just got back from line-dancing – dancing was her passion, she said – where the liveliest participant had been an 80-year-old lady, the leader of Alison's Bible study group. After Melville poured me a very welcome beer, Alison said grace before our solid supper of lamb casserole in suet pudding.

It was a cold night, the first time I got the sense that May really was winter here. The thick blanket on my bed was welcome, and I started *Thirteen Moons*, reading slowly. In the night I was woken by what I thought were trucks sounding like trains roaring up Bushmanshoek Pass, not realising that the railway from East London ran parallel with the road. The next morning Melville told me how during the Boer War the place had been occupied in 1899 by the British, to protect the railway. There were positions marked by cairns on the cliff above the pass, where many British soldiers had died after eating mussels from the river. The farm had been occupied by Lieutenant-Colonel Horace Smith Dorrien, CO of the Sherwood Foresters Regiment. Melville had framed a copy of a letter written at the farm by him to his evidently equally martial mother, bemoaning that the action was elsewhere. Melville had obtained the copy from the Regiment's HQ in the UK, and had also found out that in 1914 the Colonel, by then a General, had been one of those who wanted to shoot the British soldiers who, in a brief Christmas truce during World War 1, had left their battle positions to play football in No Man's Land with the Germans.

In daylight the farm was revealed as a sparsely beautiful place, with fine trees around the house, and grey hills rising steadily behind to protect it. The wind made it lonely. After breakfast at 8, Melville took me out to the camp in the bakkie (the Ariel had already been wheeled off onto a loading dock), with his black workers wearing yellow waterproofs riding in the truck bed, and Chummie the collie-cross farm dog running alongside and ahead, dangerously close to the wheels. As we bumped into a paddock the dog hared ahead, chasing scurrying sprinting shapes in the middle distance – meerkats. We dropped the men off to their work of cutting back non-indigenous trees which, if left unchecked, ate into the pasture. The workers lived on the farm all week, and went home to their families in town on the weekend.

Back at base, with its outbuildings and corrugated iron-roofed barns, in one a single guy (not one of the regular shearers) was slowly and not-too-expertly shearing sheep that were going off to the abattoir; he was working in a purpose-built structure with a press for the fleeces. Like the landscape, the smell and all of it took me back over 40 years to the months I had spent on a sheep ranch in Rio Negro province, Argentina, where a friend had been working and, though I had never ridden before, we had spent up to eight hours a day on horseback. These echoes were part of what would make my time at Melville's a core experience of the trip.

Then we got to the Ariel. Melville removed the broken petrol tap, and in his work shed, with sunlight slanting onto the bench through dusty window panes, produced a box of other old taps, and tirelessly searched for a plunger and a little grub screw to retain it. His scarred, work-swollen hands were strong and deft. My tap seemed to have been an aftermarket one, as none of the regular screws would fit. Later he pointed out how the reserve facility would not work, as a hole had not been drilled where it should have been (but it did prove to work eventually). While he sorted that, I got on with cleaning the bike, rich in burnt-on oil, grease from the shifting dynamo, and lots of petrol splatter. Melville provided a bucket of hot water and washing-up liquid, and most of the oil came off the exhaust and silencer surprisingly well.

Meanwhile Melville completed the tap with a plunger that fitted and, both screws now in place, re-fitted it, and fiddled for some time until he was satisfied that the direction was just right, so that it could be easily operated from the saddle. We also cleaned out the big custom petrol filter, where there was already, after about 1,000 African miles, quite some residue.

Melville then took the dynamo nut off an old BSA B31 engine lying in the corner, and I used my Loctite for the first time on the threads, to stop it happening again. Melville checked out the fractured oil tank mounting, and approved the rubber wedge arrangement, reckoning it would serve.

It was a nice morning, and a pleasure to watch him methodically at work, someone who knew what he was doing. His own bikes in the shed were testimony to that. He had a spotless modern BMW on which he went touring with Alison and mates, a magnificent red 1928 Indian Scout V-Twin, still under restoration, and a gleaming maroon civilianised 1942 Harley-Davidson WLA, the army model, which in 1945 had approached Berlin from both sides, as quantities had been supplied to the Russians as well as to the GIs. He wheeled this out, fired it up, rode round the yard and up the track in truly relaxed fashion, canvas hat in place. He told me how one of the first times he had started it up after completing the build, he had gone out for a short shakedown run and ended up carrying on for 180 miles. It was what the heavy, comfortable, ponderous side-valve Harleys had been designed for in the first place: long, long, country roads.

Melville told me a story about the Indian which confirmed the universal nature of the Cosmic Exchange Co. He had got the bike in kit form 17 years previously from someone who had had it from Uncle Ted Gibbons, Melville's brother-in-law Darryl's uncle. Melville rang old Ted about the Indian's oil pump, which was missing, and Ted said he would look for it. But two weeks later the brother-in-law had rung to tell him that, sadly, Ted had died. Spares for 1928 Indians aren't that easy to come by, so a year later when Melville was going to Port Elizabeth, he had rung Glenn Cottrell, the new owner of Ted's old place, and asked if he could drop by and look for the pump. Glenn said he wouldn't be there but Melville was welcome to come ahead, so he did. And just inside the garage door, sitting on top of an old oil drum – there was the pump.

While cleaning the Ariel, I had discovered that the nearside front mounting for the luggage rack had fractured. Melville was dubious about welding this as it had previously been brazed, and decided that we should just wire it on for the moment. I certainly was not going to suggest otherwise, as I was by now very conscious about taking advantage of his time and effort. But then he changed his mind and went ahead, grinding out the braze, after covering the bike's seat and rear end to protect them, and then doing the job with an electric welder connected to a massive car battery, producing spectacular sparks. Afterwards he sprayed it with water, but not so soon as to make it brittle. A dab of black paint, and another job done.

After lunch, Melville had to go into Sterkstroom, so we poured in a bit of petrol from a can and fired up the Ariel to ride in and gas up. The bike had started well, though there seemed to be no compression, which I had put down to the valve lifter sticking momentarily. It handled the long dirt drive happily, but on the road it immediately felt unhappy and then conked, due to lack of petrol. I leaned the bike over, so that some came from the offside of the tank to the nearside where the tap was, but that only worked for a couple of hundred yards. Melville jumped out of his bakkie, disconnected the pipe from the Ariel's tap and blew into this to make sure it was clear – it was – and then we both laid the bike all the way down onto the ground, which got enough juice over to the tap side to make the down-hill run into town.

Sterkstroom was a poor place, where the tarmac turned to dirt in the middle and the faces were mostly black. I gassed up, then went to a co-op with Melville to buy Straight 40 oil and ginger biscuits. Driving back up the hill, the Ariel was really labouring, from a combination of a headwind and the modest uphill slope; I had to change down to 3rd. The previous day had been a reality check and at this point I knew something had to be done. Back at the farm we debated the lack of power and Melville offered to test the compression. So I kicked it over while he held a bung, with a gauge on the top, into the plug-hole. The reading was only about half of what it should have been for the Ariel's modest 7:1 compression ratio! Melville double-checked it on his modern Yamaha 200 single farm bike ("this is what you should be doing your trip on, Steve"), which read double: the gauge was working correctly.

Though that was not good news, curiously it was a relief to have some solid data to go on. It was 50/50 whether the Ariel could struggle on much longer, so we "made a plan", as they say out there. I would hire a bakkie from Avis, 50km away in Queenstown, load the bike and drive the 360km/225 miles back to Port Elizabeth where I now knew a few folk, some of whom were good motorcycle engineers. I would spend much of that evening and the following day phoning or sending e-mails. I phoned the Barlows, but sensed immediately that after three nights, very reasonably, my welcome there as a house-guest was exhausted, though Tony from then on would continue to be extremely helpful in every way. I had hoped that the highly-skilled Darryll Moresby-White would work on the Ariel, but Tony told me that a) Darryll still did a job three days a week, only b) he wasn't even doing that currently as he was having radiation treatment.

Tony Barlow steered me towards a previous Kickstart Captain who did work on people's bikes, his namesake Tony Connolly, though Tony B first emphasised that Tony C would have to be paid for the work. I was quite prepared for that and told him so, putting it down to Tony B, in Kickstart Club Captain mode, protecting his members from an under-qualified Brit taking advantage of their generosity. Tony C, a Catholic from Northern Ireland, was very friendly on the phone, and we agreed that I would deliver the Ariel to him on Friday afternoon. Meanwhile, if the compression problem lay with the piston and its rings, I needed details on them, such as whether the piston was oversize. I e-mailed John Budgen, the bike's builder, to ask about that. I got no reply, so after 24 hours, texted my wife Molly to ask her to ring him and get the information. Meanwhile, Avis at Queenstown seemed happy to hire me a bakkie, even though I was a foreign national.

That afternoon, Melville and I drove up the steep Bushmanshoek Pass – I doubted whether the Ariel would have made it up there – with the emplacements and cairns of the Boer War British positions clearly visible on top of the wall of cliff above. The place was steeped in history; a little further east there were caves with San/Bushmen paintings on their walls. At the top we stopped at the farm of Melville's 78-year-old father, who with his wife was away in Port Elizabeth for a bowls tournament, leaving their Dachshund alone there until after the weekend. Melville fed the dog, and showed me a shed with some more motorbikes, pre-war Royal Enfields; the sausage dog ran in enthusiastically and got oil on its paws. The shed had to be padlocked in a complicated way because "they'd worked out a way to get around the old set-up". They? "The staff, I'm afraid. It's irritating."

Next morning it was cold and raining, though this cleared quickly enough. I tried to write, but my mind had too many irons in the fire. I intended to stay at a seafront B&B in Port Elizabeth, but with the Ariel's situation open-ended, while the bike was being diagnosed I wanted to be somewhere close. So I had rung "Myopic" Mike Wood, who was back from Johannesburg, and explained the situation. He offered to put me up, but with the proviso that both he and his wife Rialet worked so I would have to get my own food. But meanwhile he also offered to lend me one of his bikes while mine was being worked on.

That last afternoon Melville took me out in the truck, picking up his workers in their yellow slickers and overtrousers, and taking them back as it was raining again, but keeping one in the back of the truck to open gates. Then we crossed the road and entered the camp there, past a paddock with his Herefords (which never became take-away), and along a severely humped, rutted trail, with the diesel's ticking taking me back to Luangwa, as I was tossed about but tried to keep my eyes open for wild life. We stopped and walked a while, looking for signs of the nocturnal lynx, or of wart-hog. There were wart-hog tracks by a half-dry water-hole, but our best sighting was a herd of big blesbuck, one of the antelope endemic to South Africa. Melville said that wildlife came through occasionally from the Scotsman's neighbouring hunting reserve, as the baboons got at the fences as fast as you could repair them. We heard their warning bark.

In a horseshoe-shaped space surrounded by hills, with the railway track visible climbing the north-west slope, quite soon we reached the boundary fence. And that was where the government was buying the land from the previous white couple who owned it, the last ones locally, for re-distribution to Africans. "Pretty soon the new people's stock will run down," said Melville. "And then they'll start coming over the boundaries for ours, and that will be that, the finish. You just can't live like that, constant arguments, tension. But," he threw his hands in the air, "let's not think about it."

Alison said later that she would not be sorry to move to somewhere with more social life, as it had used to be there. But she said that the problem was Melville's parents, particularly his strong-willed father, who would never move from the family farm. His mother was a Boer. Alison, from the English heartland of Natal, had met Melville while he had been an agriculture student at Pietermaritzburg down that way, and he had bought her back here. I was beginning to realise that the divisions among white South Africans were every bit as real as that between say, Zulu and Swahili, and sometimes just as bitter.

Melville said if I came back he would be happy to take me out hunting, though he said he himself hardly hunted anymore. It was not the end of his involvement with firearms, however, as in his office there were recent framed First Prize awards for Bisley-type shooting, plus hand-loading equipment for ammunition. There was also a picture of him, with a slight sandy moustache, with D Company, Queenstown Commando, taken in 1992, during his national service, when the South African Defence Force had still been an all-powerful military machine ranging throughout the region. I had read Ryszard Kapuściński's surreal account of his time as a

The hired bakkie had a metal canopy welded on over the truckbed. This made loading tricky, but two strong blokes did the lifting while Melville, bending over in the truckbed, did the difficult bit of tilting the bike, adjusting the bars and tying down. So at 11 in the morning, off I went. I felt a little down about re-tracing my steps, though it was a different drive, down to Grahamstown, with steeper passes. The bakkie was basic, with wind-up windows and a "riding crop" hand brake, but OK. The hilly scenery was impressive but finally a bit monotonous. I ate the apple Verna Barlow had given me the previous Monday, whilst stopping to phone Tony Barlow from a vandalised, rather spooky shade area, with all the concrete table tops stolen, and bones, including a small animal skull, scattered under a table. On the road the heat and glare became a bit oppressive as I skirted Grahamstown and blasted on through the undulating coast highway. After 220-odd miles, I took the N2 Kragga Kamma exit and ended up back in Port Elizabeth, parked by a refuse dump, at around 3.30pm. I knew I was close to Tony Connolly's workshop, but couldn't find it, so phoned Tony Barlow who said to come back to his house and he would lead me over. Which he did, and was friendly with it.

In Tony Connolly's large garage/workshop we all had a beer. Tony B apologised that he hadn't been able to put me up, explaining that Verna had friends staying for the weekend, and I told him that I understood that guests were like fish – after 48 hours they began to smell – while Tony C capped that with "Guests are always a pleasure, either when they arrive… or when they leave". Two black guys working on a pipeline outside were called in to help unload the bike. I ran through the Ariel diagnoses, and then Tony B got me away, and drove us with truck and Cadillac in convoy at high speed to Greenacres shopping centre and the Avis office, which was just closing. The guys in Queenstown had failed to tell us that the bakkie should have been turned in not there but at the airport. But Tony B schmoozed the young Indian lady there, while at the petrol station next door I filled up the bakkie to replace the fuel used. With that, the day's jaunt had set me back a bit north of £100. (Later an Avis lady on the phone would try to bill me for £250, but when I protested and she checked, she found the Queenstown guys had "pushed the wrong button" and it was actually a little less than I had calculated.) Mike Wood was there, and we loaded up my kit, and drove off to his home in Fernglen.

PART THREE
PORT ELIZABETH

*"You may plan a trip with an old (British bike), but what you
more often get instead is an odyssey, full of detours, unexpected contests,
new acquaintances, and strange turns of fate.
It's what keeps some of us coming back to British bikes,
and others from ever reaching Ithaca."*
Peter Egan, *Leanings 2*

Chapter 13

ROCKER
TURNED RACER

Where to begin about Mike and Rialet Wood? Mike was a big man, tall and broad, with a big white beard and a big smile. He was unfailingly kind to everyone he met, and he was half-blind due to macular degeneration. The son of an Anglican vicar working in the impoverished Transkei, he was sometimes disorganised in an absent-minded professor sort of way, but always trying to see the bright side, and was possessed of a genuinely questing intelligence and considerable engineering skills.

His wife, Rialet – the name was an Afrikaans abbreviation – was a social worker with blacks, whites and Coloureds down in Missionvale, the city's ghetto (one of the shocks about Port Elizabeth was that the beggars at traffic lights would sometimes include white people). I had expected a cold response from her, as she was reputedly no fan of the Kickstart Club and its demands on Mike as editor of their newsletter, and she had not been there at the welcome party the previous Friday. She later explained that, as a relatively infrequent visitor, she feared that Verna Barlow would have felt obliged to spend too much time with her. Both women had a lively awareness of the Boer tradition of hospitality, and she laughingly chided Mike for having told me on the phone that I would have to get my own meals. She seemed warm and playful, mocking Mike in an affectionate way, her mouth as quirky as Dame Edna Everidge's. Photos showed that she had been a dark-haired beauty in younger days. Her temper, though I would never see it seriously unleashed, was legendary. Mike claimed, only half-jokingly, that it was why they didn't keep a gun at home.

The Woods lived in a rambling suburban house, single storey of course, set in a generous gated garden with a swimming pool and a pond full of koi carp, presided over by an ageing Alsatian watchdog, Mynka, who barked on and off all day, but was friendly. Their home had a very different atmosphere.

The word "positive" was actually mentioned by Rialet. They went to their church at 7am every Sunday; one of their two grown-up sons had been raised Anglican but switched to Dutch Reform, and the other one vice-versa. At mealtimes Mike said grace, and often it was moving. I am, I suppose, an existentialist with mystical tendencies, but happily accepted their Christianity, as this country seemed to demand a spiritual response, and theirs was, well, positive.

It certainly didn't make them happy-clappies, or unrealistic about contemporary realities. Inevitably one of the first things we would talk about was the crime. Mike told a story of how one weekend he had been under pressure to finish the panelling in their sitting room and had run into a hardware place in town on Saturday morning. He had known what he wanted and was going for it when a black guy, an assistant as he thought, told him no, go this way. But Mike could see what he needed and strode on, and the next thing, *BAM*, he was down on the floor – he had been hit from behind with an axe handle. "I was quite irritated." When he got up to remonstrate, *BAM*, he was hit in the chest with a Taser (like the one Rialet carried, along with a pepper spray, and now pulled out and demonstrated with a loud crack). "And that really hurt," said Mike. "Now I was definitely cross." But when he had staggered up, he was looking down the barrel of a gun. He was herded into a small room with everybody else, while the robbery-in-progress continued; and when they were done, the thieves sprayed tear gas into the room to deter pursuit. "It was terrible," said Mike, "really, really painful, and there was a little child in there, screaming."

That first night, like most others, we ate ready-meals from Woolworths. While in the UK, cheap and cheerful Woolies had just gone under to the crunch, taking a chunk of all our childhood memories with it, out here the chain was thriving, but as a different animal, a more upmarket equivalent of Marks & Spencer. Rialet joked about what a good cook she was, and later said she wasn't much for housework – despite indoctrination by a strict Afrikaans farm mother. "Some mornings," she said, "I wonder why I should make the bed?" We drank a bottle of beer or two and, despite the religion, neither of them were the least bit prudish. South African brandy had been a pleasant surprise. Wellington was a favourite – affordable and, while no *fine cognac*, a lot more palatable than the Spanish or Italian equivalents. Later Mike talked about an 80-year-old uncle of his who used to say that the proper way to warm brandy was between the breasts of a well-endowed woman. I felt at home with Mike and Rialet immediately. They put me in the spare room which looked out over the back, and I slept well.

Next morning, Saturday, Mike took me back to Tony Connolly's, driving a decrepit and scruffy Korean offering whose engine he had already rebuilt more than once. I was to find that there was no "latest model" snobbery about what you drove in Southern Africa: if it ran, that was good enough. Tony was mostly otherwise occupied that weekend, as his son, who had been brain-damaged in a car crash, was staying over with him. I met Tony's wife Frankie who, although the weather was no cooler than a warm autumn day in the UK, was sat huddled in a blanket with a couple of small dogs on her lap as additional insulation, complaining bitterly of the cold. And these were folk who had, within living memory, emigrated from outside Derry! I guess the body's thermostat had re-set itself to the mostly-clement South African climate.

Tony had already got the Ariel's tank off, and was saying that the compression was OK. With continuous kicking, his gauge's dial did seem to confirm that, but Mike later said it was because the engine had been cold, with oil in the sump. Tony, resorting to the usual mechanic's trick of slagging off the previous man, then wondered why the engine had been built with the compression so "low" to start with, at 7.0:1. I rallied at this, saying it suited my touring purposes, and used a Hepolite parts book from his shelf to confirm that this had been the standard ratio for '54 Red Hunters. Tony pointed to what he thought was a compression plate at the base of the engine, which would have lowered the compression further, and it did look that way. But Mike, beard bristling, blind as he was, *really* looked, and found it was just part of the crankcase.

We proceeded, driving round to visit Ray Wakefield, another Kickstart member, a water engineer who had arrived here from his native Gloucestershire 26 years previously but still retained his regional accent, which I found comforting. I enjoyed interviewing him as part of that month's article for *Real Classic*, since he was articulate and interesting, having moved from being a young rocker in Gloucester, to racing, both solo and sidecar, and now record-breaking – though not all the club were enamoured with his obsession for the latter. In 2008 he had had a frustrating time with a streamliner at Bonneville Salt Flats but had also, for land speed record holder Richard Noble's team, looked into the possibilities for attempts at Verneuk Pan in the North Cape, where Malcolm Campbell had done runs in the late 1920s. "It's better than Bonneville," Ray asserted.

By the time Ray arrived in South Africa he had given up on motorcycling, but he joined the Kickstart Club anyway. They told him he didn't have to have a bike, "but soon I had nine or ten," and he then started racing again at nearby East London, "a lovely track down by the sea, partly on public roads." Only it wasn't "racing". Racing licences were so expensive that he and the Historic Motor Cycle Group "paraded" their immaculately-prepared machines, with a staggered start to put people together. "John Cooper," said Ray, "was there last weekend." (John "Mooneyes" Cooper had been a UK racing legend in the late '60s and early '70s, riding what was practically the British motorcycle industry's last racing gasp, the works BSA/Triumph triples. In 1971, at Mallory Park, on a BSA Rocket 3, he famously beat seven-times World Champion Giacomo Agostini.)

Ray currently owned a Triton ("as a rocker I'd always wanted one"), powered by a 650 Triumph Bonneville engine with altered balance on the crankshaft, as well as an ex-GP kneeler outfit, and an alloy off-road outfit powered by a BSA 350 single which he took on club runs, and a 750 Norton Atlas. But the maximum eye candy for me was one of the prettiest BSA A65s I had ever seen. I might have sold mine but I couldn't seem to get away from the things. Ray had originally dug the 1969 twin out from a chicken run; now it sported a disc-brake front end, Gold Star silencers, and a lovely scalloped alloy tank. "I cut it down from a five gallon one. I wanted to make it look like a Matchless G50, hence the maroon colour, and then the cowboy in me heard it crying out for clip-ons." He had taken that one racing, with the engine "pretty well standard", but with a brilliant camshaft grind "done by a friend in Cape Town, re-profiled, but not fierce". Ray's own engineering skills had benefited Mike: on the A65 "Spock" (the fiery one), Ray had fixed the oil pump bypass valve, working out the necessary correct pressure from the spring tension and the piston volume.

When it was time to leave, Mike found that he had lost the car keys (Ray's sly Alsatian, Radar, had already nicked Mike's wallet). It was some time before the keys turned up, lying on a garden path. Driving with Mike was quite interesting too.

Chapter 14

RUN-OUT
AND T-BONE

Later I would learn more about Mike's partial sightedness. Macular degeneration is an eye condition that leads to the gradual loss of central vision – as needed for reading, writing, riding or driving. He explained that the eyeball was too big, stretched, with the pixels larger than normal, and under tension. The veins in the eyeballs were deteriorating so he could not risk having high blood pressure or taking a blow to the head. Mike's first blind spot, known as a Fuchs Spot, had been discovered 20 years before, and now he had a cataract. They had stopped the bleeding in his left eye with laser treatment, but that had left a permanent blind spot there, plus a lot of floaters, and the possibility of waking up blind or with broken vision.

The condition was incurable and meant he could not adjust his vision with lenses. And now he had a new cataract in his good eye, and a specialist at a check-up a month previously had told Mike that he could not remove the new cataract, due to the danger of bleeding/blindness. So, for the first time, Mike was admitting to himself that he might be a danger driving. Yet with all that, he was one of the most fundamentally cheerful individuals I had ever met. You could not be around him without feeling good. And on a motorbike he still rode like a lion.

His bikes were mouth-expanders too. I had only seen the smart Ariel VB outfit, but there was also a hybrid single, a BSA M20 side-valve 500 single engine in a swinging-arm Ariel frame – a desirable move, as the M20 and M21 had always featured just rigid or plunger suspension. The bike had a Japanese carb, no dynamo and a Triumph gearbox. It went incredibly well, and I later learned that the previous owner had done work on 350 and 500 Gold Star OHV singles, BSA's finest, so Mike's M20 was likely to have been tweaked with Gold Star camshafts etc. Not for the last time, I thought, *that's* what I should be riding.

There was also "Spock", the ratty red o.i.f. BSA A65 (I really couldn't get away from them). Mike had won Spock in a Kickstart Club raffle, though later Tony Connolly would confirm what Mike had long suspected, that it had been set up to let him win. He was valued for the work he had put in, despite his myopia, as editor of the newsletter, and all he had had at the time was a sluggish old BMW single (on one ride it had run over its own front mudguard, which had detached itself and gone forward around the wheel). The A65 had a load of problems. "People used to want Spock to come on runs," said Mike, "because they knew something else would go wrong." The most spectacular mishap was when it caught fire. Mike had ripped the blazing petrol tank off the bike and hurled it away (despite the fact that he rode without gloves because his hands were so big he could never find a pair that would fit comfortably). He then had to uproot a small tree to try to beat out the flames before a bush-fire started next to a game reserve. Ray Wakefield had written a poem about it. Spock was still a piece of work, with the ignition key missing and the seat unattached; the current tank was one with chromed side-scallops from 1970, which interestingly (for a BSA anorak) seemed to fit the following year's thicker o.i.f. frame spine.

These larks with Spock shouldn't imply that Mike was not a seriously talented engineer. His day job was to maintain a network of radio/TV masts, and the bikes shared a garage with the equipment he was assembling to build a machine to automatically grease the masts' support cables. This hazardous task had until then been undertaken manually by workers going up and down the high wires, suspended in the equivalent of a bosun's chair. Recently one man's harness wire had broken, leaving him dangling, and he was near to death by the time a helicopter rescued him (partly because the chopper reportedly would not take off until the money for its fuel had been transferred to the company involved). So Mike had been tasked to design and build a mechanical greaser that would crawl up and down the wires, and he said that the work was coming along well.

That Saturday evening I took Mike and Rialet out to a restaurant of their choice, the self-consciously bohemian Stage Door, next to Port Elizabeth's Opera House. The weather had turned and, after dark, rain was pushing in from the sea. It felt slightly edgy, walking along the wet street from the parked car to the inevitable security guard outside the joint, but inside was pleasantly funky, with bohos at the next table, nice food, and the metal troughs in the men's urinals entertainingly filled with ice. The bill was more than reasonable. As the menu put it, "If you don't like the staff, don't tell us: at these prices we can't afford anyone better!" We went on for ice cream at a rain-lashed parlour, down on the waterfront which Tony Barlow had counselled against walking alone. It seemed he was right. Driving home, Rialet told a story of a girl who had been snatched there by a pair of white low-lifes, raped, and then disembowelled. But despite all, she had crawled to safety and survived, and was now, said Rialet, a motivational speaker.

That Sunday was the Kickstart's monthly run out. The weather was dry, but windy enough that the captain, Tony Barlow, said he wasn't going to come. He did, however, lend me a bike for the occasion – unfortunately, though understandably, not one of his Nortons, but a little 1978 Suzuki GS400 twin. My experience with Jap bikes was very limited. The only one I had ever owned was a 1,600cc 6-cylinder Honda behemoth with six carburettors, called a Valkyrie, a naked Gold Wing – and that had been built in America. Still, anything, as long as it rolled. But first we had to get over to Tony's. I quaked at the prospect of going pillion, which no rider relishes, but Mike, considerate as ever, had thought of that, so he rode Spock, the A65, and I rode the M20, which Mike then swapped onto for the run itself.

The Suzuki started on the button, and was painless. It changed gear on the left (as opposed to the right, the British way) for each of its six speeds, and revved high in all of them, but at least there was a read-out to tell you which gear you were in – though the glare soon rendered this invisible. We filled it up with petrol, then met about a dozen or so riders, most of them on traditional BMW airhead twins, in the parking lot of Kragga Kamma shopping centre. Mike took a show of hands, and we were off.

I stayed near the front as we got back on the N2 highway heading west, watching Mike in the lead holding a good pace on the M20 despite riding almost straight into the wind. The Suzuki, though feeling bland and a lot lighter than my Ariel, handled the side-gusts well. After a while, Roy Cartvel, a rider on a faired BMW who I would soon get to know well, came charging up from behind and swerved in breathtakingly fast just in front of the M20, giving Mike a slipstream tug.

Once we took the Van Stadens turn off the highway, it was exciting. The mountain roads were covered in washed-down red dirt, but the M20 romped up them, Mike riding physically, unhesitatingly, with full commitment and skill. It was a pleasure to watch him and hard to remember his visual impairment. Close by in the hills above the road I caught sight of my first baboons, but when I mentioned this later to Mike he said, "What baboons?" He avoided the larger red rocks that had fallen into the road, but at one point his front tyre caught a smaller one and spat it out sideways like a bullet.

Then we saw a young black guy on the roadside walking towards us wearing a green blanket, his unhappy face painted in a white circle. Mike told me later that he would have been coming from a circumcision group. This rite of passage was a major event, with parents having to slaughter an ox, as well as burn all the participant's old clothes and buy him new; but if they would not do it, young men had been known to kill themselves. In Rialet's view the ritual was not good for other reasons. At the ceremonies, she said, the elders encouraged the youth to think of women as nothing and, from her observations as a social worker, she believed this increased the likelihood of rape and sexual violence.

Following several miles of up and down going, we arrived at a bridge and, as arranged, stopped to rendezvous with another BMW rider – an Aussie, Alaric Giles, who had just done 10,000km in three weeks around South Africa on a mud-splattered hired BMW 1200GS, the latest version and complete with metal luggage. Tall, fit and amusedly laconic, Alaric was the real Adventure Motorcycling deal, with a similar bike of his own back home. He had just done Die Hel (The Hell) at Gamkaskloof, 50km of zig-zag rubble/dirt road down steep hillsides to a remote valley which had been almost completely isolated, until the track had been bulldozed in the Sixties by a guy who had ended up marrying a farmer's daughter down there. Alaric headed on that day for the even more challenging Baviaans Kloof; Tony Barlow had described hilariously his own attempts to traverse this in a family car. The riders' comments on the Aussie: "He's going to pick up a lot more mud down there."

My Suzuki had been over-revving wildly when I pulled up to stop, and did the same thing when we started up again, until Mike reached down deftly and flicked off the choke lever. Oops. Mike knew the little bike well, having borrowed it and then fallen off while simultaneously riding and taking photos. He would do snaps later this day too.

We rode on, past Sunday groups of blacks, through a couple of towns, and country with bougainvillea hedges and citrus orchards, to the pleasant café/ shop where we stopped for an excellent brunch. The only bum note was when a guy I was sitting near suggested that I contact the editor of *Bike S.A.* magazine to help publicise the trip. "He's Jewish," he said, "but we won't hold that against him." It was an otherwise very good-humoured sit-down, with Mike shepherding all, and taking photos energetically for the newsletter. I got some good advice on possible routes north from the pleasant, serious, bald-headed chap sitting opposite me, Stewart Fergusson, who I was also to get to know much better.

Then we rode back again, with several people peeling off to get home and watch the Grand Prix on TV, or stop for a beer and lunch. I followed Mike admiringly, and after a stop for snaps beneath the spectacular high arch of the Van Stadens bridge, sadly a favourite spot locally for suicides, we got back on the N2 with the wind behind us now, and returned safely to PE. Mike said (correctly) that I should fill up the Suzuki before returning it. At their house we met Tony and Verna, then swapped bikes as before and pulled away, Mike on the A65 and me following on the M20 bitza, past the roadside avocado sellers and turning down beside the shopping precinct, towards Fernglen.

I was romping along on a high after the excellent day, tucked in tight behind and to the left of Mike, glad to be back on a proper bike with some real poke and a righteous exhaust note. When Mike, who had been riding with his right indicator on continuously, turned into a street, with a bakkie behind us I accelerated to tuck in closer to him – and then I was shouting "NO! NO!" as he'd braked and tilted left across me into what turned out to be his gateway! I braked hard, but there was no selection and I hit him, T-boning his bike. As I went down on my right side, I remember looking as Mike fell, desperate that he didn't bang his head in the full-face helmet and go blind.

Then the bike was on top of my right leg, and my sensors were exploring for breakage, which would have done for the trip. But the protective gear, the armoured trousers and jacket, and especially the tall boots with the metal plates at the ankle, did their stuff, despite the hot exhaust pipe. Mike was up and apologising already, as I was. How English was that! I had just hit one of the man's bikes with his other one, and *he's* apologising. As I lay there, the M20's throttle was stuck open and the engine roaring, and I couldn't remember which of its controls was the decompressor, to stop it. That annoyed me. The guy from the bakkie behind had halted and was helping, and eventually I was up, with nothing broken, and the bikes were OK, bar one shattered rear indicator on Spock.

Rialet was in the doorway watching, and said wryly, "I don't think you will want to talk about this!" and we didn't, to any of the others, or indeed to the magazine readers. "I think," said Mike, "I think we should have some brandy," and we had several Wellingtons, and a lovely evening. My right ankle had started to hurt, and soon ballooned out into a massive haematoma, which was troublesome for a week or more; my inner ankle still bears a mark, a permanent souvenir of Port Elizabeth.

Chapter 15

A MATTER OF TIMING

In the next few chapters, there is a real danger of technical overload. For any readers bothered by this, a good rule of thumb may be to skip paragraphs containing the word "sprocket". It all becomes clear in the end, especially if you use the Glossary on Page 322.

As the days passed, I bonded with Mike and Rialet more and more. The following evening we talked about an ongoing problem they had involving a close family member, which had been the reason Mike had had to leave that initial welcoming party at Tony Barlow's and fly off elsewhere. It was true he had seemed a little preoccupied that evening, but you would never have guessed the pressure he was under with the resurgent threat of more very difficult years dealing with a problem for someone they loved, with no guarantee of a happy outcome. Their faith had clearly helped, but I was struck by their equanimity, their calm.

I needed a bit of that, as contact by e-mail and occasionally phone was re-established with home. I had asked Molly to ring John Budgen to find out what over-size, if any, the Ariel's piston was, after he had failed to respond to e-mails. Telephoning from Africa was expensive, but Mike and Rialet urged me to call her; once again I had not spelt out to them the probability that Molly and I were separating, blaming any friction on the fact that she and Rosie disapproved of my trip. Molly had contacted John and confirmed that the piston was +0.060, just about on the limit, and it was surprising to me that John had not had the engine re-bored and sleeved back to standard.

But Molly told me John's wife Pearl was now back in hospital with shingles and had lost the use of her legs, and that it had been very awkward troubling him with my problems under those circumstances. She also said, "We have problems here." When I rang them a second time I was told that Rosie was having nightmares about me chasing her with a knife; Rose herself wouldn't come to the phone, as she was "watching TV".

I wrote to Rosie, a possibly over-sentimental but deeply-felt letter by e-mail

– and then the thing wouldn't send, due to a loose connection at the back of the computer. It was endearingly typical of Mike's world, but so was the fact that he soon sorted it, and the mail was sent. I had ended my message by emphasising that whatever happened I would be seeing her again at the end of July. A couple of days later I got this reply:

> "c.u. then, all is fine here, I went 2 eve's house yesterday and rode in a thunderstorm, conor who rode with us was only waering (sic) a short-sleeved t shirt, he moaned loads. Luv ya, rosie.w."

This reassured me more than any emotional outpourings could have.

On a lighter note, I was also in touch with my step-brother Raymond who was looking after things for me in the UK. My post was being forwarded to him, and among it there had been a letter on House of Commons note paper from our (Tory) MP, who had seen the brief article about the Short Way Up trip syndicated in another local newspaper. Whether it was them or him, he was under the impression that I was doing the trip to raise money not for Kawaza, but for an Oxfordshire children's hospice. Anyway, he wrote that it was "always a pleasure to see individuals pushing their limits in the name of charity". Raymond told me that the day the letter had arrived, this man had featured in the *Daily Telegraph* near the top of the list of MPs with allegedly questionable expense claims. Raymond suggested that we should write to the MP, noting his recently publicised affluence and suggesting that under the circumstances a contribution to our charity fund would be very much in order. I was tempted...

Within a couple of days, Tony Connolly had done the top-end work on the Ariel; he was known for working fast. He had found no evidence of damaged or collapsed piston rings, but Port Elizabeth had lived up to its Motown rep, with new +0.020 and +0.040 piston rings available off the shelf from a Mr Newby. But the +0.060 ones we needed were intended for something else and of slightly different dimensions, so the ring grooves on the piston needed to be re-cut. This had been done by another Kickstart person, John Peart, a bearded 72-year-old precision engineer and paid-up eccentric from Willesden, West London, with the accent intact to prove it.

John, for a hobby, machined and built from scratch 6ft-long working model steam locomotives; he had restored a couple of classics bikes for himself including a 1936 Ariel Red Hunter; he ran marathons, and regularly smashed himself up on modern superbikes ridden to the limit and beyond. A non-stop talker, John was sceptical about the excessive clearance on the Ariel's piston ("doubt it would get you back to Cape Town"). He thus added another element to the baffling mix, which included Tony C's discovery that, after little more than 1,000 miles, the rear drive chain was completely knackered – you could bend it sideways back on itself. This was consistent with what John Budgen had begun to find back in England, but it didn't explain why the chains were wearing out at least five times faster than they should have. Again, Port Elizabeth came through with genuine Renolds chain replacements, so Tony C's final bill of around £140, including the chain, and the rings plus the work on them, was reasonable.

I collected the bike and rode it back the way I had come into town, turning west before the N2, and taking a country road for a dozen miles. Soon enough I had to realise that, depressingly, there was no real change in the Ariel's performance. There is a "fog of war" element to mechanical problems on older machinery, even with things that seem simple in hindsight, and we were now seriously entering that foggy zone. Mike already reckoned the problem was incorrect valve timing, so I rang Tony Connolly again, who said he was willing to a) check the valve timing and b) get the cylinder re-lined and fit a new piston. I also rang John Peart, who was keen to help with that. I then e-mailed the leading Ariel spares suppliers in the UK, glad to be using Mike's e-mail address as some years before I had fallen out with these guys in a big way. They could supply a piston complete, but would not courier it out, meaning a week's delay and uncertainty as it came by post. Darryll Moresby-White, who was just off on holiday, took the trouble to phone with the number of an experienced Ariel contact, with spares, in the Cape Town area.

Meanwhile, two of the guys I had met on the ride out, Roy Cartvel and Stewart Fergusson, dropped round at Mike's, and Stewart, who was clearly highly respected by the others as a rider and engineer, took the Ariel out for a good long ride. He came back convinced that the power problem was not the piston; and that since we had eliminated other possibilities like the engine timing, he too believed that the problem more than likely lay with the valve timing, which would also be consistent with the low compression. In

ABOVE: *About to set off from Tokai and start the trip.*

PREVIOUS PAGE: *Across the Zambezi. The ferry is stuck in a bank of reeds, deliberately, to let a dredger out.*

LEFT: *"He didn't see nothing but road." First breakdown, outside Cradock.*

BELOW: *"Corkie" with his 1948 Piper Clipper.*

ABOVE LEFT: *Melville Price rebuilds the Ariel's petrol tap.*

ABOVE RIGHT: *Melville with his civilian 1940 Harley-Davidson WLA.*

BELOW: *Mike Wood and Steve.*

ABOVE: *Roy Cartvel watching Stewart Fergusson working on Jerry's valve timing.*

LEFT: *Steve on the rebuilt Ariel, along the coast road from Port Elizabeth.* (Mike Wood)

ABOVE: *On the road to Clarens. The mountains in the background are Lesotho.*

RIGHT: *Botswanese pot-holes on the road north of Nata have their effect.*

ABOVE: *Kazangula ferry across the Zambezi, as the sun sinks. The guy in the pale jacket is Elvin the fixer.*

BELOW: *Riding out from the 'Moorings' camp in Zambia.* (Andy Legg)

ABOVE: *Day off at Victoria Falls.*

BELOW: *Trans-Zambezi Riders escort Steve towards Lusaka.*

ABOVE: *Ginty Melvill (left), Steve and the chaps celebrate reaching Lusaka.*

LEFT: *Ginty's mechanic Cholo, with Jerry.*

BELOW: *Steve in Ginty's yard.* (Ginty Melvill)

addition, he confirmed that higher gearing was an absolute must, to counter the damaging vibration.

So I togged up and rode the bike back to Tony Connolly's as agreed. But when I got there Tony was standing in the doorway to the garage with his arms folded, and told me that something else had come up that was going to take all his time, so that he could not do the work for me. It was an awkward moment.

I rode back and, when Mike and Rialet returned, told them, kind of lethargically, fatalistically, about this latest set-back. I felt no pressure or irritation from them about my continued presence, and that was without price. Rialet had got home first, and told me that Mike said he couldn't remember a week when he had felt so relaxed, which I took as a compliment, unless it was said just to put me at my ease. Simply sitting talking with them in the evenings had been nourishing for me.

Without being asked, they sometimes addressed questions I would never have put to them, such as how good-hearted people like them had existed as part of the white elite under the apartheid regime. The answer was always that it was so deeply ingrained into their upbringing, and into the status quo at the time, that they had rarely considered it. They seemed to look back on their younger selves with bemusement. Rialet told a story of how on the farm where she grew up, she was stopped from lifting a puppy to drink from an outside tap because someone had seen a Kaffir drinking from it. And how when they were little, the hard round candy we Brits knew as gob-stoppers, because the outer layer was black, they called, quite unselfconsciously, "niggerballs". There was even a saying about them: "life is hard as a niggerball, but it's *lekker*" (nice, sweet).

We talked a lot, partly because Mike's eyesight meant that he didn't watch much TV or read. When we did watch, it was the rugby, where the top South African teams such as the Pretoria Bulls seemed more like American footballers; or the news (there had been serious flooding in Cape Town about a week after I had left there); or sometimes a soap about a newspaper office. Every evening, whatever we had been drinking, ended with one more cup of tea.

If there was any unease, it was my concern about taking advantage of Mike and Rialet's good nature. With them no "blending" had been necessary: they saw my need and opened themselves and their home to me without hesitation. It was Tony Barlow and others who asked the occasional question to check that they weren't being taken advantage of. I had intended to move out to a B&B after a day or two, but as we got along so well, and the e-mail access plus proximity to Jerry's ongoing rebuild was really useful, I offered to pay the Woods the going B&B rate of about £160 a week for staying. They consulted with each other overnight, and then said that if I really wanted to pay, they would like me to add that money to the Kawaza charity fund. So that was what I did.

Now Mike wanted to do an experiment on the Ariel. He stood it up on its piece of plank so that the rear wheel would rotate freely, took off the air cleaner rubber while I removed the spark plug, and with his thumb blocking the plug hole, turned the engine by pulling on the rear wheel, till he could just feel compression starting. Then he inserted a short piece of more-or-less straight wire down the plug-hole, and marked it at that position. Next we turned the rear wheel backwards and, using blow-back from the carb as well as a moment when there was pressure from the plug-hole, Mike was able to find, and mark the wire at, the bottom of the stroke. In that way he was able to ascertain that the inlet valve was closing between one-third and half-way up the piston's stroke – that was about half-way short of where it should have been doing so, with the engine accordingly starved of the intake of its charge of fuel/air mix. "The valve timing is so far retarded that I don't understand how the engine has been running at all!" exclaimed Mike.

I took this as a left-handed compliment to the Ariel's Colt .45-like unfussy ruggedness; that, fully loaded, it had got us this far, even with the engine so radically out of whack. It certainly seemed to explain a number of things: the lack of power; the intermittent feeling of low, or no, compression on the kickstart; the 90 miles to the gallon (because only about half the normal charge was being used); and why Melville's compression test had always shown two readings, a higher and a lower. Now we were getting somewhere. But it left the question: why was this happening?

Setting the valve timing on Ariel singles was a matter of lining up dots marked on the meshing timing gears, inside a cover at the bottom of the engine's right side. Mike energetically said that this would be simple, but reading my little Pitmans rider's manual, it didn't sound like it. And if the timing gear sprocket, with one set of marks on it, had turned on the camshaft spindle, as Darryll on the phone now told Mike that it might have, the actual re-timing would be complicated indeed. There was also the matter of pullers to remove the sprockets; Mike believed a simple bolt-type one he had used on the M20's identical Magdyno should do the trick (it didn't). But in another phone call, the Ariel specialist outside Cape Town did say he thought we should be able to strip the engine with the tools we had.

Mike had thought about it more by now, his questing engineer's mind puzzling at the "why" of it. He recognised that if this was the real problem, it would have to be addressed really carefully. So we lined up the ducks and made a plan. BMW fanatic Roy Cartvel, who lived nearby, had offered the use of his well-equipped triple garage for the work. And Stewart Fergusson, despite having a full-time job and plenty of other interests, had agreed to participate. But only after he had got the full Ariel workshop manual off Darryll, whose departure on hols, luckily for us, had been delayed until after the weekend. Stewart would not commit to doing something unless he could do it meticulously. Meanwhile I e-mailed my step-brother Raymond, who fortuitously lived in Suffolk, not too far from the UK Ariel specialist. He agreed to go there after the weekend, collect the sprocket we needed to raise the gearing, which I had confirmed by e-mail that the specialists had in stock, and arrange to have it sent by DHL out to Port Elizabeth, at a total cost of over £120.

Chapter 16

TOP DEAD CENTRE

Roy Cartvel turned up at the house that afternoon and, once I had released the gate, walked in seeming a bit distracted and looking for tea – famously he always travelled around with his own outsized flask, but he had left this somewhere. There was a zany air about Roy, and he was very well liked by the other Kickstart members. He was more tanned and weather-beaten than the rest, as he was much involved with yachts. He came round again after supper, by which time I had learned that he was a recovering alcoholic, and turned out to be an absolute hoot, so that we were all soon falling about around the table.

A typical story he told involved a bike trip he had taken with two others plus a big guy, a magistrate as it happened, called Jack Slabbert (pron. "Slubbock"). Jack had recently returned from Australia with a prize bit of biker sleeping gear called the Swagbag – a low tent/sleeping bag/inflatable mattress, all in one – which made it considerably bulky, so much so that it could only be fixed to the back of his little Suzuki 400 twin on the slant; and like that, the wind had played havoc with the bike's handling.

The first night they camped, it snowed, and Jack was discovered to be claustrophobic, so that he had to sleep with his head *outside* the Swagbag. The next morning he bought a beanie hat and an additional blanket, which didn't help with his bulked-up load. The party then took a shortcut up to that night's destination, which unexpectedly involved a section of dirt road. As Roy braked for this, Jack braked to avoid him, and went down, hitting the ground cursing out Roy, and claiming the latter's brake light and indicators didn't work (which they did). "After that," said Roy, "we called him Jack Splat."

Roy had grown up in Cape Town, and told us that the only two British machines he had ever owned were a side-valve Morris Minor and a D1 BSA

Bantam. For many of us, these little two-stroke machines had featured as a first bike. Despite lack of performance and marginal electrics, being a BSA they were sturdy. Had this Bantam tilted him towards BMWs for life? No, he'd found it a bundle of laughs – when it went down, it would spin round and round like a top, pivoting on the single bar footrests and taking no damage. On evenings out they would ride the Bantam three-up from down by the waterside, up Cape Town's hills, with the third guy having to hop off at the bottom of the final slope, run up the hill and jump on again at the top. Rockers in those days, said Roy, were known as Milk Bar Cowboys, because they didn't go to bars and drink; a favourite meeting point had been the Carousel at Seapoint.

I spent the day slowly working on a piece for *Real Classic*. Mike was to be a big, big help in painstakingly getting my photos ready to send in a useable format and in e-mailing them. He also printed out, and laminated, the photo of Rosie and me from the evening before I left, so that I had it to carry with me on the road. Later, Roy showed up to lead me on the bike round to his garage. I had been in PE for a week now, and I could feel tension building in me after the enforced passivity, when as editor Frank put it, I should have been "out wrestling crocodiles". The Ariel proved difficult to start, popping and banging when it did so because the air cleaner hose was still off.

Roy had a very big, fully-equipped and carpeted garage, also featuring, cheeringly, Nick Ward cartoons on the walls. With Mike in attendance we wheeled Jerry up onto a low wooden bench and slung the bike with webbing straps from a rafter above, to secure it. Then underneath on the bench Roy slid in an enormous tin pan, like the biggest oven tray in the world, to catch anything, oil included, that fell out as the bike was stripped. Roy started cleaning off the engine, already oily again despite its recent top-end rebuild, as Stewart was very particular. I got the socket-heads out of the bike's toolbox, where I had re-located them from the panniers in the interest of weight distribution, and began to remove the tank and seat. I discovered one of the four tank bolts was missing, as I had failed to check that it was lock-wired on. This angered me, but Rooibos tea and the banter between the other two soon got me out of that. Mike said eagerly that he would replace the bolt, and he was as good as his word, finding another in his spares hoard and drilling its head skilfully to take the lock-wire.

While we waited for Stewart, Roy fabricated a new, sturdier fastening for the oil tank, where the old one had broken and was still wedged up with rubber. He cut and bent the metal, and then it took a lot of difficult spanner-work to get the mounting installed with the oil tank still in place; but by 11pm it was done. And Roy didn't even know me, I'd only really met him that day.

Stewart Fergusson arrived and, sitting on a stool with his gold-rimmed glasses, looked a bit like a longer-faced version of the Hollywood actor Peter Boyle. He was a single man, I guessed in his 50s, though talk was rife amongst the Kickstarters of his new, serious relationship with a lady in Johannesburg. He had even asked Roy about a more ample, comfortable King- and Queen-type seat for BMWs (naturally Stewart had one), which had set off another round of speculation, this time dimensional. (I later met the lady, who was charming, and not outsize at all.) Stewart's time with us was limited; he had a responsible day job, and was also soon going to have to prepare for a classic car rally, the Continental Milligan, as navigator in a VW Beetle. But over the next few evenings he did the work with 110 per cent concentration, and always meticulously. His judgement was steady. He was the Guv'nor.

Stewart's first move was to fit a protractor on the crankshaft, and carefully mark the valve opening and closing positions, which Roy recorded on his whiteboard on the wall – and these confirmed Mike's rough calculations, that the valve timing was retarded by more than 40 degrees. He then removed the timing side engine covers and found that the camshaft timing dots had been set, not lined up, but with the one on the smaller engine pinion below having its dot one position to the left – which meant that it was one tooth *advanced*, and also did not coincide, as it should have, with Top Dead Centre. I felt brief euphoria – line up the dots and the fault would be corrected?

But this was quickly dashed the following evening, as we all three sat in contemplation for a while, and then calculated (literally, with the calculator I carried in my waistcoat) that if one tooth equalled 14.5 degrees of timing, the dot needed to be moved three teeth's-worth in the other direction, ie so that it was two dots away to the right. We knew that John Budgen had dismantled the bottom end to fit the new main bearings, and Mike speculated that John might have set the timing one tooth out to compensate for whatever was wrong with it, but that he had gone in the wrong direction. To put things right and re-time the engine correctly we needed to find out how this situation had come about.

Mike thought that the Woodruff keyway on the smaller, lower engine pinion might have sheared, and the gear welded itself to the crankshaft in the wrong position. Stewart had already struggled long and hard, so that he would be able to re-set it, to remove the upper, camshaft gear sprocket, without a proper puller to do so. The threat of damaging something irrevocably in the process was real, and so was the anxiety in the room, especially when something shifted and he said, "I broke it…" But he was only referring to the seal holding the camshaft on, and he got it free.

Now, disappointingly, Stewart and Roy had another struggle on their hands, to try to pull off the lower pinion as well, which was stuck. There were further revelations. The crankshaft was found to be moving from side to side, with end-float of 2mm, far too much – you could move the shaft sideways by hand. It seemed clear that some spacers were missing, and later telephone advice from Richard, the Ariel expert in Barrydale outside Cape Town, was to remove the engine, split it and space it up properly. But we didn't have the time, and Mike believed that the shock absorber spring was holding the crankshaft in a stable enough position on the drive side (though clearly the situation was not doing chain life any good at all). So we left it like that.

The fog continued to thicken. What of the piston that John Peart had worried about? Mike discovered one basis for his concern had been a ring gap slightly more than 12 thou. when the book said 8 thou. was the acceptable maximum; but Mike believed that in practice 12 was OK. We decided to run with the existing set-up, though Richard offered a new +0.030 piston, and re-bore facilities were available in PE. Would I regret this? In addition, with the rocker box covers removed to expose the valves, the rocker shafts were discovered not to be a matching pair. There was also wear on the little detachable end caps on the valve stems, which had dimples worn in them.

That Sunday, after a power cut and computer failure, Mike drove me downtown. I had heard him crashing around at 7am as he went off to church. He told us the sermon had been delivered by missionaries who proselytised among Muslims and helped those who wanted to become Christians. It was an activity I had heard about previously and considered well out of order. Mike too said he was "unsure of great chunks of dogma" and definitely against those who promoted their own God against the beliefs of others. We got some chain spray and chrome cleaner at an auto-shop, then dropped in at the hilltop HQ of the aerial mast company to pick up one of his cameras.

Back home, Mike dug out some rusty old sprockets to see if any of them would serve as a replacement on the Ariel. After lunch we drove to Roy's where things were soon fraught. Mike's endearing, boyishly energetic enthusiasm to get on with things meant that, though Stewart had not yet arrived, Mike wanted to see if any of the sprockets fitted (they didn't), and to do that he had to disturb the timing disc Stewart had set up on the engine – I should have stopped him. After that Mike set about removing the rocker covers to find out why the exhaust rocker was stiff, but again I was anxious as I was sure perfectionist Stewart, our best resource, might have been willing to do that but would be less likely to if we started messing about with it. The mechanical dismemberment, the removed rocker cover upside down with valve lifter cable still attached, dismayed me, and then sure enough in walked Stewart, and was clearly displeased about the disturbed timing disc.

There was worse. After he had left, telling Mike and Roy to put the rocker boxes back and measure the clearances, Mike began doing what Roy had already done for the inlet side's little valve end cap, working with the exhaust valve's end cap on a grinding machine to gently grind out the dimple worn in its top – when the cap shot out of his hand and (he thought) hit the door on the far side of the room. In Roy's cluttered workshop we were never going to find it, though we all spent a long time looking. It was not necessarily the end of the world, as I could add end-caps onto the order to the UK for the sprocket and, in addition, Roy believed that a similar cap off an Alfa Romeo car would serve. I told Mike, who was mortified, the truth: that it could have happened to anyone. We went home to a *braai* supper, and next morning Mike left on a business trip for three days and I settled in for another week's waiting.

Chapter 17

MARKING TIME

It was scarcely unpleasant, but I was losing momentum. We had a routine by now; Mike and Rialet left early for work, so I would stay in bed out of the way, listening to their footsteps, Rialet's quick and purposeful, Mike's heavy and occasionally crashing into something. When they were gone I had breakfast and went about my occasions, taking far too long to complete a first (far too long) piece for *Real Classic*, plus chasing Ariel stuff and journey contacts. By the second week I knew I was not going to be able to make the Natal Classic Rally, and let the organisers know. I deeply regretted that, as both my original South African contact, Gary Brown, and the rally organiser, Richard Sawkins, had taken the trouble to arrange temporary membership of their club, accommodation, hospitality and a rally box for me.

Melville Price had shown me one of these boxes. They were bulky things which fitted over the handlebars, blanking out the speedo and mileometer so that you had to follow the directions. He told me some people who were serious about this regularity event, after up to two days and many checkpoints, would finish only seconds shy of the designated time. All a bit intimidating, and my plan would have been to tag along behind someone and enjoy the ride and the social side, as some other riders did. But Jerry had dictated otherwise.

At Mike's, if I needed to stretch my legs I would operate the keypad and locks, say hello to Mynka, step quickly out of the rolling gates before they closed again, and walk the half mile down to the petrol station and the little row of shops, to get more Emugel ointment for my ankle at the pharmacy, or replenish beer and biltong at the bottle shop. The petrol garage had a bonus: a rare 1950s pick-up version of the little Austin A35 (just 498 of them had been built, and half of those exported), a tiny pale blue thing, well restored, with bright red covers for the spare wheel and the load bed. More

Toy Town than Motown, but grist to the mill for the car mag. Walking back, I kept my eyes open. Rialet had told me that the thief gangs laid signals outside people's gates using what looked like litter, via a coded system with combinations of empty cans and packets, meaning "house empty all day", "maid in" etc. It was potentially serious stuff. In the local paper there were always reports of fresh home invasions, and one evening when Mike and I were walking Mynka, Roy's car slid up to the curb; he was part of a neighbourhood patrol rota. I did see a can outside one house, but it could have just been litter.

Another time I was in the house when a bakkie pulled up, dumped a load of old carpeting right across the gateway, and drove off before I could get out there. Mike had told me a tale of how he had got his guys from work to dump tree cuttings in the drive of a tree-surgeon's foreman who had refused to remove them as agreed. I dragged the carpets to the side, and soon after another bakkie with its truckbed full of blacks pulled up. Mynka went onto full bark, the white driver got out and, via the intercom by the gate, explained that his guys could use the carpet as flooring for themselves. With the metal lattice gates still closed, I gave him Mike's cell phone number, and then dubiously opened the door. It was all friendly, but Mike on the phone explained that the old carpets were for Rialet, who handed them out to her social work clients in the township. They were clearly prized items, and after that I dragged them inside the gates.

I was never bored during my days at Fernglen, though the only visitor was the taciturn maid, who came once a week, and went home with a food bag as well as money. Without the Walkman (I hadn't progressed to an iPod yet), I had not listened to music while I'd been away, or missed it. The lack of libido was odd too. When I did have spare hours, wanting to conserve the so-excellent book *Thirteen Moons*, I foraged. Because of his eyesight, Mike did not read, and most of Rialet's books were in Afrikaans, but I did find a copy of Arundhati Roy's *The God of Small Things*, an excellent novel set in India, a country where "various kinds of despair compete for primacy... [and] *personal* despair could never be desperate enough", a not-irrelevant insight for Africa also. I sat reading outside on the back porch, fringed with purple and scarlet bougainvillea, where the *braai* was, with the sound of water trickling from Mike's home-rigged fountain into the pond for the coy. Occasionally it felt like slacking, sitting in a quiet sunlit garden, reading and making notes, with birdsong, a dog yapping somewhere, Mynka lying by the pool. But perhaps I had come for this too.

Indoors the water pipes sometimes made a loud moaning groan. The house was a little run-down. Rialet said Mike was always too busy helping other people, and they both knew they would have to go through it before their move to the house below Cape Town where they planned to retire the following year. That place was smaller but, though they had lived at their present home for many years, Rialet said she would happily walk away from practically everything there. They had no worries about selling the house; the property situation was evidently not yet the same as in the UK.

Rialet would arrive home first, and we would drink tea and talk about her day. One lunchtime she had had to go with an Afrikaans woman who cooked at the centre; the woman's husband, working decorating above his head in their bathroom, had fallen down dead. Rialet said the man had been overweight, but they had managed together to move him from the bath and cover him with a sheet. His 35-year-old son, also overweight, had been there too, telling himself that he must be strong, but Rialet said he was a son also and that it would be OK to cry.

The wife left the room with the corpse in it and went outside, but Rialet said she never feared dead bodies. I had only seen a corpse in the distance after an accident. Rialet said it was important to touch them or the image might linger. She said if you did this you realised, as she had with her dad, that there was no-one left. When she brought home the sheet to wash, at one point she buried her face in it – she *really* wasn't squeamish. Later, as I found Southern African women would do, she went into a *recitatif* about her nature. She was, she said, very sensitive, but you would never know, she would never show it. Growing up on a Boer farm with brothers had made her that way. She liked her space, abhorred social kissing, and so on. When we talked about their moving she dismissed the accumulation of furniture, books, etc with a wave of her hand. She said she could leave it all tomorrow. Rialet might have been a little odd, but I liked her immensely.

Mike would usually be last home, though some days he would drop back at lunchtime too. He was always booming with energy and enthusiasm, one time leaping on his M20 special and roaring off to town to see if there was a queue at the hairdressers and if not, get a haircut – "only the trouble is, I've got a deaf barber so he can't hear what I want, and I can't see what he's

doing." It was often hard to remember Mike's condition, till he held a book
or his cell phone right up to his face to peer at it. I proof-read that month's
club newsletter for him.

One evening he came back with big news. Prompted by a colleague who,
like him, had joined Sentech, the radio/TV mast company, 40 years before,
Mike decided to put in for early retirement. The reason was his progressively
deteriorating eyesight. He had said to Rialet already that he was convinced if
he tried to work out his remaining three years he would kill himself, or
someone else, in an accident – the other day he had narrowly missed two
guys by the side of the road. It was the change from light to shade that was
the worst. Recently he had walked out of a dark interior to read a number-
plate, and for 30 seconds the plate had been a blank to him. He seemed
relieved to have made a decision; and if all went well he would be out within
five months, on three-quarter's salary for the three years, and then a full
pension. We had talked it over that evening, drinking the customary endless
cups of tea.

As the second week began, on the Monday we got a lucky break; another
Kickstarter, Dennis Hibberd, had heard about the Ariel's problems. He too
once owned an NH350, though he had soon got rid of it ("too gutless"),
along with all its spares, with a solitary exception – a 23-tooth engine
sprocket – exactly what we were after; the existing one, at 20-tooth, was
just one tooth up from sidecar gearing. Dennis let us have it for £16. And
since it was a Bank Holiday in the UK, I could ring my step-brother briefly
and cancel the order with the specialist firm, saving £100 or so. That
evening, in my absence since Mike was away, Roy and Stewart had managed
to prise off the lower, crankshaft-mounted timing gear – and found that its
Woodruff key and the keyway were undamaged. Stewart was now able to
get the valve timing fairly close to what it should have been, using a timing
disc on the valves themselves.

It was the major breakthrough. But it left the timing marks two dots off
to the right, and there was only one plausible explanation left: that part of
the crankshaft, the heart of the engine, was out of whack. Specifically, the
crankpin on the timing (right) side was incorrectly fitted into the flywheel.
Mike believed that after some catastrophic failure in the past, the key in the
crankpin had sheared and the shaft had 'welded' itself fast.

Still, the valve timing was done, though that did not mean we were home free. On the Tuesday, I borrowed Rialet's car and at 8.30pm drove to Roy's. I chewed things over with him, the bike on the bench, with much of its innards in kit form. Successful reassembly was not a foregone conclusion. When Stewart arrived, he set about removing the larger of the two primary drive sprockets by hand, in order to remove the chain so that we could fit the necessary longer chain when the new, bigger sprocket was put in the following day. Stewart, sitting close to the work on an old chair, just noticed something tiny dropping into the big oil-stained tray beneath the bike. It was some of the miniscule, un-caged rollers from the sprocket's bearing. He appeared to retrieve them all.

Later we attempted to come to a decision about the crankshaft end-float. We rang Richard Hoyt, the sympathetic Ariel expert from Barrytown, and while I fretted internally, Stewart had a comfortable half-hour conversation with him, laughing at the state of the bike, and at me, chuckling, "He's looking a little despondent now." They agreed that the crankcases should be split and spacers inserted to correct the end-float. Afterwards, we three sat on the rough chairs drinking Rooibos tea and gently probing possibilities. If Roy, Mike and I got the engine out, Stewart would try to do the business. But his Milligan Rally started in just over a week's time, and Roy too was off with a mate on their BMWs to Cape Town around then. And I quailed at the thought of totally dismantling the engine, and of what we might find. Driving away preoccupied, I somehow got lost retracing my steps over the three or four blocks to Mike's house, but luckily encountered Stewart who led me back.

The next day Roy drove us to Port Elizabeth's industrial area to get the necessary longer primary chain, taking the old one with us. The area was business-like and rough, and so were the roads: we had the chain place's address, but it still proved hard to locate. Once there, I was heartened to see a faded "Renolds" sign over the workshop window, that being the pukka make of chain as originally used by British bikes. Roy schmoozed the friendly Coloured guy behind the counter, saying he had run with the guy's boss (literally – Roy had been a serious runner, doing ten miles a day regularly, until he'd had a back operation). The guy had also known Mike and been very helpful over the cable-greasing machine. He did as Roy asked and secured three extra links on the existing chain, which they determined was still serviceable, while removing the second spring link, and he did not charge us – a better result than having to buy a new chain. And Roy was consistently good company.

With movement in prospect, I got Roy to stop at the bank on Cape Street and changed $1,000, secreting the fat wad of cash in the zipped pockets of my Rohan trousers. The only blank we drew was with Roy's Alfa Romeo friend who didn't have any of the little valve stem caps that Mike had fired across the garage, the Ariel's allegedly being the same as a 116's. Finally we swung by Tony Connolly's to retrieve the holding-down straps that Melville Price had lent me for the bakkie-journey down. Tony, like Roy, reckoned we should bolt the bike together and chance the end-float; the potential damage to the con rod, and presumably the main bearings, should be gradual, especially because I would not be thrashing the bike. I had pretty much decided that, so that evening rang Stewart and told him. "O-kay," he said, several times. Mike believed that Stewart wanted with all his engineer's heart to take the engine apart and really sort it, but like the rest of us realised that we just didn't have the time.

Later I drove with Rialet to the airport and picked up the returning Mike, who my ultra-sensitive antennae read as slightly less warm and, as was I, eager for me to be off. He certainly felt the same as Roy and Tony, that we should chance the end-float and go for it. But we had a nice evening. They felt we should have drinks and a *braai* to thank everyone who had helped me. I agreed, as long as they would let me buy the food and booze. Mike also unlocked 20 e-mails for me, including nice friendly ones from Molly and Rosie, plus an excellent photo of Rose show-jumping on her horse Rocky. There were also mails from my best pals, a rich harvest, and timely, as the following evening Mike would temporarily disable the computer while fiddling with the hard drives. He got it going again the next day, leaving it sat on its side on the table, its space-filled innards, circuit boards and little whine-whirring fan exposed. The great enabler.

The following morning we were expecting a visitor who didn't show, so after lunch, on impulse, Rialet drove me down to Missionvale, the shanty-town slums where she worked as a social worker. We went past the modest but clean houses of Algoa Park. Rialet said that in the past the flats there had been deliberately filled with poor whites as a buffer between the ghetto and the better parts of town. After that the road was lined with high wire fences, festooned with "South Africa's Flower", shredded fluttering plastic bags. And then we bumped off the road onto the rough ground of the township. I was apprehensive. Rialet, who down there everyone called "lay-dee", had told me about trouble times when the tyres were stacked and burning and she had to talk/charm her way through, "can you just let me out please, I'm late…" We saw one bust in progress, but there was little overt feeling of menace, just a dull lethargy, like a grey wash over a watercolour. As Rialet had said, there were white people as well as black and brown moving slowly about; a black woman stared at us from the stable-type door of her tin one-room shack. Mud tracks, no trees for shade, the odd sheep and goat wandering, and unexpectedly nice-looking dogs. A picket fence you could step over separated the dwellings from the cemetery, which covered several acres. Over the past few years, thanks mainly to HIV, Rialet had seen it grow and fill. She showed me the modest little office where she worked, next to a soup kitchen started and run by a local resident lady, where you had to bring something – anything, old cans, bottles – to qualify for food, a tiny beginning of self-reliance to counter the hand-out culture.

Yet across the road there was a fairly new hospital and, further on, smart university extension buildings, and at the bus stops, gaggles of home-going school children in clean uniforms. Not too far off was a high-rise block of flats for the police, who Rialet said suffered a high casualty rate. She added ruefully that she was afraid the condition of the building had deteriorated since the police had become predominantly black/Coloured. I sat stunned as we drove home. The drive took less than 15 minutes.

Chapter 18

READY FOR THE OFF

Much of Friday was spent driving around with Mike, collecting the big cast-iron cooking vessel from a friend, traditionally a *voortye* with tripod legs, for *Potjie* stew, and the mutton which it required from a particular butcher, and presents for Roy and Stewart, which Mike suggested, gently making sure I did the right thing. At a giant MAKRO store we got an angle grinder for Roy and a voucher for Stewart: it could have been five times as much and still wouldn't have covered the value of what they did for me.

We then spent Saturday getting ready for the party, cleaning the house and preparing the food. Mike sat with the borrowed pot balanced precariously on two rods over a banked-down fire in the *braai*-pit, nipping at brandy and coke, but there were no foul-ups, and he also made bread in a second pot. I was well impressed. The secrets to a winning *Potjie* were: browning the meat, removing the onions early on and only putting them back in the final minutes of cooking and, an hour before it was ready, putting in half a sweet potato with the veg, to thicken the mix in a natural way. The result was truly delicious, probably the best (white-cooked) food I would eat in Africa.

Eleven people came, including the Barlows. Tony B looked piratical, with an eye-patch and a bloodshot eye beneath: it was just three days after he'd had an eye operation and he couldn't drive yet. It struck me, not for the first time, that where travelling before used to involve new music, romantic encounters and riveting gossip, now it was more likely to feature ailments, and problems with children and elderly parents. This cropped up again later. Tony Connolly was there with his wife Frankie, and at one point, expanding on the fact that I didn't *seem* like a biker, she told me that I had "a voice like a vicar". Mike too had written down something of the same in the club mag, describing me as a "fine English gentleman" with a "quiet unassuming personality".

But wasn't I the guy who had once walked backwards down the table-top at a Dordogne village rugby club dinner with a bottle of wine in each hand, pouring it over the seated guests, while a determined attempt to de-bag me led the Chief of Police's wife to cover the eyes of the Mayor's wife, crying "Don't look! Don't look!" Hadn't I fist-fought a paratrooper in a pub car park, and won? Ridden my Norton Commando on acid? Made love to three separate women in one 24-hour period? Well, yes – but the Sixties were a long time ago now, and like the De Niro gangster character Noodles, at the end of the movie *Once Upon a Time in America*, for the past 15 years I had "gone to bed early". In the ourselves-as-others-see-us stakes, I preferred Bruce Kirby's description of me in the Cape Town TOC's mag, as "the courageous crackpot" – in all correspondence after that I signed myself as "Captain Crackpot". The courageous bit was clearly off the mark. At the party and elsewhere, more than one person told me they thought I was "very brave", when you could practically see the bubble above their heads reading "Thinks: very stupid".

Afterwards I would make the mistake of complaining to Mike about Frankie Connolly saying I talked like a vicar, and had to back-track hurriedly as I recalled, too late, that Mike's brother and father were Anglican men of the cloth. His father built his own churches and taught himself Land Rover mechanics, to be of more real service to his flock in the Transkei. For all that, the party was excellent, with the gifts presented to Stewart and Roy, and some great laughs around the dining room table, dominated by Tony B. However, I had been assuming I would be back on the road the following Monday – Rialet had noted a little ruefully that "now he has a bounce in his walk" – but during the evening I heard about some final complications with the bike which would delay the off for another couple of days.

On Monday evening we were all back at Roy's garage. While I was absent, much had gone on. Stewart had timed up the valves, fitted the new engine sprocket and reassembled the casings, using the gasket set from my spares. Good: something had come in useful. Roy had made up a more solid bracket for the horn; they had found that all the nuts which held the cylinder to the crankcase had been loose, so there were worries about stripped threads, and no available spanner properly fitted them. In addition they found one of the exhaust rocker cover bolt heads was a different size from the others. Also, to try to make the infernal exhaust valve lifter operate correctly, Tony Connolly had shortened the cable's casing where he should have shortened the cable itself; to redress this, Mike was cutting a groove into the cable's adjuster and putting in a spacer. That made me very nervous, because one wrong move could mean I would be starting an engine, now with full compression, without benefit of the valve lifter – lifting which was also the only way to stop the motor.

With nothing for me to do, I paced about, surplus to requirement. Mike, tasked with setting the tappets, had discovered that the exhaust valve rocker shaft was longer than the inlet one, and believed that was the reason why the exhaust rocker was not freeing up properly. With Stewart only available in the evenings, this could have delayed departure yet another day, but Mike decided to take the next day off work, cut the hardened spindle to length himself and, after reassembly, go with me on a test run for Jerry.

Meanwhile I had been looking at a period *Motor Cycle* in-depth description of the 1954 Ariel VH engine, which Darryll Moresby-White had supplied along with the workshop manual. It included one of their incredibly detailed and accurate exploded line drawings of the engine and its internals. When Mike came to study this he suddenly realised, as did Stewart, that if, as we believed, the timing side crankpin was misaligned (which was the probable cause of the valve problem), then the oil passage in it to the vital big-end bearing was likely to have been cut off, or at least reduced. It was one of those moments: we all sat down and considered, hard. The fact was, as with the crankshaft end-float, that I and the bike had got this far. So oil must have been getting to the bearings somehow. There were engines, like the mighty Panther, which relied on simply oil-splash and mist for cylinder lubrication. Mike speculated that maybe just the overflow of oil from the cam chamber passage was enough. It explained why the oil tank had always remained cool and the engine oil clean, even after hard work – only a fraction of its contents had been circulating as it should.

It was after 11pm and we went home to sleep on this. There was really no selection – I had been in Africa for a month now, and I had to get going and take a chance. I would just have to ride from then on with the Damocles' sword of big-end failure hanging over the enterprise.

Bright and early next morning Mike got the exhaust rocker spindle in his lathe and ground off part of the collar section with an angle-grinder. By 11am the Ariel was fully reassembled, wheeled back down the ramp, and I kicked it into life. And, miraculously, like the fine weather that day, all was well. With Roy on his BMW and Mike on the M20 bitza, we rode to the sea. It was glorious, after two weeks of confinement in the city, to turn right at a country T-junction and finally see and smell the ocean. We ran along the coast, past the mouth of the Maitland River, with sand and spray and golden light ahead.

I was not entirely comfortable with the bike's front-end handling, which at first I attributed to Roy having put too much air in the tyre (it wasn't – the steering damper had just been tightened down a touch too much). But there was no denying that the bike was transformed, pulling properly now and, with the taller gearing, keeping up with Roy's big twin, cruising at 50-plus. "Going like a Boeing", as Mike put it. There was only one moment, when we had stopped on a down-slope, overlooking the ocean, and lazily I rolled downhill and bump-started the engine, producing a horrid metallic clank from the bottom end, which I guessed was down to the crankshaft end-float. This would reoccur, occasionally, when kick-starting. Mike had his camera and was snapping away one-handed on the move, which yielded at least one brilliantly impressionistic picture of Roy and me riding towards an ocean that seemed to be sweeping up over the land.

Eventually we turned inland and ended up sitting outside at a place called Eliphant's Walk for lunch. Other bikers turned up, including Willem Pelliboer on a G12 Matchless, who had reportedly had some problems on the Sunday run a fortnight previously. Mike and Roy latched on to him. This was a time of transition for the Kickstart mob as well, since both Mike and Tony B were stepping down. So now they sounded out Willem about taking on the role of Captain. He was not unwilling.

We rode back to Roy's and made final adjustments to the Ariel. Then at Mike's it was time to pack, and enjoy a last supper. It was a relief not to have to wait another day, but I drank beers, wine and brandy to help keep the nerves at bay. Mike said grace for the last time. He asked for "Travelling mercies for Steve and Jerry". The phrase would stay with me. The evening was somewhat disrupted by Roy arriving and making himself at home, and then Stewart dropping in. We were all off shortly, Stewart to the Milligan, and Roy on the BMW for a long weekend in Cape Town, and if their presence meant no final moments of intimacy for me to express my thanks to Mike and Rialet for their unbounded hospitality, at least we could celebrate the comradeship of the rebuild. I made a last phone call to Molly, who gave me the unwelcome news that our beloved black Labrador Zoe was not well. I e-mailed to Rosie the picture Mike had taken of us riding by the ocean, and then had to sit up until midnight as he kindly, obsessively, put a picture label on the second photo CD which he would post, with others, to the UK (I had left the money). Rialet was standing in the doorway of the study making jokes.

I was up at 6.20 the next morning for a bath, before Mike cooked an egg and bacon breakfast. I was on the edge of emotional when we finally said goodbye. Rialet left for work first, Mike would have stayed but had a work appointment, though he said he would try and get back. On my own I was feeling pretty doomy but kept busy sending a last few e-mails and persuading my big bag, minus the sleeping bag which I had now secured separately under the rack, into the Pacsafe. Then I pushed the bike outside the gates, posted the keys back, fired up and set off, with Mynka barking me on my way. My start mileage was 1,661.

Further on I thought I saw Mike's car passing in the opposite direction but didn't stop. I was rolling. About 2,500 miles to South Luangwa – nothing to it. The date was 3 June.

It was a cold morning, overcast, and windy from the north once I got on the N2 coast road again. I rode along, numb with foreboding. This lasted until the N10 turn, left to Cradock and the north. A mile beyond it, the Ariel's engine died.

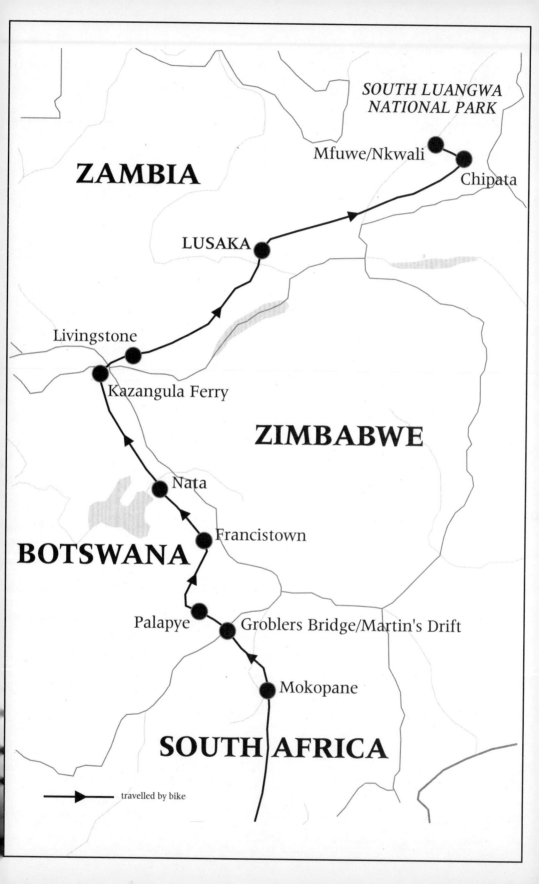

SOUTH LUANGWA
NATIONAL PARK

ZAMBIA

Mfuwe/Nkwali

Chipata

LUSAKA

Livingstone

Kazangula Ferry

ZIMBABWE

Nata

Francistown

BOTSWANA

Palapye

Groblers Bridge/Martin's Drift

Mokopane

SOUTH AFRICA

travelled by bike

PART FOUR

PORT ELIZABETH – ZAMBIA

"All that road going, and all the people dreaming of
the immensity of it … The road is life."
Jack Kerouac, *On the Road*

"Where better to be than on the road to test day by day the assertion
that the hardest thing in life is to remain constantly attendant, especially
since it gets harder to do the further along you go?"
Charles Frazier, *Thirteen Moons*

Chapter 19

PRESSING ON

That cold morning, it seemed like the end of everything. I began rehearsing failure; the biggest worry, apart from being a laughing stock, was paying back the publisher's advance. I checked the oil and petrol, then kicked the bike over three or four times and it re-started. I decided to check the spark plug – and found the plug cap on at a funny angle, and the plug itself only screwed in loosely. Phew! I changed the plug for a new one, pushed the cap on firmly and, although it took several kicks to start, we were rolling again. I half expected another halt, but made it to the gas station at Paterson, had a coffee and a monster muffin, and then needed to kick several times under the eyes of a group of schoolgirls before Jerry condescended to start.

We bashed on, the winding mountain roads OK, the straights monotonous – I was going to have to think of ways to pass the time. The bike was willing enough, but backfired pulling into the Cookhouse petrol station, as it had starting out. I would try another change of plug. It took just 3.6 litres – we were averaging about 70 miles to the gallon. There was some oil blown back from the rockerboxes, but way better than the last time.

I carried on to Cradock, arriving in the early afternoon, and found a nice B&B in the same antique-looking street as the hotel I'd stayed at last time but half the price, and with parking in its compound. Normally I would try to cover around 200 miles a day, and start looking for somewhere to stay about 4pm, as the sun went down quickly at around 5.30. The ample landlady wanted to know all about the trip; in the end she said she would pray for me, and I was unironically happy to hear it. I needed all the help I could get. Several people in Port Elizabeth had said the same, and exposure to the vast landscape again convinced me that living here required some spiritual acknowledgement.

The landlady knew Darney Gerber, who I'd phoned from PE with a view to doing an article on his collection for the car mag. He arrived outside in a 4x4 and took me back to walk me through his classic cars ("I can give you an hour"). He was a short, no-nonsense businessman in his sixties with no time for negative attitudes. "Do you see anyone outside here with a machete or a machine gun? No. As soon as I get to semi-retirement, my wife and I plan to drive as much as possible through Africa, we love it." He, like Stewart Fergusson, was about to compete in the Continental Milligan Vintage Trial; he chose a different car to enter each year, which was one way to keep his collection well-fettled. This year it was to be a '38 Ford V8 Super, Bonnie and Clyde's conveyance of choice, its side-valve engine rebuilt with piston rings from a 2R Toyota. He had period bakkies, British classics and Yank tanks from the Twenties to the Fifties, including that 1948 Hudson 6. He said bluntly that American cars and trucks had sold well in South Africa "because the British ones were very flimsy for our conditions". But the cream of his crop was a long-bonneted, beautifully flowing Thirties British drophead coupé, a car I had never heard of, a 1935 Railton. "Reid Railton used the mechanicals from a straight-8 Hudson to try and beat the Bentleys, because he reckoned the Hudsons were faster. This one, done by the coachbuilders Carbodies, has an all-aluminium body bar the steel running-boards. It was definitely intended for racing. It's the only one of its kind in South Africa. I found it in Port Alfred at the back of a garage full of car spares and swapped it for a 1935 Alvis. The restoration took three years."

After Darney dropped me off, I ate early at the same steakhouse as before – as much as anything because I needed a drink. Back at my digs, though a hot shower and en-suite loo were included, sound-proofing was not. The African in the next room made phone calls all evening, then at 6.30am put on a charismatic Christian radio station. I was awake, though I had slept for six-and-a-half hours straight; the 180-mile ride had been tiring. At 7am my neighbour prayed loudly for ten minutes, and then sang a bit. I think he was travelling for one of the churches. Well, I'd prayed myself the day before.

I changed the Ariel's plug again, and taped round the edge of the rubber connector to the air filter, which seemed to help with the back-firing. After an hour's anxiety and dread, packing up and preparing, I hit the road north again, not the main N10 but a cut-through to Hofmeyr and then Burgersdorp. Tony Barlow had printed off a route he had worked out for me all the way to the border, avoiding motorways and cities; I used this as a basis, since he had taken the trouble to indicate towns where there were definitely places to stay – up towards Lesotho there were quite long gaps between these. In the event I would only book ahead once, and things worked out fine.

The country just outside Cradock was a really good valley, which raised hopes of more varied landscapes, but soon we were back on the long straights and stunned again by the distances, as well as uncomfortably strong side winds. Still, the sunshine was good, and the Ariel thumped along (actually it only thumped on uphill sections; otherwise it was more tocks and rattles). The speedo told me that performance fell off as the day wore on. One diversion, as on the previous day, was the number of monkeys running across the road, which hadn't happened on the previous abortive trip – was it the season, or the weather? In the paddocks by the roads there were now huge termite mounds, which more than once I took to be the humped backs of animals.

I stopped for lunch in the little town of Burgersdorp. I'd parked outside a garage intending to buy a pie, but two beefy Afrikaner hunters came over, checked out the bike, and told me there was a better place just up the road. This was the Hagenhuis coffee shop. I parked beside the hunters' bakkie, in the shade of several tall trees opposite. Suddenly the wind dislodged a cascade of yellow autumnal leaves and I stood quietly among the falling shower, a magic moment. Inside was a lovely bohemian atmosphere with a well-considered antique layout, nice things for sale, just excellent coffee and delicious savoury pancakes, one tuna, one ham. "Better than a pie, eh?" said one of the hunters as they left. It was a shame that I over-did the praising of the place to the staff, and saw the owner lady turning off. But the few oases like this meant disproportionately much in the midst of the physical and cultural wilderness.

I pushed on north. I had filled up, topped up the oil and checked the bike over after lunch, noticing it was giving too much oil from the cylinder head and tightening down there: some had reached the rear tyre, which you don't want. Later, accelerating from a stop, the speedo needle suddenly bounced round to 120mph, then settled back again. After the stop I had wiped petrol from the top of the tank; it was back again when I next stopped – was this a split in the tank? If so, the Ariel boys had recommended sealing it by rubbing soap in, and I had a bit ready in the tank bag. But luckily it was just imperfect sealing from the petrol cap, again.

Early in the afternoon, I reached my intended stop of Aliwal North, where a metal bridge takes you into the Orange Free State, but I didn't like the look of the place so I pushed on the 40-odd miles to Rouxville and Zastron. One thing I had noticed all day was how good (and traffic-free) the roads were. Along the way there were maintenance crews, litter pickers, verge cutters, a couple of roadworks. Now, beyond Rouxville, there were signs warning of pot-holes, but these had usually been temporarily filled in with yellow dirt and rubble, which at least made them easily visible, and avoidable by a bike. Overall they were *nothing* compared to the state of the roads in Oxfordshire.

I took the turning off to Zastron, a long town in a valley with the air of a holiday place out of season. There was nowhere obvious to stay, but signs for a place off to one side. So I asked directions in a shop and rode up there, the last couple of hundred yards on a dirt road that steepened as it went towards some strikingly beautiful mountainous bluffs.

In the extensive holiday complex, eventually a girl came slowly to the desk, looking at me in surprise. It really was off-season. I was the only guest, but they rented me a chalet in a block a couple of hundred yards from the main building, beneath the bluffs, and the girl managed to get the water in the chalet turned on, though the system remained temperamental. But there was tea- and coffee-making stuff, with biscuits that included a packet of *boerebeskuit*, which I pocketed for future use. I rode the bike onto the nearest hard-standing, and then at 6pm, after night had fallen, walked back down into town. The last thing you want to be doing after a day in the saddle is to kit up again and ride in the dark, and then do it in reverse after a few drinks.

But – African night! Carrying a fat wallet! So I belligerently pocketed... a penknife. I used to travel with a switchblade, but wiser voices from the knife culture of Argentina had long ago convinced me that getting into it with someone who knew what they were about with a blade was nothing but an invitation to rearrange one's facial features or worse. Still, anything can feel better than nothing. I had a friend who discouraged some Sicilians' amorous advances on his girlfriend for hours with just a blunt-ended fruit knife – and my Mauser Swiss Army knife also boasted a very serviceable bottle opener. It was a long walk down, but the street lights soon began, and everything was tranquil except for the barking guard dogs, doing their job.

Nel's Restaurant, which I had spotted earlier, proved to be a delightful catch-all: a bar and takeaway, with a few nice tables for eating in. Outside, a Boer with a Sonny Bono haircut talking with mates hailed me as "Oum" ("Uncle") and said a few words of Afrikaans. The incomprehension was mutual but polite. Inside, the young blonde landlady (Nel?) was very friendly, and I sat at the bar and had a couple of beers, enjoying the background music. On the well-stocked shelves was a liqueur called "Fokol", which was up there with the name for Boer moonshine, "Witblits". The Boer drinkers ignored me, so I chatted to the only other guy in there, after initial apprehension as he was wearing earrings and drinking cider, which I read was considered by some to be sissy. But he was OK, just a young black taxi-driver waiting for his takeaway, whose dad regularly drove a meat truck to Zimbabwe, a journey he said took 13 days each way.

My meal – sole, chips, vegetables, and white wine – was good, and then I staggered happily up the hill. Nel's had been another oasis. Later Mike Wood phoned to see how I was doing, and I talked to Rialet. The most amusing news, though not for him, was that Roy Cartvel's big BMW had developed a fault, shortly after he had set out for Cape Town, and he'd had to abort. Should have done it on an Ariel?

But it was a peculiar night after that. I woke at 1.15am. There were noises, pipes contracting, a thump on the roof. I began to consider my situation, alone in the hut block, not knowing if the other two doors into my section could be unlocked. I put the light on but must have gone back to sleep. Normally the vivid dreams and reveries that travel often unleashes are a bonus. This time I woke again at 3.15am, mildly horny, and thought lazily about a girl back home.

I think I drifted off again, because when I was conscious once more, I found myself thinking deeply and in detail, as I rarely do now, about my mother's death and the anguish of it, and more particularly how, as a typical disorganised first-year student, I had missed the train I should have taken from Oxford to London and been late arriving to see her at hospital. This meant that it had not been as she had planned, so that she could maximise her dwindling resources of strength for us to talk properly. It had been the second last time I would see her, and there had been other derelictions. She had been younger than I was now, it was all nearly fifty years ago, but I craved, and still crave, forgiveness.

Next day maybe some of that lingered, because the first 40-odd miles, to Wepener, were utterly miserable, despite bright sun having burnt off the frost on the grass and the bike, which Mike had warned me to expect. The bike had had no compression when I started it, and on the road, deep vibration was back at an indicated 50, with permanent low-level shakes at the 45mph I was cruising at. My right thumb was still sore from the tumble outside Mike's. As the flat miles unreeled, the question was once again, could I do this?

But after a petrol stop, a cold drink and a chat with a tattered guy in a little truck down from Lesotho, things picked up. So what, I thought, if it's 45mph – that was actually about right for the pot-holed two-lane blacktop. We were running well with adequate power through this magic (if monotonous) landscape. After around 75 miles I turned off the road to drive into Ladybrand, a busy little town, and ate a rubbish lunch in a Chicken Frango, but it was good to take a break. Then it was back on the R26, as Tony's route recommended, which ran along the curving north-west border of Lesotho. Ever since leaving Cradock I had been anticipating with each lot of distant blue mountains spotted, the towering flanks of "the mythical mountain fastness of Lesotho", as I had played it ironically in my head. In fact the independent Lesotho had only come into being as a refuge from attacks by land-hungry Zulus and whites, and by 2010 was so poor that it was asking to become incorporated into South Africa. Beyond Ladybrand, I finally got a sight of the real mountains, and they were worth the wait.

After another 40 miles or so to Fouriesburg, I turned off the R26 and headed for my destination, Clarens, an arts and craft centre in a beautiful setting, about which I had read good things. The only downside was that it was now Friday, and reportedly the town got totally full over the weekends with project workers down from Lesotho itself. So for once I had phoned ahead. All the local tourist board could offer was the relatively expensive Maluti Mountain Lodge, so that was where I was headed. And the 20-mile ride from Fouriesburg was the best so far. The road had curves, and soon there were the fantastic red and ochre Lesotho mountains and valleys off to the right. I stopped to take pictures at a picnic place opposite a sign for the

"Surrender Hill" trail. In the Anglo-Boer war, Fouriesburg had ended up in 1900 as capital of the Orange Free State, and the Hill was where in 1902 they had signed the treaty surrendering their independence.

It had been a short day's ride, only about 140 miles, and we had made good time so it was still only 3pm. We rode on, past a rock outcrop shaped like a sphinx. The outskirts of Clarens initially disappointed, being another mini-township/shanty town. I took the second turning off the main road and we drove uphill along a tree-lined avenue, past galleries and coffee bars. At the top was a substantial square of grass, with a self-conscious "pub" on the corner, where a rank of Harleys were already parked up. I rode around and stopped to get gas, buy postcards (quaint, I know, in the age of e-mail), and get directions. A white guy admiring the bike obliged, and I rode back down the hill, further along the main road again, and there was the big, almost Alpine hotel off on the left.

I was about the only visible punter so far. There was a split-cane shelter for vehicles, so I parked up and went inside to check in with a garrulous young white guy with Harpo Marx hair. He took me to a row of rooms behind the main building, with glass fronts and sliding doors. Not too bad – there was a bath – though the TV had been ripped out, and later I saw an "AUCTION" sign from the previous month outside. The place had just changed hands.

I was tired. It was a little further from the centre of town than I had hoped, maybe a mile and a bit's walk on a dirt road running parallel to the main one, where there were also several "FOR SALE" signs, and I got dusted by 4x4s in the process, before turning back onto the road up the hill. I wandered around in the dusk – there were some nice-looking shops but they were closed, and some of the restaurants seemed to be too. I went into one which the *Rough Guide* had said offered 107 different kinds of beer. But they were not in evidence, and the place was tepid, with just a smattering of loud white customers, so I had a beer and left. After another check around I gravitated towards the eatery on a corner of the square called The Highlander, where there seemed to be a bit of life.

And how! Inside I was early enough to get seated, by a nice large black lady in a red headscarf, at a table by a half wall dividing the restaurant from the bar. I was not observed but could watch the action as the posh crowd got loud in the bar while a more boho, arty and exuberant mob flooded the dining bit, which was soon packed out. Attention focused on a large birthday party nearer the entrance, with tables pulled together. The birthday girl, judging by frequent impassioned girl-on-girl hugs, in between standing on a chair and eventually dancing on the table, was a lesbian or, to borrow from Raymond Chandler, would have been "if they could have just got her quieted down a little".

Then, as I sank a couple of beers, the Harley bikers came in. Their party included a massive black gent in full leathers and a leather cap who sat down with the only other visible outsiders except me, a slightly nervous Indian family with whom he chatted away expansively till his table was ready. My food when it came was outstanding: a Natal curry, served in black iron dishes with all the chutney/bananas/coconut trimmings. It was a riotous evening by proxy – just what I needed.

After ice-cream and coffee, I walked home in the dark, being rung on the cell phone by Mike as I reached the bottom of the hill and turned onto the dark track. "They'll kill you for your phone", I'd been told, but was past caring. Mike quite properly brushed aside my incipient whingeing about vibration and diminishing speeds, emphasising the positive: the Ariel had got me nearly 600 miles further north, and I was in good heart. I kept the call brief as I stumbled along since I was becoming uncomfortably aware of the urge for the loo (the curry?) but, despite at the last minute being waylaid by Harpo, I made it.

Next day was the most beautiful morning so far, and at breakfast the hotel really came good. The panoramic windows of the dining room, which was near-deserted bar one surly young Boer with bruises at the side of both his eyes, and his foxy companion, gave the sweep of view of the Lesotho rampart mountains to the east, a solid, low, grey-brown range, with one hill further on coming to a peak. Clarens was quite a spot, and there were also the hills of the Golden Gate National Park, where I was headed. When I had looked out at 7am it had been cloudy and I'd recalled a comment overheard the night before, that it could snow shortly nearby. But now, with the mist burned off, the sky was pure blue.

Chapter 20

BOEREBESKUITS
AT BETHAL

I did a little bike maintenance, including adding a pint of oil and tightening the front brake one click of the adjuster, and I was glad of that in the Golden Gate National Park. I rode there and had my name taken by a stern black lady warden at the entry. The Park consisted of a wilderness of very, very beautiful sandstone bluffs and rock formations, though at the start there were quite a few camps/lodges, and some tiresome speed bumps through canyons and round hairpins, plus a 30mph speed limit, which two cars in front more than obeyed. Once they had stopped, the bendy roads through the sandstone valleys were most welcome after days of pretty much nothing but straights. On the map I had seen there was a short cut north to Kestell, but when I got to the turn-off it was a dirt road and steep and so, with the fully laden bike, I decided against it.

Exiting the Park with regret, it was immediately back to South African reality, ie interminably long, straight, switchback roads for 15 miles north to Kestell, with bad side winds from the east just to keep things interesting. The bike was going well, though the speedo said not, and by the end of the day it would have packed up entirely. Thank God the mileometer still worked, it was what kept me going, cutting things into little increments, how far to the next stop and so on; as well as letting me calculate when fuel was running low, though luckily I had a range of 250+ miles from my four-gallon tank.

After a petrol stop and checking the map, there were 40 more miles of endless switchback, running through fields of mealie corn, to my turn-off for Warden. I was taking A-roads north rather than the N3 Highvelt toll route, so as to miss the heavy trucks and swing well to the east of Johannesburg, which by reputation was Crim Central with traffic to match. Warden was a country town with lumpy roads, and I followed signs to "On

The Move Pizza" which seemed to be a mostly black truck stop with very loud patrons, but run by a washed-out young white girl, and the pizzas were made fresh in a brick oven. I needed to rest my weary backside, and sitting outside in the wind and dust till the grub was ready allowed me to enjoy the passing scene. Two laughing boys riding a white horse, tractors with trailers filled up with smiling excited folk – some were field labourers, some just hitching a ride. The pizza was OK but the crusts were too thick, so I gave the last quarter to an older black guy sitting opposite me who was discontented with his meal, and agreed to give pizza a try.

Then I carried on, with the wind intermittently bad and the sky clouding and clearing, slogging all afternoon through 80 miles of arable fields through Vrede to Standerton, where there were plenty of signs for B&Bs. But I had only done 170 miles. It was 4 o'clock, so I gassed up and asked the young Eddie Murphy-like attendant which was the road out to the next town, Bethal. The guy couldn't understand where I was talking about (not uncommon), so I showed him on the map, and he said "Ah! Beth-AL! You got to use all your mouth when you say it."

It soon seemed like Beth-AL might be a bridge too far. It was another 40 miles, the sun was going down on my left and mist was gathering. I was reluctant to put my lights on (an old bike reflex – dynamos usually had a problem putting out enough charge to sustain main beam headlights/brake lights etc for very long), but I did stop and fix my wonky bar-end mirror with an Allen key, and thus justified the presence of the set of keys in the tank bag. Things got worse. I was weary when I reached Bethal, which was set in coal mining country and not elegant, but above all displayed no signs of accommodation at all. It was after 5pm by the time I had driven through the place. The light was fading fast and the next possibility was Middelburg, 50 miles further on – and I *really* didn't want to drive at night. I stopped by the last petrol station to check the map, and looked up and spotted a solitary B&B plaque up on a lamp-post. I rang, and a lady gave me directions, easy because of the grid layout of the town. *Big* relief.

A bearded, paunchy guy was waiting at the gates and saw me in. His parked car had a marijuana bush sticker on it, and he told me he was sorry that there would be no breakfast as his wife wasn't feeling well (funny, she'd sounded OK on the phone). The room was basic and cell-like, and festooned with hand-written notices about what visitors must and must not do. But the bed was OK, and there was a kettle and a bath, and after 210 miles I didn't care. We talked a little about the bike and then, as recommended, I walked back through deserted dark streets to a large Wimpy Bar, another blast from the past – the one in Swindon in the late Fifties had juke box installations on the tables and made us feel extremely cool. Here the black girls serving seemed happy to be in this sterile, brightly-lit environment, as I was that evening, though it was hardly the Real Africa.

Back in the room I had a coffee and a nip of Wellington. With 800 miles covered, two-thirds of the South African leg, I passed the time by doing, for the first time, a proper Botswana/Zambia itinerary with the routes and distances. This was sobering but, with the bike going like it was, did seem possible. When I turned in, it was a cold night, and I was glad of the extra blanket.

I was woken, as my host Chris had warned me, at 5am, by the sound of Bethal's most prominent feature, thousands upon thousands of pigeons which belted out an unbearable chorus that Sunday morning. I bathed and then furtively, with a bag to catch the crumbs, ate – one of the absolute Don'ts – the *boerebeskuits* from Zastron which, with a cup of tea, were very sustaining. The Wimpy didn't open till 9am and I wanted to be off by then. Diabetic pills, malaria tablet, clean glasses, clean visor, pack, and then slip outside for a bit of maintenance. After wiping off a solitary piece of pigeon poo from the saddle – we had been lucky – I put the bike up on its plank so I could spin the rear wheel and lubricate the drive chain, checked the wheels' spoke tension and the tyre pressures, and then loaded up. As I brought the last load out, there was mine host sitting outside smoking a cigarette and reading the papers. Unprompted, he remembered he had offered the previous evening to give me a hand removing the screw-on inspection/filler cap for the primary chaincase, which the PE guys had fastened too tight for me to undo. This chap had trouble too, but eventually his monster screwdriver and my mole grips did the trick. Just as well, as the case was dry. My helper sold me some oil and I topped the case up; the primary chain was already a little loose, but acceptable so far. So the B&B hadn't been too bad after all.

The 50 miles to Middelburg ran through country dominated by coal mines, with the roads gouged by the big trucks, a few of which were even about on a

Sunday. I wasn't feeling too good, which I blamed on the scratch breakfast. At Middelburg I pulled in for petrol, and the tall bearded attendant got chatting. "England, you have a Queen, right? England is a monarchy." I said we were a constitutional monarchy, and that the Queen was only a figurehead. "Why?" I told him that we had had a revolution about 300 years ago to make it so. He was undeterred. "Say hello to the Queen for me," he grinned – but the elevated political conversation was then undermined by Jerry refusing to start for a while.

I cruised Middelburg's main drag and pulled in at another Wimpy. It was still early and there weren't too many customers, but the crew seemed unfocused and a cheeseburger took 25 minutes to materialise. A whole new take on fast food. But the good-looking young black lady manager brought it over herself and chatted, smiling, until she asked, "Are you staying in Middelburg?" and I told her no, I was on my way to Zambia, at which point she walked away. A bat-squeak? My attention was diverted by a stocky, totally confident white guy who had walked out, a semi-automatic pistol stuck high in the right side of his belt, and scrutinised the loaded Ariel minutely. A cop – surely?

The guy in Bethal had said rain was forecast, but as we left town it became hot; we were now in South Africa's northernmost province, Limpopo, and had come down gradually from the Highveld to the lowlands. It was the only day I would feel seriously overdressed in the Cordura jacket. We also now hit the main road north to the border, the N11, which I had thought would be boring, but not so. Before the next town, Groblersdal, there was the Loskop Dam and reservoir off to the left and some good up and down riding, with the Ariel feeling quite spirited.

I went on another 15 miles or so from Groblersdal to Marble Hall, where I stopped, though I wasn't hungry, but just to stop, as it was now seriously hot. At a market I parked in the sunshine where I could have been in the shade, and as I was doing so an older white guy with a Breton face, wearing a large jade crucifix (no atheists etc) came over. He was ex-Rhodesian from Bulawayo, of French extraction on one side, and for the past 15 years had been travelling all over South Africa. Checking out the Ariel, he said his father had told him about Square Fours. In the KFC, I randomly ordered a wrap from a kind patient lady, and guzzled a cold Twist lemon drink, absorbing the market comings and goings (and its noise), feeling frazzled and tired. Across from me, an older black guy in a homburg hat got served a KFC meal that included two whole medium-sized loaves of bread, which he went to work on.

When I came out, a ragged boy trying to sell me oranges said seriously that the Ariel was beautiful. But Jerry, ever-wilful, had not been starting as reliably as usual (the change of altitude?) and now, with our admirer plus four of his mates and a large guy in the next car watching, several kicks brought forth nothing, and some of them had lacked compression – that pesky valve lifter again, I hoped.

The crowd grew. The large guy, and a security man, kindly offered a push, but curiously I was sure that this felt like just a temporary glitch, and kicked on. There was now someone giving a running commentary. This should have been Embarrassment Hell, but somehow it didn't get to me. When the bike finally fired up I gave a (one-handed) *et voilà* gesture and rorted off with as much style as I could muster.

At Roedtan, 30 miles on, I stopped again at a petrol station for yet another cold drink to sip standing in the shade, and a tubby young black guy came up to chat, having clocked the British road tax. He had recently returned from seven years in Surrey, as a hospital porter and DJ, and was just delighted to be back in Africa – "the food!" His sister came over too, and when I asked him, he taught me the handshake/clasp/handshake, which from then on I could really do. After they'd gone, another young black guy asked "wot'll it do?" type of questions. I had adjusted the valve lifter at the engine end as best I could and now, with him and his pals watching as I mounted up to leave, I strictly observed Standard Operating Procedure, turning on the petrol at the last minute, ignition a fraction retarded, find the compression with the valve lifter, invoke Travelling Mercies, and kick – and it started first time.

There were then three tedious sets of roadworks with alternate one-way traffic, where you had to wait in the heat for up to 20 minutes. The road surfaces had got worse that day, but nothing chronic. One thing I had noticed was the way bicycles (*injingas*) would be riding towards you on both sides of the road. The last works were un-manned, so I and a couple of cars just waited till oncoming traffic finished and then went for it. But I had forgotten that while we were waiting, I had prudently switched off the petrol. When the amount in the carburettor ran out, despite flailing for the tap under the tank, the bike died, on the "wrong" side of the road. I re-started frantically under the bemused gaze of a solitary road worker, pushing his lonely barrow in the middle of nowhere.

We slogged on to the last big town before the border, Mokopane (formerly Potgietesreus – the government, as was their right, had started reassigning African names to towns, though this cheesed off the white tribe who had grown up with the colonial names). The going had not been nearly as monotonous – some hills, some bends, some bush. Riding into town I passed a tempting-looking hotel and some B&B signs, but kept on rolling, looking for the bank I hoped would change my traveller's cheques into the dollars I believed I would need for entering Botswana (the internet had advised $125), and beyond that Zambia ($175 US had been mentioned, and I didn't know if I could change money in Botswana). I saw a bank to visit the following morning, then rode on and settled for The Sleep and Go Motel, at the far end of town, a compound with a barrier, surrounded by blocks of rooms, with a solitary cell-like little structure in the middle – my accommodation. It was badly lit, but there was a TV and a shower, the bike was secure and there were no noisy neighbours. The downsides were no breakfast (there was a Wimpy not too far off) and a long walk back into town, with even longer to that bank. But it was a walk that I was going to have to take as I was out of Wellington and had failed to stop at a bottle shop en route, and now was *seriously* in need of a beer.

I ended up walking literally miles, following one bum steer after another. "Go to the Spar", "Go down to the meat market" etc, but Mokopane seemed to be in the grip of Prohibition. As dark came, I was conscious of the wallet, but I had to have a drink. I got more and more frustrated until finally I spotted a drinks chiller with beer behind the counter of a Nando's. I ordered two Amstels ("bring them both now, please") and ate good chicken and rice (the mild version, but it was hot enough). On the long walk home after dark, two ladies crossed the road to my side but didn't accost me, and a couple of genial guys tried to sell me dope (or they might have been selling the girls). The lack of menace called to mind a car which had slid up to the kerb one night in the Melbourne suburb of Saint Kilda, with a guy sticking his head out of the window and enquiring politely, "Would you have any drug requirements this evening, sir?"

Back at the motel, at the desk I bought cold bottled water which was disproportionately wonderful; talked on the cell phone to Mike and Rialet; and then Roy Cartvel rang to say well done. I'd covered about 1,000 miles so far, and the northernmost border crossing at Groblers Bridge/Martin's Drift – chosen to minimise the time in Botswana, which was expensive – was only about 130 miles away. I did some sock-washing and prep for the following day's border crossing (the advice I had been given was to allow half a day for borders), while Zuma, or "Zumpy" as the radio comedians called him, gabbled on the TV, and then the weather forecast said it was going to be wet up this way for the next couple of days.

I rang Ginty Melvill who was drunk, but seemed suitably impressed by my progress, told me the current exchange rate for Zambian kwacha, and how the ferries at Kazangula from Botswana to Zambia ran every half an hour, and advised me to buy a Botswanese SIM card for the phone. He said again that he and some of his club, the Trans-Zambezi Riders, would come out, maybe the 300-odd miles to Livingstone, and ride me into Lusaka. So it was a useful, heartening call. After that I watched the movie *Spider Man* on TV, just about the first "entertainment" for five weeks. Under the circumstances, it felt well weird.

Chapter 21

FIRST BORDER

I was up early, as the motel check-out was at 10am, and I had to do the thing at the bank which didn't open until 9am. After a Wimpy breakfast, I took the long walk into town and hit the bank. Queuing, an elderly Afrikaans speaker behind me said, "Just the two of us, eh?" gesturing at the otherwise black queue and, on hearing I was going to Botswana, declared loudly, "It's good there – not like with this lot here." I collared a bank lady who directed me to another queue around the corner, though there was no indication that it was for a Bureau de Change. She told me to use Window 1 or 3 (of 8).

During ten more minutes of queuing I tried to exercise African patience. When I finally got my turn, at the mention of changing traveller's cheques to dollars, the unsmiling black lady teller got up without a word and disappeared for more than five minutes. She finally returned with a little guy, and they got ready to do the change. I signed the dollar traveller's cheques, but of course they would only give me rand. I called for the manager, a Coloured man, but he wouldn't budge, claiming to have no dollars in the building. I went on a bit, but finally walked away with the signed cheques, a questionable move as, because they had to be countersigned at a bank in front of a witnessing teller, they were now theoretically useless (in fact, at a later bank I would pretend to be signing them, and get away with it). I was more worried about the immediate lack of dollars. The ones I had brought from England would cover the border into Botswana, but what of Zambia? At that point, if there had been a T-shirt for sale reading "MOKOPANE SUCKS" I would have bought it (but not with dollars).

I was cross, but not unduly and, back at the motel, got away by 10.15. But I was probably a bit shook up, and was shortly reminded why I went to the bother of wearing silk inner gloves under my gauntlets, as for once I left them off, knowing I was stopping for petrol, and at the gas station, when I pulled off my right gauntlet, its inner lining was pulled inside-out by my damp hand. I was very awkward with that, with the petrol cap and with getting coins out of my pocket to pay. I apologised to the elderly attendant, who was extremely gracious, saying he was in absolutely no hurry, he had been there since dawn, and he would be there till dark. That gave some perspective, and I calmed down. The glove's errant fingers took five minutes to sort out.

The 130 miles to the border were very monotonous, the weather windy and cloudy. Sometimes birds would fly up at the noise of our exhaust, including hornbills like the herald bird Zazu in *The Lion King*. When I got to Martins Drift, I thought about staying. There were lodges and safari places fairly close, and if it was going to take half a day to get through the border… but Martins Drift was a dusty hole where I ate half a vile roll, brittle from the freezer, for which the security guy still had to cancel my receipt with a pen, in a dusty outside area with a maniacally noisy black family at the next table playing a dice game. However, next to the café, behind a locked gate that only let in one person at a time, beside a large sign reading 'NO GUNS', was a Bureau de Change. There, in a cell-like room, a world-weary but sharp young lady changed rand to the required dollars at a fair rate, and I also got some Botswanese pula. So all that drama in Mokopane had been for nothing. Still: result.

I hit the border. There weren't any queues of trucks; I collected a gate pass, then parked further on, conferring nervously with a couple of other white parties, and entered the elevated Portakabins for passport and vehicle document checks. Behind the mesh above the counter, the border personnel were all black; some were OK, but others seemed more interested in joking about with each other or getting off shift than in seeing to us. I had a good guy for the passport/visa stuff, but was half-way outside again when I remembered (duh!) the *carnet*. For that I drew a young guy who had just arrived and was clearly unfamiliar with the document's multi-layered yellow sheets. An older guy came and explained it to him, and I reinforced this by saying, "That's it, stamp it just there." Possibly a mistake, as when the older guy went off shift, the younger guy shoved the untouched *carnet* back to me, and told me to get it stamped at Kazangula. Tense and confused,

I half-thought this was just up the road, and was outside again before I realised he was talking about the exit border from Botswana.

With trepidation I went back in, waited for long minutes until another window came free, in the meantime learned patience from the black trucker in front of me as his endless duplicate/triplicates were grudgingly stamped. When it was my turn, this second official had no problem with the *carnet*, stamped it, dated it, and we were done. Outside there was a final wait for the customs inspection, and I chatted distractedly about the bike to an intermittently interested cop, until he developed a sudden obsession with wiggling his little finger in his right ear.

I and the bike were waved through customs, and before I knew it we were riding across a Bailey-type bridge over the Limpopo River, which was green and greasy but not great at that point – another missed photo opportunity, along with the South African road signs with CAUTION and a picture of a wart-hog. The whole South African border thing had taken an hour at the most, and then I was on the other side and in Botswana, which was initially just a car park and an administration block, with a gate at the far end.

I dismounted and walked to the building with some fellow travellers, including a couple of friendly, if slightly sceptical, South African mining engineers. From *The No. 1 Ladies' Detective Agency*, I knew that Botswana people were proud of their country and its relative lack of corruption and, from gossip, that they could be a little self-righteous about it. The passport lady did seem quite fierce. I filled in the necessary little form but then she asked where I was going to that night. Feebly I couldn't remember the name "Palapye" – all I could offer was "It begins with a 'P'..." Ignominious moments like that are why I prefer to travel alone. One of the mining engineers supplied the name and then asked me innocently, "This your first time in Africa..?" At the customs desk, a young man stamped the *carnet*, no problem; he didn't date or sign it, but in the interests of a simple life I could do that myself.

Queuing for the final road permit/road fund window with the South Africans again, when they said they were there to work on the diamond mines which are Botswana's chief source of income, I told them I'd read that the mines would begin to be worked out in five or six years' time. They just said these were the largest workings in the world for gemstones, rather than industrial diamonds, and the problem at the moment was that the market for gems was depressed. They knew Palapye and told me that the exotically-named Desert Sands Motel was the nice place. At the desk ahead of me they were relaxed with the fierce lady dishing out the permits. It occurred to me that so far there had been no mention of the $125 entry fee. When it was my turn, I asked for third-party motor insurance as the engineers had, but was told haughtily that it was included in the £20 all-in price, which also covered road tax and the permit, and was good for 90 days. And no $125 entry – that must have been if you were flying in. God bless Botswana!

I rode out of the gate and stopped at a nice petrol place/shop on the other side. It looked much the same as South Africa – borders here seemed arbitrary – but the atmosphere was different. The assistants were truly helpful, I got good coffee, a SIM card for the phone and a flask of VO brandy in short order. I chatted to the short, ample South African driver of an "Intrepid" sort-of minibus which was full, from their accents, of English "Travellers" who were also heading for Zambia.

The driver told me about a cheaper place to stay in Palapye, down behind the train station. I thought not, but wouldn't have been so snooty if I'd known the Desert's £40+ prices. He also recommended the Northgate Lodge at Nata, the town I was hoping to get to next, and confirmed that the long stretch of road after that, beyond Nata to Mpandamatenga, as I had already heard, was so pot-holed that the Minister of Roads had lost his job over it. The driver amplified: it seemed that the President of Botswana had been up in those parts and, after seeing the highway, had summoned the Minister, who arrived late and, when asked why, said "Because of the roads…" Which pretty much did for him. The driver said I should be OK on a bike, but I resolved to get up early the day I did the 200-odd miles from Nata to the Kazangula crossing into Zambia.

Heartened, I fired up again for the remaining 60 miles to Palapye. I had vaguely been expecting desert and had filled the Camelbak, but it was pretty much the same bush. There were no police cars in evidence as in South Africa, but there were more animals wandering on the road: donkeys, goats, a cow. The wind was behind me now, where before it had been from the east, strong enough to slowly shove the magnetic tank bag into my lap. Towards Palapye, with dark clouds building all round, oncoming cars flashed me, presumably telling me to put my lights on. But I was conserving them as I already had doubts about whether the battery was charging as it should. I beat the dark and I beat the rain, but only just, riding into the strung-out town of Palapye, with its approximate signs for the motel; the Wimpy Bar next door was the giveaway.

The Desert Sands was large and smart enough, and had a particularly sparky reception lady. It was a relief that they had a room, though the price, at around £40 without breakfast, confirmed Botswana's reputation as expensive – but hell, it was only for the one night. There were several blocks of rooms with tall glass sliding-door fronts and long drapes to cocoon you inside. In mine, stupid with fatigue, I nevertheless got the new SIM card in and texted the fresh cell phone number to Molly and to Mike; I would buy a card with credit the following day. When I came out to eat at the Wimpy it was lashing down with rain. I had left the poor Ariel in the courtyard between reception and the Wimpy as the desk lady had suggested and, after I had eaten, returned to the desk to ask about phone cards. The girl confirmed that the wet weather was completely unseasonal and unheard of. I expressed concern for the bike and she, God bless her, told me to push it ("Don't ride it!") into an unfinished conference room behind the reception area.

Just as well. The rain would continue hard for the next 12 hours or so, and damp getting into the electrics and control cables was the last thing I needed. I can only apologise to any future conference delegates who look down and see oil spots on the tiles. The lady also suggested that if the weather kept on like this then I'd do better to stay another night. Back in the room I drank brandy and warm water, probably too much, and watched TV till I fell asleep.

Chapter 22

HAPPY BIRTHDAY

In the morning, though the rain had stopped temporarily, it was still very windy. The receptionist's words had planted a seed, and I decided to stay. After breakfast at, you guessed it, the Wimpy, I walked back into town, skipping over puddles and performing the customary stumble across African paving stones, got a phone-card and found an alternative eatery for that evening. It was cold out. Desert!

I spent the day washing clothes, catching up on the journal, route-planning (I hadn't realised till then that after the Kazangula crossing into Zambia there was still another 60 miles to go before reaching Livingstone), and finally a spot of bike maintenance. The rain was soon hammering non-stop on the roof again, but aside from the cleaning ladies who had been banging about outside since 8.30am, it was OK to be warm and dry. The spannering didn't go too well. After a check round for loose nuts and bolts, I went to adjust the slack rear chain, but a) with an attack of brain-fag, couldn't work out why the adjuster-bolts weren't turning until I remembered that, of course, you had to loosen off the rear wheel spindle before they do, and b) when I tried to loosen the spindle, I found that the PE guys once again had done it up too tightly for me to shift, even using the big spanner and, for the first time, the mallet. The chain was quite loose, though I knew it would tension a bit more with me sitting in the saddle. I cleaned the bike off as best I could, but it was depressing working in there, with the odd cleaning lady peering in, and a door banging loudly, unpredictably, in the idiot wind.

Next morning it was still raining, but I had to get out of there before I choked on Wimpy-food, even if at the bottom of their bills was printed the word 'BLESSINGS', and they gave away boiled sweets which I stashed in my waistcoat. Also I had to get on to my rendezvous with Ginty in Zambia, so I told myself it was just drizzle now which I wouldn't have thought twice about back in the UK and, after using some of a tube of AFC1 anti-corrosion stuff, plus a couple of squirts of WD40 to help waterproof the magneto, I paid, pushed the loaded bike out from its haven, gassed up and headed off north on the 90-odd mile main road to Francistown.

The rain was fairly light at first, but one thing I hadn't packed was the anti-fog spray, and a misted-up visor soon meant no rear vision, and only a really limited view to the front, for a good while. I had turned on the lights but, as I suspected, they quickly dimmed so I turned them off to preserve the battery's remaining juice for the rear brake light. Still, things were OK. I stopped as per usual after 50 miles at the only option, an African joint where inside you put your order through a hole in the wall to a kitchen. I was the only white face but, despite my Creature-from-the-Black-Lagoon appearance, with wet jacket and flapping overtrousers, attracted little overt attention. I was probably too far out to be relevant, I thought. I stayed drinking coffee till the place was rendered untenable by a local comedian who recited in his native tongue so loud in the cramped room that it actually hurt your ears.

As I squelched off for Francistown again, the *real* rain began. Soon I was riding with wet sleeves, soaked gloves, damp boots and, for some reason, the belly of my waistcoat soaked. This was where the old Brit-bred discipline of wrapping everything important – wallet, camera, address book, phone – in clear plastic bags, paid off. With my lack of lights there was lots of self-righteous flashing from oncoming cars, including the police – daytime headlights for bikes were evidently the law. I slogged on, indulging in at least one injudicious piece of overtaking. At Francistown I took the ring road round to the west, and, soaked through, stopped for petrol and a local energy drink called "Burn" (or was it "Hell"?) which did later seem to do the job. The young attendants were warily friendly, and one girl, when she saw how soggy I was, took my silk inner gloves to the hand dryer in the Ladies.

It was only 11.30am so I bashed on for the 140 miles to Nata, mildly worried about snatch from the loose rear chain, but as the rain slackened off we made a good pace. I had noticed all along that there were no deep puddles or standing water, so the roads were well drained and the surface wasn't too bad, though as we got further north, the pot-holes were no longer announced as they had been, and there were more of them. At lunchtime I stopped at a "Lay-bye" (sic) with a half-full garbage can surrounded all about by discarded tins and bottles; some things are the same all over the world. Water, biltong, biscuits, but I forgot to take my diabetic pills. For the final 30 miles, just as everything had been dried by the wind to an acceptable level, the rain came back with a vengeance. No fair! The date was 10 June, so that was how I spent my 66th birthday.

It had slackened off as I arrived at Nata, which was a long drawn-out town with a frontier feel, the roads leading north-west to the Zambian border and due west to the Okavango Delta. There was a petrol station opposite the Northgate Lodge compound and I stopped to gas up for the morrow. Then the Ariel wouldn't start. It was the worst refusal so far, and I immediately started fretting about the same thing occurring on the bad road to the border, though the probable cause was that for once I had forgotten to switch the petrol off when I stopped. I was reluctant to push Jerry over the road and park up with the problem still in place. One of the young attendants gave me a push-start, but with the bike fully laden it was awkward and we didn't get a result. Finally a kick brought it to life. Meanwhile the guys and girls, when they heard I was riding to Kazangula, told me the final 100km ran through National Parks. "You will be chased by elephants," chortled one. Another added, "And lions!"

With the bike running again, I rode across the road and parked under a thatched awning for cars. Before I went into the compound I asked an older security guy where the nearest garage was, as I knew I had to get the rear chain tensioned before tomorrow's bad roads. Then I squelched into reception and was brought up short by the prices (over £70, but that did include supper and breakfast) so, to conserve dollars for the border, I opted to pay by MasterCard. I carried my bags and the panniers to Hut 6-66 (scary!) and then, leaving my gloves to dry out, I rode off a little way up the highway to J and J Engineering.

There, a suspicious but friendly Mma sent for her hubbie to check out the Ariel, and he eventually assigned the nicest of the mechanic lads I had been chatting with to loosen off the rear wheel. In the open-fronted garage a sandy-coloured puppy which I had petted now followed the bike around wherever it was pushed. The lad brought a very long ring spanner which did the job and, with Jerry up on its piece of wood, I could now tension the chain, noting that my futile efforts the day before had bent the adjuster bolts, but that they still worked. I over-tensioned the chain, then re-did it, and the lad checked it with me in the saddle, saying it was OK, though I thought it might still be a little tight. Finally I did the big axle nuts up myself, so I knew I would be able to undo them.

In the shop, after hilarity and disbelief at how old I was that day, we talked about the bad road ahead, and the Mma confirmed that the pot-holes were "like dams". But she could supply me with white front and red rear adhesive reflectors, which the South African AA data had indicated were mandatory for getting into Zambia, and which I had been worrying about. So I was feeling good, and back at the Lodge, at a shop outside the compound, I bought beers, brandy and crisps. In my *faux* African (but nice) thatched hut, I got out of my wet clothes, showered and, in the last of the light, sat out on the raised veranda and drank the beers, looking over bougainvillea and barbed wire – the Lodge, despite its pretensions, was set beside a noisy truck depot/turnaround. But it was the only place I would stay at where there were a couple of complementary condoms artfully arranged on the bedside table. As darkness fell, I went inside and watched BTV News, which was mostly incomprehensible, but did let me know that the weather the following day would probably be OK. Then the cell phone went. It was my brother Julian, who is punctilious about birthdays, but I can't pretend I wasn't touched.

In the near-empty dining room I ate a decent supper on my own with a couple of glasses of wine, and went back to lie in front of the TV, so was asleep/passed out when Rosie and Molly rang. Rose had had an exam at school that day; she was OK. When I enthused to Molly about reaching Zambia shortly, with a few well-chosen words ("Oh, you always do what you want to do") she deflated my mood, and capped it with ongoing news of Zoe, our Labrador who, from happily walking two miles or more a day when I left, had lost the use of her back legs and refused food for three days (a really bad sign with a lab). The vet, after giving Molly three days' morphine tablets for her, had said, "And after that you'll have a decision to make." How had all this happened? "Steve, she's getting old," I was told – but 11 wasn't that old for a Labrador. I could see it from Molly's point of view: one more responsibility to have to shoulder single-handedly in my absence, along with Rose, and the house, and her own ailing mother in a home nearby. But the sadness in the news ended an otherwise successful day on a slightly low note.

Chapter 23

ACROSS
THE ZAMBEZI

Next morning the sun was shining but, despite my early-start resolutions, it was 10am before I got away. The bike was OK after its night under the canopy, where it had got a bit wet from blown spray and drops, though not deluged. It cheered me to find that I had misread the map and the whole journey to Kazangula was only about 180 miles, but I still half intended to stop after 120 or so and stay at Mpandamatenga.

The first 30 miles were fine but then, at a livestock quarantine barrier, the fun began, heralded by a lorry at the roadside which had spectacularly shed its load. The pot-holes were pretty much continuous for the next 80 or so miles. On the bike, it was mostly fine as long as you didn't go too fast to weave between the holes, a bit like trail riding. A few times I slipped up and rode into a hole with an almightly bang from the suspension that made me very mindful of my original 350's broken frame, and the extra stress from the Big Bag at the back. The concentration on my line took my mind off the way the bike was feeling as the morning wore on. It always steered well, but there was a jerky feeling to the power delivery. At my first stop it occurred to me that I hadn't slackened off the rear brake after adjusting the chain (really, really Not Mechanical, right?). So I did that, using pliers on the brake rod's knurled adjuster wheel. The back wheel had spun freely and the rear hub hadn't been hot, but things did seem a bit smoother after that.

However, a metallic jingling noise was still definitely coming from the engine, but the pot-holes took my mind off this and it was an interesting morning, with oncoming trucks in the distance edging from one side of the road to the other, to miss clusters of holes, their cabs rocking and bouncing like elephants plagued by an unseen swarm of bees. So it wasn't really bad for me, but with the necessarily slow speed it was a long road, and the weather became hotter and hotter.

Towards Mpandamatenga the road began to improve, though you still had to watch out for the deep holes. "Panda" proved deeply unpromising, no real town at all, just a collection of buildings, warehouses and workshops, and a petrol station with a) a mob of black students/travellers off a coach milling about, and b) no petrol. But thanks to the Ariel's frugal habits, I still had easily enough to get me the last 60-odd miles to the ferry. So I parked in the shade and, since it was nearly 2pm, went to investigate a store which proved to be serving food out of a kitchen at the back. After plenty of confusion while getting a ticket and explaining what I wanted (but didn't get), the unsmiling cook served up an initially unpromising winner, a mound of rice with coleslaw and beetroot (eeugh!), topped with fried chicken.

The chicken was absolutely great, a world away from KFC, and so, amazingly, was the coleslaw, really appetizing and full of goodness, and I ate with pleasure at a table outside in the warm afternoon, sipping a Sprite and watching the Africans. It was a good break. I topped up with oil and we rocked on for the remaining miles to Kazangula, where I planned on spending the night and hitting the ferry and the border fresh in the morning. The road was monotonous, but then began to be fringed by the forest of the National Parks, though the only animals I had to keep an eye out for at first were goats and donkeys on the road. It was warm, and the bike wasn't sounding quite right. I told myself off for paranoia, and though I knew I should stop, droned on intending to do it in one hit. And then it happened – the engine note deepened, and with an audible metallic rattle, the engine died.

Words cannot describe … with 3,165 miles on the clock, I only had 25 more to do to get to Zambia. I was so near! I had no back-up plan for Botswana, bar the number of one biking lady who lived outside Gabarone, at the other end of the country. It was Thursday and I had arranged a rendezvous with Ginty on Saturday night at a camp 200 miles the far side of Livingstone, though he had said more than once that if I had trouble he could get a bakkie down to Livingstone itself. So it all pivoted on getting to Zambia.

I got off the bike, looking around for wildlife. It was boiling hot, and for the first time, as I blundered into the bush seeking shade, I was besieged by a multitude of flies, real bastards. Filled with dull dread, I took a drink from the Camelbak, then returned, took a look at the bike – nothing obviously out of order – and before long, to get free of the swarming flies, I tried kicking it over – and it started. I let it cool for a little bit longer, then started it again and set off, very, very slowly, for Kazangula, praying all the way. Because of the noise I was thinking of mechanical mayhem, maybe a broken valve spring. The miles on the odometer turned over interminably slowly. Then before long I had to pass the best photo opportunity yet, a big bull elephant standing quietly by the road, far enough away for safety. But I wasn't stopping for him or anyone, I just edged onwards, the bike rattling thinly, and finally reached the outskirts of Kasane, the town adjacent to Kazangula.

And then – I pratted about. The enforced halt had thrown me badly. The logical thing would be to find a place to stay, and there were signs for a Lodge, but getting to it looked to involve more off-road riding down a track than I was prepared to do, mindful that the bike might break down at any minute. I rode back to a petrol station on the corner where the road ran on to the ferry. I parked up and went in and they confirmed that yes, there were hotels in Kasane, a mile or so away, but I still faffed about indecisively (and in the process, even omitted to fill up with petrol). Then came the moment. I fired up, and embarrassingly, actually cried aloud, "Go for it!" and turned the bike round to the ferry, despite it now being after 4pm and the sun being low in the sky, the Zambian border reputedly taking up to half a day to negotiate, and with another 45-odd miles then to ride to Livingstone, on a sick bike with no lights and low on petrol. Go for it indeed.

The Botswanese border post, housed a mile away in extended Portakabins, was as brisk and as friendly as you could wish. I was in and out in ten minutes with the *carnet* done up right and sage words ringing in my ears: "Don't give any money to anyone until you are on the other side." I confirmed with a white car driver that the ferry was straight on. When I got there the place was muddy sand, with random vehicles and taxis parked haphazardly above it, and the "ferry" visible on the far side, just a flat-bottomed pontoon. At least there was no queue of heavy trucks, though hundreds were parked on the far shore. The Zambezi, a thrilling name, was muddy and maybe a quarter of a mile wide there. I was on my own. It was a beautiful evening, with the sun low to the left behind trees and sparkling on the water. On the other side of the gully that gave access to the pontoon, a deep, muddy trench with river water sloshing in the tyre tracks, women with burdens were silhouetted against the light. It was a scene full of nature: tranquil and dangerous.

I was sweating like a pig in my jacket. At first I tried to ignore the attentions of the inevitable fixers, and one in particular, a smooth guy in a pale leather coat with sharp eyes, but he was quietly persistent. Ginty had given me the name of the fixer he used, so I told pale-coat, and he said he knew this man but he wasn't there that evening. I only havered a minute longer, then took the blue form he was offering and filled it out. I told him I was writing the trip up, hoping publicity might equal leverage, and he handed me his business card; it said that this was Elvin M. Simonsuna, Operations Manager of The Tower of Success Business Centre, Dealers in Clearing and Forwarding and suppliers of spares, computer parts etc. For $5 payable at the far gates, Elvin was my man.

I moved the bike on request to make way for a taxi, and then the pontoon arrived and Elvin and others urged me to get on. Thank God the bike started first kick. It was a real trials ride on the laden bike, down into the rutted, muddy approach, with a car also coming in from the left, but I gave it a handful, the Ariel's pedigree came good and we shot through the mud and bumped up onto the pontoon, braking hard to pull in next to the front car. Elvin came aboard and we were soon underway. Pay the ferry man? No, it was all taken care of. Elvin, despite his sharp eyes, was really solicitous, telling me slowly and carefully what to do. In mid-stream there was a moment, as we ran into a tangle of driftwood and reeds, but this turned out to be deliberate, to stop the pontoon, as a dredger was coming out from the far shore. With all this, and the ladies sitting patiently in the front with their slung flour sacks and babies, finally we were across to the Zambian side.

There was another off-road moment leaving the pontoon and riding through the massed trucks to the customs offices. Prompted by Elvin, I parked up and entered the building (quick! quick!) and after looking round, subconsciously, for a white queue, joined the line for the passport/visas, and in short order was relieved of $50 for a three-week entry visa. On to the next window where the guy knew *all* about *carnets*, so there was no problem and, armed with the stamped document, and again prompted by Elvin, we walked round through the throng, *very* fast (this seemed important) to the other side of the same office. En route, I asked Elvin about insurance, and a shark appeared from nowhere wanting me to go to his office. But Elvin said it was all taken care of, don't listen to this man, and we went straight to a window where a lady, shown the *carnet*, promptly produced a permit/ insurance documents, and in less than half-an-hour we were done.

Outside I started the bike and rode to the exit gate just ahead of a truck. Typically, as the cops were checking the papers, Jerry – who normally ticked over so unstoppably that the valve lifter would no longer stop the engine, and you had to put it in gear and let the clutch out to do so – chose that moment to die, so I had to push it through the gate, to the amusement of all. Then I met up with Elvin and his crew, and he used his phone to calculate that I owed him $110 plus his $5 fee. With the visa at $50, this totalled $165, $10 less than I had been told, so I paid willingly, though there was a moment. Because I didn't have the money prepared, I would have to get it out of the wallet with the crew clustering round. Elvin said it would be cool, so I went ahead, with only slight apprehension of a possible car-block further on up the road.

It was 5.15pm now, the sun was setting, it was nearly 50 miles to Livingstone and I had no lights. After changing my remaining pula to kwacha (luckily), I said goodbye and set off. The light was going fast, but the road surface was good. After a few miles in the dusk, I came on what would become a familiar sight, a broken-down lorry or coach with people milling about, traffic down to one lane and a cop standing there. I kept going briskly, avoiding eye contact and driving past the cop's raised hand, then heard a loud "HEY!" from behind, but rode on. I just didn't have the time.

After about 15 miles I knew I had to do something about a back light at least (I did have my front and rear reflectors stuck on, though naturally no one at the frontier had paid any notice). I pulled into a lay-by, and the light went dramatically as I fumbled around in the tank bag and found the LED emergency cycle lights, then couldn't read their instructions (this was the first time they had come out of their packaging), and somehow lost the plastic back of the rear light. But I duct-taped it up, and more tape secured it to the rear carrier, the only drawback being that I could switch it on but not off.

As I was struggling with all this, without the benefit of the Maglite which was deep within the strapped-on Big Bag, a lorry pulled into the lay-by. Two guys got out and walked past saying Hi, and as we got talking – "How are you?", "I've been better" – I looked down and realised that the kickstart was missing! But I had the spare! And reaching in my pocket for the adjustable spanner, my fingers found something I'd forgotten about, the tiny LED torch that I'd attached to the keyring, which proved brilliantly bright. Chiding me gently for lack of preparation as I fumbled around for more tools, the two guys fetched a big spanner and used it to hammer the kickstart onto its shaft, then I tightened it with the adjustable, and by George, we'd done it. Without losing anything else.

There was more. They suggested they would drive behind me and light my way. They also said that when we got into Livingstone there would be a major T-junction with a petrol station, and if I turned right, just a little way down the road was a backpackers' place to stay, called Fawlty Towers. That sounded about right. I double-checked the details, Jerry started first kick and we set off into the darkness.

It was fairly hairy. The light from the big lorry behind was not the brightest, though at least when the light became brighter that told me there was a car overtaking. The guys had said that the loaded truck was not fast (just as well). We trundled along at between 20 and 30mph in top, and even then, on the first long switchback climb I lost them on the up-slope and ended in total darkness at the top, weaving along in 2nd with my legs down till they (and a car) lit me up again. I took it even steadier after that, but was still all over the place on the first of three signed "Bends" along the way. There came swimming up in my mind a piece of advice from my mother 50 years before, when we'd ridden in a feebly-lit Vespa/Morris Minor convoy down to Rye one night: to watch the verge rather than the white line. On that verge, people walking loomed up in the African way, as well as unlit bicycles and the occasional goat. Then, going by a village, suddenly there was a police Land Rover parked on the left and an amplified voice crackling through a loud-hailer, with the only words I could make out being "…VERY DANGEROUS…" I rode on, but a night in the cells seemed a real possibility; that would solve the accommodation problem, I thought fatalistically. But after a mile or two, no one was pursuing – maybe they were low on fuel too. Far worse was the glare from the lights of oncoming vehicles, with bus drivers in particular seeming keen to tell me off with dazzling high beams, leaving me dangerously blinded.

The wavering ride seemed endless, but I was expecting even more, when street lights came into view, and then a "WELCOME TO LIVINGSTONE" sign: I punched the air as we passed it. Under the sodium light I pushed on briskly and reached the T-junction, looking around the deserted crossroads until the truck pulled up beside me and the driver pointed out the (unlit) petrol station, and Fawlty Towers beyond it. I told the guys that I wouldn't forget what they had done for me, and the driver said he would try and look in to check on me at the Towers. Then they were gone, and I was parking up outside the tall double gates, when a gatekeeper emerged and said to come in. I'd made it.

I parked up in a corner of the spacious yard and walked straight into the big empty bar with its pumping music, monster TV screen, dark wood, comfortable sofas and armchairs, library shelves in one corner and a friendly black barman. Rooms with showers were $45, so not cheap. There were budget alternatives in an annexe across the road but I felt I had earned a couple of good nights. I gratefully took the room and sat, feeling bemused and sipping my first Mosi, "The Beer That Thunders". I had enjoyed it at Luangwa, the name referring to "Mosi-Oa-Tunyi", the native name for Victoria Falls, just up the road. A plump white lady manager on the next stool told me about the free Fawlty shuttle bus to the Falls at 10 the next morning.

After a couple of beers I was shown the room, one in a row in the far side of a big internal compound of lawn and swimming pool. Then, still slightly dazed, I walked cautiously out to one of the nearby restaurants which the manager had recommended, down the – previously very intimidating – dirt road opposite, and next to a church. It was a funky Italian place, Olga's, with a big, curiously quiet black family party at a long table indoors, an attentive waiter (glass of wine please!) for my table on the terrace outside by a glowing brazier, and soon, kicking music – in particular a cholo/Mexican anthem in Spanish, spattered with Anglo obscenities. Sitting there with my ears ringing after the day, the pot-holed road, the unscheduled stop, the ferry, the night run – it was beyond surreal. I ate *tagliatelle carbonara* and afterwards got chatting to the young Italian guy who was running the place as part of a charitable programme. Then I tottered back and slept for eight straight hours.

Chapter 24

FAWLTY TOWERS

Next morning, after showering, I went for breakfast, which was being cooked in a communal upstairs area of the main building. I shared the table with a very taciturn young English guy muffled in a thick red and white woolly scarf, and later a jolly mixed-race English girl, as well as a young black guy who filled us in about Victoria Falls. Then I made my first sortie on foot into Livingstone, needing money. I was down to about $100 plus the kwacha I had changed at the crossing, and needed to cash a traveller's cheque. The footpaths and pot-holed streets into the city were dusty, and there was a constant hassle from people wanting to sell stuff or asking you to change dollars, though some were friendly and, flatteringly, called you "big man". I even exchanged names with one of them.

Eventually I found and went into Barclays Bank. I queued for a quarter-of-an-hour, fretting about the bus for the Falls leaving at 10am, and finally got a nice teller who was fine about the cheques – but wanted the receipt from when I had bought them before he would change them. In all my travels I had never been asked for the receipt, and had discarded it back at home. Frustrated, I stamped back to Fawlty Towers and caught the minibus.

I sat next to an extrovert, well-muscled 23-year-old guy called Rob. At first I slightly discounted him as just another backpacker, but then got talking and discovered he was a martial artist and a pilot, out there on a contract. There was a group of young American girls who were interested in my trip, and the jolly mixed-race girl was also there on her way to bungee-jump off the bridge that crossed into Zimbabwe. When she said she was going to start later that year at Leeds University, it turned out Rob had graduated from there. I was able to chip in about what a live city Leeds had always been culturally. I had visited, after a Beat magazine there called *Ludd's Mill* once published a short story of mine which no one else would touch (and which went on to be the genesis of a four-book sequence by my best mate, the writer Carey Harrison).

We passed a police checkpoint and bumped onwards to the Falls. Rob was also due to bungee-jump, but was kind enough to keep me company, walking from the busy tourist market/taxi bit at the top, down well-signed paths through forest, with the falls already a deep out-of-sight rumble. The guy at breakfast had advised about hiring waterproof ponchos: the place where they rented these was muddy underfoot from drifting spray as the roar got louder – were the ponchos really necessary? By the time we got down, over bridges with grinning Japanese coming the other way, to reach the main falls, we couldn't hear each other speak from the continuous thunder, and every inch not covered by the poncho was drenched. Rob, in sandals, did better than me with the walking trainers, but they dried out. He took a picture or two, capturing both the background rainbows of spray and me looking like Granny Gummy with the poncho hood drawn tight.

Shaken and satisfied by the spectacle, we went down together to the Boiling Pot, the big pool round the corner from the Falls. The climb down through the trees was quite long, and at the bottom there were still streams of water and slippery rocks to negotiate. So when a mild-mannered guide fell in beside us, I was not proud about taking his hand to steady myself on the tricky bits, though it cost us some kwacha later. We ended up by the big pool, looking up at the bungee-jump bridge over into Zimbabwe which – thanks to Peter Godwin's book and Tony Page's outright refusal to set foot in the place – seemed like a no-go area to me. We watched a couple of bodies jumping, and then arcing back up and down again until the bungee lost its bounce, but my urge to jump off things had waned. The climb back up was steep, but we made it with just two stops, Rob being very considerate.

He was an interesting young man, from a poor background in Batley, Yorkshire, and everything that he had achieved – university, pilot's licence – he had done on his own. Rob rang the girls and fixed a rendezvous; he wasn't too bothered about the bungee jump, which they said closed at 1 o'clock and had an hour-and-a-half queue. At a track on the top we met baboons close up, causing me slight trepidation as my mate Carey and another friend of ours had once been savaged by the Barbary apes on Gibraltar, but these guys were merely grumpy-looking. When we met the girls, the one who had just done the jump ran up and embraced, still high on the experience, crying, "Hug it out!" We checked out the market where there were some handsome copper bracelets, and Rob pointed out the little Mnyame-Mnyame figures, the lucky Zambezi river God. Then we got a taxi back.

A bad afternoon followed for me, wandering around in dusty Livingstone trying to get money. One of the only two light spots was meeting a nice mild hustler who called "Steve! Steve! It's me, Elias?" He was the one I had exchanged names with, so I bought two Mnyame-Mnyame figures strung on thin bootlaces, one for Rosie and one to go round my own neck. But its luck didn't extend to the Visa card which, at a hole in the wall, was rejected: "insufficient funds". Embarrassingly, this turned out to be true. The editor of the classic car mag had failed to run the pieces I had stacked up for him, and the delicate web of my overdrafts collapsed temporarily into unauthorised hell. The other good thing that afternoon was buying a SIM card for yet another new phone set-up from a nice girl in a petrol station, who installed it and put on credit. Zambia's ZAIM network was not great, however. Texts to Mike in PE wouldn't go, and a single conversation with Ginty used up three-quarters of my credit, so I had to buy more the next morning.

But otherwise that conversation with Ginty was nothing but good. He reassured me about changing money, and everything else. He said he would bring the necessary kit in case a valve-spring had broken, as I had half-guessed to begin with about the breakdown in Botswana (though now I doubted it, as we probably wouldn't have got as far as this if it had). We arranged to meet the following day at Moorings, a campsite a day's ride away, on the road to Zambia's capital, Lusaka, which was an easy 120 miles further on after that. And if anything did to wrong in the meantime, Ginty would "send a vehicle". This was good. I was sorted.

I still needed to change money though. It was 3 o'clock and I was feeling woozy, so I walked down the road and had a pizza, and then continued the dreary round, going to try the traveller's cheques at the Bureau de Change next to Fawlty Towers, who sent me to a bureau down the road where the ladies said no dice, "the boss is away". So it was back to the first one to at least change the $100, but the guy there said they were out of kwacha! I changed some small dollar bills, then went back down the road where the contemptuous ladies changed the $100 at a derisory rate. This, too, was Africa. As was the alien street life – what had the girl behind the pizza counter's sulks meant? And the fact that half the time I couldn't understand what people were saying to me? Or to each other? But I didn't experience that sense of how everything changes when you might not have enough money. If pushed, I could still pay for some things with the MasterCard, and after the following evening, Ginty was going to help sort me out.

I went back to Fawlty Towers to drink a Mosi by the pool and watch the comedy of the many, many pool tile layers dicking about with the American girls in bikinis lying on recliners. The girls, with impossible naivety, were asking the guys solicitously if they'd Had a Nice Day?

When the sun declined and the midges came out, back in the bar the big screen TV played concert footage of Kiss loud and proud, and soon, good golly, Bad Company, a favourite band from back in the day. Rob and the crowd spilled in from a sundowner booze cruise on the river, some of them fairly pissed, though Rob said most people hadn't realised how short the cruise would be and didn't get into the free booze quick enough. Working on another Mosi, I eyed them all indulgently, paternally. It was good to hang with the younger folk for a bit, but there was no spark for me I'm afraid, even when the abundant mixed-race girl came to squat behind my armchair and gushed how she'd wanted to talk to me ever since Rob had told her I was an author, and that she really wanted to get into politics but also do a bit of writing and could she have my e-mail so she could pester me when she got back home? I provided it in a courtly way, but subsequently remained un-pestered.

A young guy then sat down, pretty pissed, asked if I was the one with the bike doing the charity ride, and began to talk about his father's friends, who apparently included Pink Floyd, and might be able to help. I gave him the website details but he was boring, so I went to the bar by Rob, got another beer and chatted with him for a while. He told me about the fighting culture in Batley, how you knew there would be a ruck every time you went to a pub, how guys sat with their arms folded and you were working out where the knife or bottle was, and how things had only changed for him when he went to university at Leeds. This was interesting stuff, but then Rob said, "I think I'm going to have to talk to her," and I said, "I think you should," and that was that.

Everyone was going down to the pizza place, so I sloped off quietly to a restaurant opposite and had fish and chips and a glass of wine, marvelling at how I was spending possibly my last money. I knew the next day's 200-mile drive was likely to be problematic. Everyone said the road after Livingstone was bad and, since the stoppage in the jungle the day before, I hadn't ridden the bike at normal speeds. How was it going to hold up?

Chapter 25

MEETING
MR MELVILL

Next morning I got myself together methodically, had breakfast early, not eager to see the others, and talked to a pair of out-of-place South African underfloor heating contractors who were looking for business in Zambia. To get there they'd crossed Zimbabwe in one 1,400km hit at speeds of 120-140kph, but actually they were OK. I bought more phone credit; it was a warm morning as I carried my load bit by bit to the bike. I had enough money to settle up, then pushed the bike out to the petrol station and filled up. It started fine, which was a relief, and we were off.

The town traffic was cut and thrust, the main offenders being the swarms of minibus taxis. These were frequently un-roadworthy camper-sized vans, belching diesel fumes and crammed with humanity (while I was there, one was stopped in South Africa and found to be carrying 47 passengers), with armed ticket-takers, and the assumption that other traffic would give way. The taxis often kept their indicators on when parked, so it was impossible to tell when they would lurch back onto the road.

But the real trouble, from the edge of town onwards, was the road surface. The Chinese were re-doing the road to Lusaka. I was aware of Chinese commercial activity in Southern Africa from news items like the one the previous year in Robin Pope Safaris' wonderful e-mailed newsletter, *It's Monday*. Normally full of safari tales and stunning photos from Luangwa, this time they had written how the costs of school-building at Kawaza had risen as the price of concrete had doubled, due to a shortage because of the Chinese buying in bulk. You couldn't blame China, now on the ascendant, for seeking to open up markets and corner mineral resources – we had done the same thing previously, with considerably more use of overt force – but the perception was that they had little interest in benefiting local communities as they went about their business. The Chinese strategy involved securing rights from African governments in return for projects such as this road, which would benefit their activities as well.

On the ground, right there by Livingstone, the result was pretty bad, as they had started the new road from the Lusaka end. Though Chinese vehicles and crews were all around, the pot-holes on this section were bad and getting more so, and as we weaved in and out of them the situation was complicated by near-new 4x4s coming up fast from behind. But there was worse to come. After about 20km the road under construction ahead was blocked, and traffic was diverted into the forest on a red dirt track.

Naturally there was no indication of how long this diversion would go on for, and it turned into the Ariel's off-tarmac baptism of fire, with surfaces ranging from washboard to deep dust berm wallows and, the worst, gravel. With the laden bike, I took it very steady, mostly in 2nd, and it was a tiring, grinding, anxious experience. The worry was mainly for the bike, as the forks topped out with a characteristic clang, and I tried not to think about the fractured (again) front pannier rack mountings I had discovered in Livingstone, although they seemed to be holding. The occasional truck or bus overtook me from behind, but that was OK. Even in the deep forest there were people standing along the way, and trackside stores with tattered plastic sides and roofs; you wondered about these people's lives.

Eventually, after nearly ten miles, the track emerged and ran alongside the new, pristine, unopened road (the temptation was to jump up onto it like Steve McQueen), and then at Zimba, the tarmac road, perfectly good, began again. Just like that. I didn't fancy the town, so stopped by the roadside further on, in some rare tree shade, with people on foot passing along paths further into the bush, but only the children looking at me. I drank water and ate biscuits. It had been very tiring, and I only hoped that the other stretch of "bad road" I knew about, the last 60 miles up to Mfuwe Airport and Luangwa, wasn't going to be all like that.

I fired up and moved on again. The bike seemed to be behaving itself, and by now I was completely comfortable riding it, despite the heavy load and the low speeds. (Later, other people's speedos would record our cruising speed as exactly 40mph.) The roads were more interesting and varied, with fewer long straights, and there was lots of uplifting response from the roadside, Zambia being the best country so far for smiling and waving. The waving came in different styles. Little girls would flutter their hands at you, while young guys pushed out a palm, like Go Man Go. I stopped for petrol about half-way, at Kalomo, and brought a Sprite and chocolate-covered peanuts from a jokily stern Indian matriarch, then sat in the sun on the attendant's bench, consuming them and fielding a couple of polite enquiries about the trip. I rang Ginty as arranged, and confirmed our rendezvous.

It was a thoroughly pleasant day, running across a plateau and passing the first villages with round thatched huts. There was a rattle from the primary chain, but the bike was going pretty well. Almost there, I stopped for a final fill-up in Monze, a university town, so I would be ready for the next day's run. A foxy lady and a cool guy parked their car too close to where I'd left the bike resting, and were sitting talking, but then the guy came over and started chatting, and they left before I had to start the bike. I knew Moorings was only a few miles further on: later Ginty would be astounded that my rip-proof Reise Map of "Sambia", sourced at Stamfords of Covent Garden, was detailed enough to note every petrol station and camp, including Moorings. It would be one of the few pieces of my kit that impressed him.

I still managed to miss the turn-off due to misinterpreting the sign that said "Moorings 2km" as meaning 2km further up the road rather than down the track, and not wishing to linger as there was a crowd of people selling stuff by the roadside. It was 4pm. When I had obviously gone too far, I asked some people, came back, took the correct path, crossed a narrow gauge railway track, and at the camp's barrier had just finished having my hands anointed with disinfectant for quarantine by the guard when bike lights appeared up the track. It was Ginty and his friend Andy Legg, who had arrived half-an-hour earlier. They still had their helmets on and, crying "Ginty!" I greeted Andy like a long-lost brother, until he gestured to the figure on the red Ducati Monster and the penny dropped. Well, it had been nearly two years since Ginty and I had met on the Isle of Man. With that sorted out, I took stock.

Ginty was a short, thickset 69-year-old. His wrinkled, sun-darkened face had a cluster of tiny warts round one eye, and a discoloured patch. His hair was unfeasibly bright for his age, and from time to time over the next few days I'd look at it and speculate, until we later had a haircut together at the Intercontinental Hotel and seeing it shampooed convinced me the colour was all his own. That day, after a 120-mile ride out to greet me, he was instantly friendly, but impatient. He had already been bitten on the boot by a blue heeler dog, and slipped on a mat on a veranda, bruising his knees and badly grazing his right hand, which would give him grief the following week as he took the spanners to Jerry. He claimed to be slowing down. He still had three or four British bikes, but had sold his Norton twin café racers after a series of get-offs – in favour of the 600 Ducati. We set off down the track. I was still new at dirt roads, though I would find that well-graded ones held few terrors. I was leading, and mercifully doing OK, when the red Monster twin, which was hardly a trail bike, came by and disappeared ahead, with Ginty riding smoothly and as fast as on tarmac.

At the end of the track we turned left, passed a central bar building with a stone terrace, bumped over lawns, and stopped by a tree, outside a chalet with a tent pitched next to it. Andy Legg got off his modern Harley 1200 Sportster and took off his helmet. He had a friendly open face and, like Mike Wood, was the son of a missionary. He was now the director of Multicrop in Lusaka, a firm which specialised in irrigation, and immediately seemed a pleasant, sensible guy. Despite my protestations, he and Ginty insisted I slept in the chalet and they went in the tent.

We were soon walking over to the bar. Ginty was in no way an alcoholic, but when circumstances permitted he did like a big drink in the evening, and the drink he liked was Scotch – he'd dropped beer, he said, as part of a successful weight loss programme. You didn't see very many overweight Anglo whites in Southern Africa, where not staying in shape was actively frowned upon. Ginty bossed Philip, the black barman, around; later he would explain that he had been coming here for years and knew Philip well, but it still sounded pretty peremptory, and Andy and I exchanged raised eyebrows. It was great to sink a couple of Mosis, but then when the only other people there, a party of Indians in the area behind us, got too loud, Ginty said audibly, "Bloody nigger noise!" All I could think of to say, feebly, was, "Steady Ginty, the night is still young!"

Orders were taken for a *braai* supper with nshima, though we wouldn't eat till considerably later. A portly, smiling Irish lady, who lived and did nursing work locally, arrived and joined our party, together with her Palestinian husband and a young Irish girl volunteer who had only been in the country a couple of days. When the Indians departed, and we went to sit round a table on the terrace, Ginty became outraged at the mess they had left. "I won't have this, living like bloody..!" He ordered Philip and his boys to clean up and re-jig the chairs, cordoning off that area, and to bring fresh braziers against the night chill. The Irish lady had a go at Ginty about how he was treating the help – "I'm an old Colonialist," he grinned crookedly – but when they left she invited him to drop in at their place any time, "there's always a bottle of whisky". Ginty did, undeniably, have charm.

As we sat waiting for the grub I was told about the lady now running Moorings who was also a doctor. She and her husband had done a lot of charitable work for the neighbourhood, but a year previously her husband had been shot and killed on his doorstep by some men who had turned up to rob the place. A tragic incident which was, they said, very uncharacteristic of the area and of Zambia in general, where there were certainly thieves, but they were rarely violent. The following morning we would meet his widow, a very brisk and dignified lady.

We drank on. Ginty's every other word now began with 'F', and I don't mean 'Freedom', with his anecdotes turning to sexual stuff, particularly the behaviour of a bunch of Welsh girls on the ferry to the Isle of Man. Eventually I felt I had to keep my end up and recalled a beautiful young waitress in Colombia with whom I had spectacularly ended a long dry season spent on the ranch in Argentina. Ginty eventually said sardonically to missionary's son Andy, "I don't suppose you've done much like that?" But Andy, happily married, remained unprovoked. The food came, and we turned in soon afterwards, to be up at 7 for a 7.30 breakfast.

Chapter 26

TIME OUT
IN LUSAKA

Andy brought me a cup of tea early, and before the 7.30 breakfast which, as Ginty observed, turned up at 8.15 sharp, I did a bit of maintenance on Jerry so as not to let the side down on the run into Lusaka. I checked the nuts and bolts and the tyres, and got to use the mallet, to help get the screwed cap off the primary chaincase and top up the oil in there, to try and cure the rattle. I also consulted the Pitmans book and then successfully adjusted the clutch. We hit the road and it worked OK despite their larger, more modern bikes, with Ginty out front, me in the middle and Andy tail-ending it. My bike was quieter and felt much better. After a first stop, soon there were single headlights coming towards us, and it was Trans-Zambezi riders Hans and his pal on sports bikes, who had come out to meet us. There was the customary wonderment at the Ariel which, by the time we had got to Lusaka, would have covered nearly 2,000 miles since Port Elizabeth.

We rode on in convoy, and later another pair of bikes passed, though only one of them joined us, Len on a modern Hinckley Triumph US-styled twin he had imported from Australia. We turned left at a T-junction onto the road up to Lusaka, with some good up-and-down riding, and at one point I asked Andy to go on ahead with my camera and get a shot of us riding in a group, which he did. We crossed rivers and railway tracks (which Ginty said you should always stop at), and pulled in for a beer some 15 miles shy of the city. The owner of the joint apparently chased out the locals from the *rondavel* where we took up residence; someone said, "It's usually the other way round!" It was good to talk with these large, fit guys on modern bikes who had been extremely tolerant of Jerry's 40–45mph, which would barely have been out of 1st gear for them. One of them was even kind enough to compliment me on a bit of bend-swinging on the hilly approach.

Then we rode on and, sooner than expected, Ginty was signalling right –

I'd known he lived that side of Lusaka but hadn't realised it was 12km out, and overshot slightly due to my less-than-perfect brakes. It was a private-type road with a manned barrier, and its own polo grounds further up. Ginty's place was really nice: several acres converted by them in the previous five years from bush to grass kept fresh with sprinklers. There were rose bushes along the drive, lemon and avocado trees, exotic hens with "trousers" and their chicks, a big warehouse-like workshop where the bikes lived, and another long open-fronted car garage with Ginty's classic Daimler. Parked nearby was a bus converted to live in, and as a bike transporter, for the rallies all over Southern Africa.

You could not fault Ginty's hospitality. I was a near-total stranger, despite our two-year correspondence, and he put me up without charge in "Kate's Corner", a handsome separate guest house which his wife ran as a B&B for visiting business folk. This had its own kitchen, shower room etc and a main bedroom with a tall, traditional reed-thatched ceiling coming to a high point. It was looked after by their maid Margie (with a hard 'G'), and I would eat with Ginty and Kate in the main house. That first day, after beers on the veranda, the lads departed and I met Kate, who looked a little like the singer Annie Lennox, and was extremely nice, well mannered, funny and friendly. She and Ginty seemed to be a case of Beauty and the Beast – and endearingly, they called each other "Doll".

Ginty was not what Dickens' Magwitch called "a dainty feeder". Neither am I, come to that, but he had a habit of restlessly rubbing his face, and coughing unrestrainedly, perhaps as a result of Lusaka's dust and diesel fumes – I would develop the same affliction while there. But the thing that got him told off by Kate was his habit of absent-mindedly removing his front teeth in the middle of a meal. It was Kate some years previously who had insisted in putting down a relatively modest deposit cheque for the land their home stood on – a sound move, as properties on the road had increased in value to the extent that it was now known locally as 'Millionaires' Row'. One evening she would also tell a good story about the war days back in Southern Rhodesia, when she had worked for the army in communications. She and a pregnant colleague had taken on a shooting team of men from the British Army Instructors down there and, with the pregnant lady firing from a seated position, had comfortably won the match and a crate of beer. Kate was far from just a pretty face.

After a cold lunch, I rested up until a visit from Ginty's son-in-law Terry who, with Debi and their children, lived further down the road. As did Ginty's nephew, who we visited later. He had recently suffered a bad bike crash, sustaining nine compound factures in his lower legs; despite having physio equipment, the prognosis wasn't great for him being able to walk again. Terry was tough, an ex-pro polo player in Argentina among other places, and we discussed possible routes back to South Africa, maybe involving Malawi or Mozambique. I was getting to the end of *Thirteen Moons* – eventually I gave the book to Kate – and, to spread out my own reading matter, I had started reading Ginty's copy of Peter Godwin's *Mukiwa – A White Boy in Africa*, about growing up in Rhodesia. It includes descriptions of his service in the counter-insurgency/liberation struggle, the "Dirty Little War" as he called it, that had dragged on until 1980 and independence. When Terry realised I was interested, he said he had a small library of books about that period. I told him and Ginty about a Rhodesian friend of mine from school who had been killed shortly afterwards doing his national service: they said they would try and get details.

The following day, Monday, after breakfast Ginty marshalled me to begin work on the bike. In this we were greatly aided by Cholo, one of his several garden boys, who doubled as a mechanic. As well as the Ducati, Ginty's own bikes included a Matchless single, an Indian-built Bullet, and his P and J, a Triumph Speed Twin. Later Ginty would write that he didn't know if I held a spanner like a quill pen because he never saw me with a spanner in my hand. It was true that I rarely got a chance to work on the bike while I was there, as Ginty would either impatiently take over tasks himself or depute them to Cholo, who he addressed curtly, like a subordinate, without looking at him. Cholo was a friendly but understandably reserved young man, and a natural mechanic. He quickly removed the Ariel's lock-wired tank and complicated seat, and it was he who discovered that of two long rear bolts which held the underneath of the engine to the frame, one had lost its nut and fell out just as we got a spanner on it, and the other had gone missing already. Maybe that helped explain some of the vibration. It was Cholo who reputedly asked Ginty if the Bwana from England (me) was very poor, because of the state of the paintwork and chrome on the Ariel's petrol tank, as well as the fact that I only seemed to possess one pair of trousers.

I made a start cleaning off the bike's wheel rims, but next morning Cholo had cleaned the bike completely, as well as straightening the rear brake rod and detecting and correcting several other faults. We replaced the engine bolts together, though it was mostly him, and I guiltily gave him some kwacha for all his help. When I told Ginty about that he bristled, and it was the closest we came to overtly falling out. Ginty had bought Cholo a house, as he had for their servant Margie, and I think he believed that gave him exclusive rights. One time he let Cholo test ride the Enfield Bullet up to the gates and back and the young man was clearly a natural: lithe, careful but quick.

Despite what seemed to me an unfortunate manner, once again I could not have hoped for a more helpful host with fettling the bike. Ginty still worked part-time as an agent for SeedCo Zambia Ltd, but spent most of the next week driving me around in his battered bakkie (again no status symbol autos here), tirelessly chasing down solutions for Jerry's many problems with all his restless energy, and showing me Lusaka in the process. We removed the rear carriers that day as they needed welding, both the front mountings on the pannier racks, and the side front braces on the carrier (Melville Price's work had succumbed by now). The following day we took them to Andy Legg's workplace, at the gated, well-organised Multicrop HQ, full of irrigation components, on the way into town, and Andy welded them himself. His repairs would last the duration.

Oil changing and chain tightening were accompanied by a lengthy investigation into the lack of lights. I couldn't believe that the dynamo itself was at fault, given how well the rebuilt magneto was performing. Ginty explored inside the headlamp shell and soldered an earth wire which he had found loose in there; he also cut out the pilot light holder and replaced it. Meanwhile I put the trick battery on charge, then quickly realised I had got the polarity wrong. When none of that produced light, the dynamo was removed and the first of several tests on it were run by Andy Legg, who established that it was not a fault with the Boyer regulator/rectifier, but that the dynamo itself was not charging. Ginty was thrown by the fact that on the Ariel, the dynamo was driven by gear rather than chain.

The next day we plunged down the wide highway from the west, past industrial estates, gas stations and The Castle, Ginty's local Indian-run supermarket, and into the diesel-fumed outskirts of the city, dodging swarms of the feckless blue and yellow minibus taxis. The skyline was dominated by two tall sky-scrapers near a main junction. In one, said Ginty, the lift had partially malfunctioned and never been fixed, so that the attendant had to sit on the roof of the cage to operate its controls. When the building had caught fire, the operator had been stuck there and burned to death. The other building housed radio and TV stations, and again had suffered a fire which had trapped a number of personnel, including journalists, on the roof. There, still broadcasting, with helicopters unable to rescue them because of the up-draught of the flames, they too had perished. This was Africa.

Lusaka was a mixture architecturally. With most of the colonial infrastructure still more or less intact there were some fine buildings, particularly in the diplomatic quarter, but it also had Dickensian street markets spilling over into some of the main thoroughfares like Lumumba Road (formerly Queen Elizabeth Drive). The traders sold everything from produce to large unruly piles of second-hand clothes, which Ginty said "the Taliban", ie Muslims, imported in bales, mostly from the UK. He said that the authorities were planning to move the market from the central area, which would cause a riot for sure. Driving through the market we locked the bakkie doors from inside, stowed anything tempting under the seats, and drove with just the top of the windows open, as that way it was supposed to be harder to shatter the glass and reach in to grab something. We once saw a wheelbarrow being pushed along with five or six live goats trussed up in it. "They have no feeling for animals," said Ginty.

We hit a mall, got pictures from my camera card put on disc, and then made an unsuccessful attempt to change some traveller's cheques at Ginty's bank. There was no joy as they too wanted the receipt, so Ginty took the cheques himself and gave me several hundred dollars from their joint account. He was sure he would be able to put the traveller's cheques into his account. I had experienced this once before, when a slippery literary agent had sent me off to New York with my royalties in the form of traveller's cheques: I was in mid-air before I realised that he had countersigned them himself, so they were useless to me. My American publishers had very decently stepped in, given me cash and paid the cheques into their account, without any problem. Embarrassingly, when Ginty and Kate tried to do the same, they ran up against the requirement for the original receipt for the cheques. I was back in Blighty by then and, although my bank was able to produce a copy of the receipt, in another display of techno-boobery it took me a couple of weeks to successfully fax it to the Melvills. All was eventually well, but it had been a poor way to repay their generosity.

After the mall we visited a couple of backstreet workshops to source, or get made, the missing engine bolt and nuts. This was like a scene from a Britain that largely seemed to have passed, where things were actually manufactured. The city was small enough that Ginty knew virtually everyone. Navigating the side streets, we pulled up at a workshop and met Reg Morrey, the head of a machine shop which provided nuts with the correct, old thread for the engine bolts – superior Nyloc ones too – and used the existing bolt as a pattern for turning up a second one from suitable rod. I liked the polite way that Reg dealt with his African staff, and he turned out to be an interesting guy. Later we would visit his house for lunch, and hear tales of his days back in the UK, restoring the oldest known surviving Rolls-Royce, helping to get a Bugatti back from Czechoslovakia when that country was still behind the Iron Curtain, and working as a senior executive for British Leyland. He had some riveting insider anecdotes from the last chaotic days of the independent British motorcar industry, which had made him decide to get out and start a new life in Africa. His tales would form a good basis for another article in the car mag.

Ginty drove me all round town, including township-type areas. I noticed, at one nicknamed "Soweto" that, unlike in South Africa, the close-set shacks at least benefited from the presence of shade-trees: the Crown colonial authority had apparently insisted they be laid out that way. The citizens had a way with words: we passed "Mucky Radiator Repairs", the "Thick Madam Restaurant", and the "Blood Brothers Barber Shop".

Ginty said crime levels were nowhere near as bad as in South Africa, though they were increasing due to the influx of desperate people from Zimbabwe. It had been bad back in the Eighties, but then a Neighbourhood Watch was formed to patrol the city streets at night against gangs of robbers with guns. Unlike the patrols in South Africa, this one was armed and had a German ex-SS officer in charge who, Ginty said, had been "very eager to shoot someone. The wounded were turned over to the police, the dead were dumped at hospitals."

In 1964 Zambia had achieved independence peacefully under Kenneth Kaunda, and off one of the main drags there was a monumental statue of a black man with his hands raised above his head in the moment of pulling apart the chains that shackled him. "Round here," said Ginty, "we see that and say, 'They can break anything.'"

Our drives would usually end up at the bar of the Gymkhana Club. This was a green oasis in the middle of the bustling city, with a cross-country circuit around the edge running under trees and through bush. The big annual gymkhana, usually marked by cold weather, was coming up at the beginning of July. It included traditional elements such as pig sticking (but not with real pigs) and hitting a pivoting shield with a lance like knights of old. Ginty showed me where a bush used to grow, behind which writer Alexandra Fuller (or was it her mother?) had been sick, as described in her disturbing memoir, *Don't Let's Go To The Dogs Tonight*.

The bar was a dark, pleasantly run-down place where the members, a combination of posh and louche, sometimes shouted at the barman when the drinks didn't keep coming quick enough. I only ever saw a single black member, an immensely dignified ex-ranking officer from the army or police, who would stand at the other side of the horseshoe-shaped bar from where we were.

Ginty usually hung out there with his blunt mate Alan Obst, who I had met briefly on the Isle of Man. They all deplored the way that the fields, virtually Lusaka's only green lung, were being eroded by new building, often with no planning permission. There were some good-looking women in the club, but most were as hard-bitten as some of the Pony Club mums back in Blighty. Although the drinks were good, the club could be a pretty depressing place, pervaded by the feeling that things were on the slide. Ginty usually picked up the tab, though I managed it a couple of times, before we rolled home. One night at the wheel, talking about African attitudes to the white tribe, Ginty blurted out, "They just want to take all our stuff and kick us out".

There were regular power cuts. One happened the day after the government announced they were no longer buying electricity from South Africa. Back at Ginty's, after dark I would walk over from the guest house to the lamp-lit main building, illuminating the way with my Maglite. One evening, somehow the torch went missing in the living room and, despite an extensive search, never turned up again. Losing that and also mislaying my phone, which meant having to buy a replacement for £12, reinforced irascible Ginty's opinion of me as a duffer, and possibly fatally incompetent.

With contact to home and elsewhere re-established, there was more bad news about Zoe, the Labrador. As we drove out one morning I told Ginty about this, but his only response was a clipped, "Yes, it's very upsetting". I guess he considered discussing topics with an emotional dimension to be what the equally macho Argentine culture deprecated as "breathing through the wound". Yet a kinder, more sensitive side to Ginty did sometimes emerge: in correspondence when I was home again after the trip, he always asked after the dog.

In the middle of the week there were a couple of business people booked into the guest house. I offered to move to a camp nearby but Andy Legg invited me to stay for two nights at his home, which was also just outside Lusaka but in diagonally the opposite direction. Unfortunately his wife was unwell, but Andy and I sallied forth for a Chinese meal, which was just excellent, with the restaurant full of Chinese businessmen who bounced up and down again from their chairs to exchange toasts.

I enjoyed the company of Andy. He was a highly competent engineer with a positive attitude, unfailingly helpful and a bit less complicated than Ginty. He had quite a number of interesting bikes too, in various states – a '53 AJS single, a pair of little Honda "Monkey bikes", a Norton Twin, a Russian 350 water-cooled 2-stroke, a Panther 120 big single, a BSA Bantam plus a Bushman variant and, in addition to his modern Harley, a magnificent 1940 WLA. I was later able to help him in minor ways, locating a source of spares for the Bushman, dating the Norton from its engine number, and checking the availability of late Panther engine bits. On my second evening with him we went to an art exhibition, with a cosmopolitan crowd, and much of the best work was inspired by the South Luangwa Valley where I was headed.

It was another take on the city, as was an interview to talk about my trip which Ginty arranged for me at *The Post*, the newspaper in opposition to Zambia's ruling MML Party. Corruption was a problem here as it was almost everywhere in Africa. Former President Chiluba had been prosecuted and convicted in London of siphoning off tens of millions of pounds, some of it during a deal over the country's primary resource, copper; though he had appealed, and in August 2009 would be acquitted in Zambia, allegedly thanks to the influence of the new President, Rupiah Banda. The deal, insisted upon by the IMF/World Bank during a slump in the market, had privatised the copper mines, leaving them in foreign ownership. Zambia received just 0.6 per cent of their turnover in royalties, which was a scandal in a country with 50 per cent unemployment and an average life expectancy of 38. Chiluba's successor, President Levy Mwanawasa, renegotiated the deal in 2008 to take advantage of a world boom in copper. Under his regime, however, corruption had not gone away. Early in 2009 European donors froze their funding to Zambia for the fight against HIV/Aids, which affected 1 in 11 Zambians, claiming that too much of the money was being hived off by corrupt officials. When Mwanawasa died late in 2008, his successor Banda continued to favour privatised mining companies, often owned by, you guessed it, the Chinese, who supported his government but whose treatment of the local labour force has sometimes been controversial.

I didn't talk politics with Sydney Mungala, the smooth young journo in the modern offices of *The Post*, other than making sure that it would be OK to emphasise, when talking about the charity side of the trip, how the initiative by the South Luangwa Safari Operators had dramatically improved education in the area. As far as Sydney was concerned that was fine. After conducting endless interviews myself for the bike and car magazines, I found it funny to be on the receiving end. We provided a press release and photos, but publication of the article was delayed so that it could appear in an educational supplement, and I never saw it.

By the end of the week, back at Ginty's, I was well rested and ready for the final push. A major breakthrough had been a phone conversation with Robin Pope's wife, Jo, who was back at Nkwali in South Luangwa. Early on, a vague arrangement had been made that Tony Page and I could doss with RPS for a night or two when we got there. But now, in typically generous fashion, Jo – who seemed to have been impressed by the fund-raising and by the solo run itself – said that I could stay as their guest for as long as I liked, at no charge. This was the equivalent of being handed the keys to a suite at the Connaught, with an open-ended bar tab. The only bad news came when I asked about the 60-mile stretch of road linking the last town, Chipata, and the airport we had flown into, Mfuwe, the gateway to South Luangwa. Back in my office at home I had studied that white line of road, wondering just what it was like: in Reise map terms, plain white was not even "secondary road – asphaltic/ dirt road". It was just, ominously, "other" road. Now Jo Pope said, "It's bad".

Chapter 27

TROUBLE BY
THE BRIDGE

It was Sunday 21 June (happy birthday to my brother Julian) and, after a week in Lusaka, time to go. The evening before, Ginty and Kate had taken me up the road to their daughter and son-in-law's home. Debi ran an upmarket furniture business using fine native wood, and was also a computer whizz who helped me a lot in sending articles and pictures back to the UK. Terry showed me his collection of extremely interesting books on the Rhodesian war and life there before Mugabe, and then cooked us the best *braai* yet. This seemed to be a time of change for many of the people whose lives touched mine on the trip, and that was true for Debi and family: they were about to move to South Africa for the children's education. Debi and her mother were close, and it was going to be a wrench, particularly for Kate.

I had drunk too much coffee and, after staying up to write postcards in a slightly "We Who Are About to Die" mode, the night was punctuated with pee stops. But I was organised, breakfasted with Ginty and Kate at 7am, and then loaded the bike with cut-down gear – no panniers. Everything I felt I would need for the 900-mile round trip was in the tank-bag or the black hold-all, bungeed to the rack, which I had borrowed from Ginty. I filled up the Camelbak, and then the others arrived. Ginty had arranged a ride-out to see me off, including Alan Obst who was borrowing Ginty's Norton ES2 single. Ginty was on his 1959 unit Triumph Speed Twin (and good luck, as in my experience 5TAs of that vintage were evil-handling creatures). My one regret was that I then didn't have time to say goodbye and thanks properly to Kate. She was off to Zimbabwe shortly to sort out her late mother's flat in Harare and would not be back by the time I hoped to return.

We rode off in good style, but within a mile I had to suppress a smile when, after his obvious disparagement of the state of the Ariel and my spannering skills, Ginty's Speed Twin conked out. But it was just a loose electrical connection and, unlike me, Ginty could fix it quickly by the roadside. A couple of miles on the Triumph died once again but Ginty rapidly traced that to muck from the tank in the fuel pipe, and cleared it. These were just shakedown things and I was in no position to be sniffy, as after the second stop the Ariel wouldn't start for a while, and there were painful mechanical clunks from the bottom end with every kick. We rode on and stopped for petrol, and that time the Ariel started OK.

Battling the traffic (those bloody blue minibuses), we went straight down the main boulevard after the towers, which on a Sunday was a much quicker route to our shopping mall rendezvous than Ginty's normal traffic-beating detours. There were about 20 bikes at the mall, including Andy Legg on his 1940 hand-change, foot-clutch Harley WLA. One of the tall young guys from the ride-in turned up in just about my favourite classic car, a maroon Citroën *Traction Avant* "Onze Légère". We had coffee, and some ate breakfast, including Norton-riding Alan Obst who pointed to his baked beans on toast and said, "Here's the turbo!" Andy's non-identical twin Jeff was most helpful taking snaps, though my camera had chosen that moment to display a "battery low" symbol.

Both Ginty and Andy had insisted that I make a short speech to the assembled throng, but luckily Ginty bustled off somewhere when I rose to do so, as I adapted the American pumpkin joke, supposedly based on a true incident. You may know it: a guy, in this case Ginty, stumbles out of a country bar one night, the worse for wear and horny with it, sees a field of ripe pumpkins swelling in the moonlight, finds them strangely seductive, cuts a hole in one and gets to it. A female cop, in this case South African (but not for long, as my attempts at the accent met with derision), sees movement, stops the cruise car and gets out, illuminates the guy with her flashlight and asks him what he thinks he's doing. When the guy doesn't answer, she says, "Sir, you appear to be having sexual intercourse with a pumpkin". And Ginty cries, "A pumpkin? What? Is it midnight already?"

This went down OK, though half-way through I realised that one guy was there with his teenage daughter. They didn't seem to take offence though. It turned out that the guy's dad, a policeman, had originally ridden Ginty's Speed Twin as a job bike. After more photos, we rode out to the Great East Road, which was just two-lane blacktop, but wide and with a good surface to begin with. I ended up chuffing along on my own, as Andy was riding his WLA Harley deliberately a little slowly, while the recent Enfield 500 Bullet from India, which Ginty had originally been given and lent to another friend for the day, was 10mph faster. We stopped for petrol 30 miles out at Chongwe, and I was glad of it later as there would be no more juice for another 165 miles. Riding on, after a few miles, Andy came by in good style and indicated me into the verge for a final mass photo opportunity with a good vista in the background. I said goodbye to Andy and Ginty, and rode off; Len on his Hinckley Triumph, plus a couple of other "moderns", came a few more miles, and then I was on my own.

After a bit of fretting about mechanical issues – we never had cured the dynamo, so I was just back with taped-on cycle lamps – it was good. This became one of the best roads so far, with hills and bends, thatched villages, tree-covered landscapes and friendly folk on their way back from church. Kids smiled and waved, though a couple of them held out their hands to beg or ask for food. With smoke rising from occasional fires off in the trees, and red dirt beside and on the road, this was my vision from that Piper Cherokee back in 2007, I was riding my dream. Road conditions continued OK, except for intermittent massive pot-holes, a couple of which I couldn't avoid; and there were long scars in the tarmac, running in the direction of travel, which made the Ariel's skinny tyres white-line.

Forty miles on, at 12.15, I stopped in a shady lay-by, sucked at the Camelbak (you bit the mouthpiece to release fluid), and ate a biscuit and some still-good biltong from Port Elizabeth. Starting again, everything was going swimmingly and the unloaded bike pulled well. My destination for the night was Luangwa Bridge Camp. It was by the same Luangwa river I knew and loved from Nkwali, but while the river went snaking off from the bridge pretty much due north-east to the National Parks, the only road ran more easterly, parallel with the Mozambique border, to Chipata. To reach the Parks from there, you had to turn north-west and take that "other" road. As Ginty wrote, "Kenneth Kaunda was from the East, but since his demise, the area has been on the forgotten list ... the last whitey left [Chipata] in the mid-20th century..."

I was about 35 miles from the Bridge when I slowed for a village and a bad rattle developed. Part of the African spiritual dimension had been my increasing superstition, and I couldn't help noting that the mileage was

3, **666**. Going up a hill, the noise got worse, we lost power, and the engine died before we made it to the top. I got the bike on its stand by the roadside, and experienced the usual thoughts: the shame of it all after the ride out from Lusaka, and whether this would screw up the book? I thought it might be the primary chain so, under the eyes of women and children wandering down from the huts on the crest, I managed to get the chaincase's threaded cap off by hitting a screwdriver with the big adjustable spanner, and put some oil in. More women walked past, some silent, apprehensive, but I think that one said "Thank you". An older man came, asked "Breakdown?" and walked on. Boys walked past, staring back unsmiling. I might be in the middle of nowhere but I was far from alone.

I tried a bump start downhill. No dice. The engine just chuffed without a hint of ignition, and something hit my leg as it fell off. I stopped, walked back and found it, a 4-inch long cylinder of metal with a threaded end. Looking at the engine I realised it was the whole shaft for the inlet rockers. This was disaster, but I tried to stay calm and, surprisingly enough, succeeded. I wondered about re-inserting the shaft. At first I tried from the wrong side, the off-side, even trying to tap it in with a spanner. I realised my mistake and slipped it in from the near-side, wiggling it to get past an obstacle, and then tightened the threaded end until part of it protruded from the oil banjo on the off-side, where studying the other, exhaust rocker box, showed me that the nut to hold on the shaft had gone AWOL.

I now had two problems: how to keep the shaft from unthreading and falling out again; and what to do about the oil feed, which was intended to lubricate the inlet rocker, but would now be discharging all over the bike. For the first, I rummaged in my tank bag and, in a small yellow tobacco tin full of odds and sods, discovered a solitary, tiny Jubilee clip, an old-fashioned one held together by a tiny nut and bolt, which might serve. (I had a better selection of new clips – but they were back in one of the panniers.) There was a fresh bunch of kids watching now, keeping their distance but doing a running commentary. I didn't really mind, but after a while they were gently chided by an older boy passing. I got the clip correctly aligned on the shaft with a screwdriver, fastened it over the shaft's threaded end, being extremely careful not to drop the clip's tiny nut until I got it properly threaded onto its little bolt, and then began tightening the clip over the threaded end, hoping hard that the threads wouldn't be damaged by the clip. Once it was well tight, I dabbed the clip's little nut and bolt with Loctite to help keep it done up.

I then turned to how I could seal up what was presumably an oil hole on the end of the shaft, which its missing nut would have aligned with the banjo fixing to lubricate the rockers. I considered the two-pack, but for a simple life deployed for the first time some magic double-sided rubbery black tape, claimed to be oil-proof, which I had bought from a catalogue. I cut three or four 2- to 3-inch strips and, stretching them so they overlaid, bandaged the clip and the end hole. The questions were: if it restricted the oil coming through the end of the banjo, how important was that? And was the clip going to hold the end of the shaft in place?

I took a last pace about, carefully across the road and back several times, looking for the nut, though I knew in my heart it must have dropped off earlier. The boys were amused. Then a family came up, a wild loud girl ("Are you here to buy the lodge?" she cried), and simple guys (no chance of finding out how far the bridge was from them) who were all over my gear, innocently I think, but I reluctantly rugged up, bump-started the bike, and we were running again.

I was creeping along in a daze. It was 3 o'clock by then and I had neglected to take my diabetic pills. Struggling up hills, were we down on power, or was I just being cautious? The bridge was ten miles further than I had calculated, and they were nervous miles. As we approached, the verges ceased to be cut back, so that tall grass pressed in on the road – the kind, I thought, that lions leaped from. When I reached the bridge, the market and shops didn't look hopeful and there was no garage visible. I followed the sign to the Lodge, and turned right down a track that ran past native huts and beside the river, a rough rubble-strewn bit of dirt road which I navigated with increasing ill temper as it went on for two miles. The bike was rattling loudly, but when we finally got to the turn to the right for the last steep uphill climb to the Lodge, it powered up the track in good style.

Lindsay, who ran the place with her partner Will, walked out to greet me. Ginty had booked me in. I babbled on about the breakdown as I checked the bike – the "bandage" seemed to have held, and there wasn't too much oil spattered back. So I followed her round to a tall first floor verandah supported on tree-trunks, with a bar at the back, looking out over a swimming pool and beyond, to a lovely bend in the river. On the far side, the forested slopes opposite were Mozambique. It was a magnificent spot, but the word was that the couple were selling up and hoping to move back to Seapoint in Cape Town; it must have been a very isolated life. Another reason was that Will, who reputedly liked his "turbo cabbage", was unwell (a bad leg, if memory serves). As I walked to the bar he was lying half asleep on the sofa.

A couple of cold Mosis were very welcome, and eventually I tried to pick Will's brain about my mechanical problem: would the lack of lubrication to the inlet rockers damage them seriously? He was non-committal. Soon I was led down a path covered in dead leaves to my "chalet", with its native thatched roof. It was rough and ready as Ginty had described, but rough magic too. There was the smell of burnt charcoal from a boiler cylinder just behind, and in the dark you could see the fires glowing on the slopes across the river. The washbasin had cracked and been glued, the curtain through to the wash area was falling down, and the bed was rock hard. But the shower water was warm, and I could plug in and charge the camera battery before the generator went off. Ginty and then Andy rang, and Ginty texted.

I walked back to the verandah for more drink and a steak supper; as Ginty had said, the food was "mushi" (good), and Lindsay friendly and attentive. Sitting reading at the table, I looked up to see a lizard in the wicker lampshade, waiting on the insects that the light would draw. I turned in early, crawling under the green mosquito net, because who knew what tomorrow would bring?

Chapter 28

SWISS ANGELS

The bad news was that the magic tape had all failed, despite having done so well on the way there – perhaps because of the warm engine, which would have cooled overnight. I tried fresh pieces of tape, before wiping my hands off and eating a Continental breakfast. The total bill including supper was about $70.

Two South Africans in a Land Rover, who had been staying at the Bridge campsite down at road level, got chatting and said there was a Swiss couple there who were going my way, and they would mention this to them. After I finished my checking and fiddling with the bike (wire to hold the Jubilee clip on, an unsuccessful attempt to use linked cable ties to keep the shaft in, and one I was quite proud of, undoing an inspection cap in that rocker box so I could spray it in WD40 to supplement the rockers' lubrication), I rode gingerly to the road down the steep track, looking in on the campsite and saying hello and maybe see you later to the Swiss guy, who was cleaning his teeth. I was making as early a start as possible since it was just over 200 miles to Chipata, the weather was warm, and I was under no illusions that it was going to be an easy ride.

I trickled slowly back up the track to the main road and the bridge, where I was stopped by an official, but only because a truck was coming across from the other side. Then I rode over the wide Luangwa and onto a wonderful road, swinging up into the hills – no wonder the Bridge was the destination of choice for Lusaka bikers. So it was a nasty shock to look down and see the oil gushing out from the open end of the shaft. This clearly could not be sustained, and it was the moment at which the Hood trousers, though they had been smudged and spattered previously, became permanently two tone green and (oil stain) black. The only shade was half-way up a hill, in front of a school. So the inevitable large crowd of kids began to gather (time in the classroom appeared to be a low priority), as I took off my jacket and considered my options for sealing the hole at the end of the shaft. The tape was a no-no, which left the two-pack putty that hadn't worked on the petrol tap.

As I was applying it, a metallic dark blue Land Rover drove up, stopped, and out got my guardian angels, the Swiss couple, Daniella and Martin Haenz. With the "Angels" bit, I am not speaking entirely metaphorically. I had been the beneficiary of too much good luck to think it was entirely coincidental. The couple had taken a year off to tour Africa and, being Swiss, were carrying every conceivable mechanical aid, "and yes, we also have Swiss Army knives!" laughed Martin. They were very friendly, and Martin quickly began admiring the Ariel! Since I had applied the "putty" I suggested we ride on a bit to see if it worked and, kitting up, after a reluctant start I roared off in spirited fashion, bend swinging on the curves of the mountain road.

But four miles later there was oil everywhere. I stopped and so did the Swiss, with Martin saying I had been going so well through the bends that it had made him want to come back and do it on his BMW GS1100. Then he got out a tap and die set, carefully tapped a thread on the inside of the shaft's hollow oil-leaking orifice, and stoppered it with a suitable screw and PTFE tape. Amazing. There were still drops of oil from the banjo and elsewhere, but it was an infinite improvement. And then they said they would be happy to stay with me all day, all the way to Chipata.

With the delays it turned into a long, hot, 210-mile ride. The road at first was good and interesting. Then, after I stopped to gas up the bike at Nyimba, the surface deteriorated quite badly, enough to slow us down. There were unannounced speed humps going into villages, the constant human traffic on the road (if you build it, they will come), pot-holes and "rain grooves" which wiggled the Ariel's rear wheels. There were increasing signs of Muslim presence: mosques, covered heads and green scarves. At a petrol stop (for them) at Petauke, Daniella said she was glad they were travelling at my 45-ish speed, as it was best on these roads and gave her time to look around.

It was lunchtime and I proposed eating, but they said not there by the gas station, as there were too many people and they would start to beg food, so we backtracked to a little walled "camp" just off the road, with a hole-in-the-wall bar and, in a glass box, frankfurter sausages and boiled eggs being kept warm by a light bulb. Dodgy, and I'd had the runs the previous evening (probably nerves) and taken Imodium, but I risked the food and a can of lemonade, and got away with it. A couple of genial educated Zambians came to chat, as a line of small children squatted at the gate and watched us eat. I produced my biscuits and tried "Anyone for Tennis?" (which is what the biscuits were called). The Swiss, God bless them, laughed at all my stuff.

It was now 2 o'clock and we had 100 miles still to go. Evidently energised by the grub I went for it, riding straight on through a road under construction rather than taking a diversion, and cranking it on, hammering along at 45–50mph through the hot afternoon, as the road got a little better. This was the slog of riding, and I could do it. Just after 4pm we were through Katete which, slightly smarter, looked like a fun town. We stopped about 10 miles on the far side. I was dog tired and, with the glowing sun going down to the west, braced myself for the final 40-odd miles. Then Martin noticed that my faithful little Jubilee clip with the square nut had broken, releasing lots of oil from the unsecured shaft. From his spares he provided another, sturdier clip, gently chiding me that I should keep a better eye on my bike.

Then we cracked on. The miles to Chipata seemed endless – straight roads, with the morning's forested curves feeling a long way back, and off to the left the sun sinking faster. It was a close-run thing. We got to the outskirts of Chipata as dusk was falling and I'd already been flashed for the lack of lights. I hadn't realised the town was on the border to Malawi. I should have filled up at that point, but the bike was feeling hot, so when the Land Rover pulled up beside me just beyond a busy turn-off signed to Mama Rula's, the camp where we were to stay, I said, "Let's forget the petrol and go for it." This meant I would be doing the last 90 miles on about half a tank – which was OK unless the bad road used up more fuel than usual.

As we went to move off, I couldn't change from 1st to 2nd. Eventually I booted the gear pedal viciously, and we were away. The turn for Mama Rula's came up soon, and after 2km of moderate red dirt road we were there at the camp gates; big relief. The compound for accommodation was delineated from the campsite where the Swiss were going to stay, but the gate guy let both vehicles into the compound, and just as well. I mentioned the gear-changing glitch to Martin; he squatted down in the failing light, and pointed out a gearbox cover bolt half-way out of the case. I'd tightened round the timing side case-fixing screws that morning, but neglected those on the separate gearbox, which we now screwed in all round. There was more gentle chiding from Martin, and I knew he was right. If the Ariel was his, it would be properly, carefully, looked after.

Martin and Daniella went off to the camp, and I pushed the bike into an open shed full of wooden frames, found the South African wife of the owner and got a room, dinner and breakfast. She warned me that there was a "guard donkey" which might disturb the night. The registration was done by a tired, gently humorous, mixed-race lady with expressive eyes, Isabell, probably part Portuguese. Despite the warm evening, she wore her coat buttoned up to the neck. I took my stuff to the room, in the single-storey row surrounding the compound, and showered in a maze of tiredness. I had rung Jo Pope at Nkwali from the roadside, got the camp office, outlined my intended movements to them, then missed a call back from Jo, so now I rang again and got a black guy in the office who handed me over to the Senior Supervisor. It was Kiki, our guide from two years previously! Laughter all round. He said that the road to the airport was not too bad and that it had been graded and should take me two-and-a-half hours tops. But Kiki was the optimist's optimist. He said that there would be a guide, Fred, waiting for me in a vehicle at Mfuwe Airport from 8am. I told him I wouldn't be leaving till then, he said no worries.

I arranged for a 7am breakfast, and then went looking for the bar, which fronted onto the campsite. I walked through the dark site and found Martin and Daniella at the far end, beyond the two trekking buses, which were feeding their traveller folk from field kitchens built into the former ground-level baggage compartments. The Swiss were cooking their own supper, so I went back to the bar to wait for them. Going in, I tripped on the entrance ramp and fell sprawling face down into the empty bar with a loud expletive, and this was *before* I'd had a drink. Isabell, behind the bar, was concerned. As I recovered with a Mosi, she joked deadpan about my taking all her change. I was still having trouble with the money, and twice that day had paid for stuff costing five kwacha or less with a 50 kwacha note. I sat at a table, enjoying the beer as bus people came and went, and I watched the big-screen TV on the BBC World Service, too loud and weird after the day. I had arranged to have my dinner there and it was good, with soup. The Swiss arrived; as promised I bought them drinks, and we had a pleasant time before all turning in early.

Chapter 29

BAD ROAD

I didn't sleep very well, mainly because of nerves about the following day, though it was the guard donkey that woke me at 3.15am. I didn't get much real sleep after that, lying there in the dark of the night listening to distant cockerels crow. At one point later I got out from under the mosquito net and peered through the window; I could see some mist in the pre-dawn. I was still wearing the black Ariel T-shirt to save a clean one for Nkwali, and it was streaked with white sweat marks from the day before.

At 7 o'clock I went across the courtyard and ate in the proper dining room, where another guest was absorbed on her laptop and a party of Americans were discussing business and the financial potential of charcoal. I ate up and left, went to the bike in the shed, squirted WD40 into the inlet rocker box, renewed the duct tape around the edge of the air cleaner's hose, checked tyre pressures and spoke tension, and tightened down engine bolts and case screws. There were workmen around, and the old white-moustached South African owner drifted in and told me they were making beehives to step up production of honey for export. Zambian bees were free from the varoa mite infections that were decimating the European hives, though the native strain were vicious, with terrible stings, and you could only work with them after dark.

It was just past 8am and I was impatient to be off, but he asked me where I was headed, and then gave me good information about the turn-off to Mfuwe airport, which was marked by a green Wildlife sign. Jerry, possibly sensing what was in store, proved reluctant to start, but fired up fourth or fifth kick, and we were away. Back up the dirt track and turning right onto tarmac, with people and traffic, heading north-west. The tarmac ran out after two or three miles, and we were into it.

I knew it would be bad, Jo Pope had told me it would be bad, but we were both wrong – it was beyond bad, the worst road I have ever ridden. Work had begun to renew this road over a year previously – most of the former surface had been torn up, though sometimes irregular patches remained, and some of the road had been graded – and then the work had stopped. We had encountered something similar two years before in Malawi, where the final 50 or so miles of the EU-funded road down to Lake Malawi, excellent so far, had been abandoned in mid-renovation. Here, from Chipata, this partially-done road had then been ripped up by lorries and 4x4s whose solution was to speed over the irregularities. The result became unspeakable. In my head I thought of it, and cursed it, as "Once-was-road".

The day was already heating up and the surface was pretty bad from the start, punishing and jarring. Oil was soon visible again, streaking the right side of the bike, which I hoped (vainly) was just the WD40 seeping out. I was soon trying to stay on the extreme edge of the road, where the snake-tracks of bicycle tyres followed the narrow dusty berm that had built up beside the half-graded corrugated carriageway. There were people along the way, many of whom waved, and at that stage I could still wave back.

After 25 miles I stopped, beyond one of the several villages with schools along the way. There was a rare patch of shade, and it was quiet, with a breeze in the trees. The engine was coated in oil and red dust. Checking, I found out the Jubilee clip provided by the Swiss could now be rotated easily by hand, and couldn't be tightened any further. It was a real worry that this would break and fall off. And the screw they had tapped in to seal the end of the shaft was now loose on its thread. But we were OK so far: that was all I could think, and I knew there were fully-equipped workshops for vehicles at Nkwali.

The traveller buses from Mama Rula's whizzed by, raising dust, as had several 4x4s further back; I had seen one local raise a cloth to his mouth. I got going again. Soon there was tarmac, and my spirits rose, but mockingly this only ran up a hill and down the other side, and then it was back to the red "graded" surface which got progressively worse: bone-jarring, teeth-rattling hell. Would the Ariel hold up? Would I? Then I spotted a single headlamp in the mirror and soon a young black rider on a red Honda came by – all motorcycles are called "Hondas" by Africans, but this was an actual Honda XR250 trail bike, with enviably long-travel suspension. He seemed to know the road, so I tried to follow his line, though he was going faster than I liked, and went all over the road, often swinging over to the far right side, even round blind bends. Crossing from one side to the other involved more major jarring and smashing. When he pulled in somewhere, I continued more moderately, seeking that berm of dust on the side, which unfortunately wasn't there much anymore. I was just thinking to myself that this tactic had its drawback, since if you lost concentration for a moment you would start to slip into the roadside ditch – when exactly that happened. Down in the ditch we went.

I managed to stay off the brakes and, once into the bumpy ditch, to keep upright, but I ended up stalled down in the dust, about five feet below the road level. Then the Honda rode up. By gestures and words the rider encouraged me to follow him again, saying "It's not so bad now". Revitalised, I kickstarted the bike and aimed it diagonally at the bank of the ditch – and the Ariel's engine pulled us straight up without hesitation, right back onto the road. That was one of its finest moments. We went on together, though still a bit faster than I was comfortable with. Jarring, crashing, I began to pray aloud for tarmac, and couldn't conceal my miserable expression from those watching gravely from the roadside.

It went on and on. There was a real fear that something would break. I cursed and swore aloud, and the distance became irrelevant. My efforts to keep up with the Honda caused a couple of hairy moments with the rear end fishtailing on the edge of control. I let him disappear a couple of times, but then he waited for me. Eventually in a village he turned off, and I stopped; he rode up and told me he was home now, and said the airport turnoff was "about 20km".

I thanked him and carried on, but the road instantly turned even worse before a bridge, and I was shouting aloud "No Fair!" My right hand in particular had lost all feeling and at one point I couldn't work the front brake until I had shaken out the pins and needles in my fingers. Then there was another teasing bit of tarmac; this must go to the airport, I thought – *wrong* – and some particularly bad bits followed. I was bashed, shaken up, fearful for the bike, in sorry shape.

Eventually, after 60 miles, the green Wildlife sign to the left which I had been told about turned up. But the track was *still* dust – though sometimes the surface colour changed from red to grey, mockingly mimicking tarmac. I pulled up to ask a man with a wheelbarrow, and he said yes, it led to the airport, but I didn't quite trust him, and when another guy on a little MX bike came up, I asked again and then followed him. It was a narrow track, soon running along the airport perimeter fence, and we wallowed into dust holes, and changed down to 1st where loose rubble had been dumped on the tops of concrete culverts. My concentration in picking lines wasn't great, and there was more than one unnecessary bang.

And then, we reached a short tarmac strip which led to the Mfuwe airport building and its car park, and there was the RPS logo on one of their light khaki Land Cruisers, and I'd made it.

I never really became "as one" with Jerry, the way I had done in the past with, say, my 750 Norton Commando, when man, machine and road had sometimes fused into a single fluid entity. But the Ariel had done amazingly, living up to its legend, which I had rehearsed to myself along the way to keep my spirits up. These things had coped with World War 2, with the bad roads of the Forties and Fifties, with scrambles and trials, and they could still do it, 50 years or more after they had been built. That instant thumping climb up out of the ditch, like a tractor! I felt a burst of deep admiration for the oil-spattered Red Hunter.

Freddy, the guide from Nkwali, was a big guy and endlessly patient with me as I drank half a bottle of his water, and composed myself. It was twenty-five to twelve – it had taken me just over three hours. "Only" three hours. I told Fred somewhat peremptorily that I rode very, very slowly, and that I would need to fill up with petrol. He said there was a station, which I hadn't remembered from before, about 20km up the road. So that was a plus, although actually there was still plenty of juice sloshing around in Jerry's tank, despite my fears that the rough, low-geared going might have used more fuel. Fred was giving a lift to several other people, including a Zambian teacher who looked like a wry young Morgan Freeman. They all beamed at me and let me take my time. I stowed my luggage in the truck, and we set off in convoy.

We trundled at maybe 30mph along the almost familiar strip of road. I remembered how alien and crude it had all seemed in 2007 when my wife, daughter and I had arrived here for our safari holiday. Now, after spending the last two months in Southern Africa, the conditions seemed perfectly normal, and I just blessed the tarmac, despite the pot-holes. There was more traffic, more bicycles and more of the small shops that advertised themselves as "investments" – "Wency's Autoworks", "CAPTAIN BIGGIE" and of course the "OBAMA PUB". Later, Jo Pope would tell me that the population had risen dramatically compared to 20 years previously, while the relative prosperity was mostly due to the trickle-down from the safari tourism. The bike did well at the stops as Fred dropped people off, but stalled when we halted for petrol. After that, the last passengers got down, including the teacher, and we drove on, to the bridge over the river and into the National Park, but turned left just before it. Nkwali sat on the other, east, side of the river, from the Park, and RPS and their vehicles usually got over the water on a pair of pontoons hauled across by wire, worked by the ferrymen. We soon turned off the tarmac and hit the last five miles of dirt track to my goal, Nkwali.

We weren't there yet. Although it was dusty I stayed behind Fred and the Land Cruiser because I wanted his tyre tracks. I had a couple of dodgy moments as the track was sandy, a tricky surface off-road on which you have to keep up your speed and momentum, and the Toyota's weight at least made the tracks firmer. Then I missed a right fork, going straight on along the sandy track, halting, and then having to blast out at high revs with a rooster tail of sand, under the eyes of a local carrying a load of wood. I got across to the Land Cruiser, but stalled behind it. And then couldn't start the Ariel, though Fred got out and held it steady from behind. But he was tactful and understanding when I put Jerry on his stand, and took a breather. The bike fired up quickly after that and, since I declined Fred's offer to go in front (those tyre tracks), I got completely caked in dust, with my jacket open too. We passed the big baobab I remembered, and the visor and spectacles were fogging up on me as we finally drove through some bushes, round a bend, and there was the office. The bike celebrated by dying, so that I rode through some low-hanging branches and leaves, freewheeling to a halt by a fence.

I recognised Jo Pope from her pictures in the *It's Monday* newsletter. A winning mixture of Joyce Grenfell and Lara Croft, the genteel and the intrepid, with Grenfell's inner warmth, she delivered a short welcoming speech to me, using blush-making words like "the spirit of adventure" and "magnificent". There were jolly girls from the office and guides there, and for a second I mistook one for Kiki. But then there was the man himself, and we both burst out laughing.

It was a moment. I had expected to be housed in one of the well-appointed huts, but Jo said I was to be staying in Robin Pope's House again! When she checked that I knew where everything was there, I joked that I knew where the drinks cupboard was, and that they'd probably never see me again. In her jolly-hockey-sticks accent (which gave a delicious twist to the decidedly un-ladylike language that she sometimes resorted to), Jo judged that for now I just needed "to chill", and Kiki, perceptively, took me off "for a cold drink" to the outdoor bar, which was sometimes frequented by elephants. I had the Mosi to end them all – Made It! After our first visit I had sent Kiki a copy of the car magazine carrying the Land Rover article with pictures of him in it, plus some photo prints and, showing off, one from the bike mag of me riding an A10. He confirmed that Robin had passed on the magazine and that he had also received the picture from "the newspaper", so when he had heard from Jo that someone was coming on a bike, he'd thought, "Yes! He's the motorbike man!" More roars of laughter, and I agreed to go out on that evening's game drive with him.

Chapter 30

MEMORIES
BY THE RIVER

Then Kiki walked me to the palatially-dimensioned house by the river, with all its memories and echoes. It was strange to be there without Molly and Rosie. My gear was brought, and I checked everything out. The bar and fridge were fully stocked, though I would make a point of not helping myself. Instead I filled the claw-footed bath, and while I was lying soaking, a gecko ran up the shocked white wall, and then froze.

Afterwards, as I lay on the monster four-poster bed with its canopy of mosquito netting on rails at the top, a platoon of baboons, including mothers with little ones clinging onto them, and the big guys interested in the ladies with red fannies which Kiki had pointed out earlier, crashed in and out of the trees opposite the window – I didn't remember that from before. They parked themselves in those trees, and later, when I was sitting on the sofa, one of the babies noticed me there. I stayed perfectly still, and it stared at me, moving its head from side to side, keeping on staring.

This was fun, and a reminder that, as someone remarked, at Nkwali the humans were the zoo exhibits for the animals. There were gaps in the game fence to let the elephants in (and stop them breaking it down), and for that reason staff would come and escort visitors everywhere within the compound. The animals' presence was all part of the magic. Then from the river side of the low fence, an impala's head and graceful neck stretched across to eat some leaves. Beyond, the slow river sparkled in the afternoon heat. Paradise regained. But my mood was – funny. Verging on hollow. Are all victories hollow? I did know it would take a little while to recover from the tensions and efforts of the last couple of days.

My namesake, Wilson the watchman, in his grey greatcoat and beret, came to take me to the area around the bar where there was tea and delicious cakes, and more staff to meet, including the guides Jacob and

Braston, and our hostess Melissa Powell, an apparently uncomplicated blonde Australian from around Sydney, and clearly very good at her job. The other guests were John and Fiona, a retired Scots couple, still glowing with animal encounters at Tena-Tena, another RPS camp where they had been fly-camping and "bundu-bashing", ie bush walking. On one walk they had come face to face with a male lion at about 15 yards; it had stared for a long while before they gradually eased back. All that week they had been a magnet for lions. I was envious, as lions had been pretty much the one thing we had barely seen on our previous trip. But Kiki said there were two prides in the Park now and, perhaps as a consequence, there had been fewer leopard sightings for a while. The remaining guests were Daniel and Elizabeth Dwyer, a young American couple currently pursuing their professional lives in London, as corporate lawyer and banker respectively; their house was in a secluded corner of Kensington, just a few doors away from where my brother's first wife lived.

For the evening game drive I rode in the front with Kiki, where Melissa kidded that I would be on the lamp, before the house servant Jones joined us to do that. We drove back out along the familiar approach road, in a very different style from my arrival that lunchtime. We stopped for a perfect family group of giraffes, so graceful; they walk, as Kiki pointed out, like camels, with both legs on one side going forward at once. We bumped down to the small river that ran parallel to the track and were shown the fish dam with its gaps full of traps; we watched birds, including a wonderfully alert grey-headed kingfisher, sharp in the lenses of my little binoculars. I felt a small stab of justification: it had definitely been worth bringing these despite the extra weight. We drove slowly on, bouncing through impenetrable bush. And the magic returned. I was entranced by two or three of the trees, just perfect shapes, statements you couldn't quite interpret though you knew what they meant; like the posture of Africans. And the evening light, the whole *tootie*.

We came to the pontoons over the Luangwa. One evening during our first stay, as both pontoons were crossing at once, Kiki had proposed a boat race. (When visiting the UK on his travels he had been to Oxford and Cambridge "to see which one I should study at".) I said we were "Oxford", and Oxford won, mainly because Kiki got a spare stick of wood and supplemented the efforts of our two ferrymen as they stuck their sticks in the wire and ratcheted the pontoon forward. Hippo heads glistened in the dusk out in the water, though Kiki said their numbers had been depleted by an outbreak of anthrax. Fewer crocs were visible around Nkwali, though they had not been affected.

To John and Fiona I pointed out the pylons on the far side, constructed especially for the Presidential Lodge on a hill in the distance, with their power lines still drooping or down and dangling, as they had been in 2007. The Scots, surprised, asked how long I had been there before, and I realised again that, though it had only been a few days, I had remembered so much. The top of one of the pylons had been bent down by the 2006/7 floods, and I pointed out to Kiki how it looked like a giraffe's head. Then, conscious of talking too much and boasting, implicitly, about past experience, I clammed up.

We stopped for sundowners, listening to the baboons bark at a leopard. Later by lamp light we saw a zebra and the odd hippo, but it was a long bumpy go with nothing sensational, until Kiki switched off the engine, Jones turned off the lamp, and we sat listening to the night noises, and gazing up at the silent sky full of brilliant stars.

I had a lie-in the next morning, though perversely I hadn't slept well. In mid-morning Melissa took me to see Jo Pope at the office, so Jo could find out what I needed. Nothing was too much trouble. The pesky traveller's cheques were changed to dollars with no worries. I got the use of the phone in the office (after a lock had been removed from its old-fashioned dial) to call home, and we arranged a visit to Kawaza School the following afternoon. I wasn't too upset that Jo talked me out of riding there, saying the bike's presence wouldn't mean anything to the kids. It was a true relief to be the recipient of unstinted help from such a well-oiled operation. For the bike itself, big Fred led me and the filthy Ariel down to the extensive workshop, where the manager was absent, but I explained to Brighton, the workshop foreman, about the leaking bolt and the tapped screw.

I went back later in the day to meet Rob Clifford, the manager, and found one of the guys starting to wash down the bike. Rob was a short, friendly, Teutonic-looking ex-Zimbabwean, and said that he would see what he could do about securing and sealing the inlet rocker shaft. I also explained that the oil in the forks and the gearbox needed topping up. I heard later on the rumour mill that Rob was going to take over the running of Nkwali when

Robin and Jo Pope retired the following year. This was sobering news, because I wanted Nkwali to stay the same forever. But nothing ever does.

When I got back to the house, my dirty washing had disappeared, and later would come back clean and folded. Even my trusty boots would be cleaned. I worked on my journal outside by the bar until the others came back, excited about seeing more lions close up, and were greeted by Melissa with cool flannels. Jo joined us for lunch. All the food was delicious, varied, really well cooked, with clever use of nuts and seeds, and brilliant baking and puddings. Key Lime Tart that evening was a particular high point.

Jo, though patrician in manner, laughed a lot and was down-to-earth. She explained that an Empowerment initiative by the government meant that next year RPS would have to bid for the lease on their own camp at Tena-Tena for the first time. Would other operators bid against them and each other? Or might someone outside get it and RPS then have to negotiate to run it for them? Jo understood about the need for empowerment, but … Kiki said, "It's Robin Pope's, and that's that".

Jo also talked about Government teachers, unsatisfactory and unmotivated, who taught by rote, or would write a lesson on the board in the morning, and then go off and leave the class to copy it out. Not unnaturally the kids too would go off after a couple of hours. David, the headmaster at Kawaza, was unlikely to permit that, and the extra teachers RPS paid for would help keep class sizes manageable, but it was still disturbing.

That evening we went across on the pontoon again. Nothing too dramatic appeared, although Kiki pointed out three porcupines, a mongoose (and there had been a rarer marsh mongoose in the camp pond), a cat-like serval, scrub hare and, close up, an elephant shrew. And we had sundowners – no drink tastes so good – on "Presidential Hill", the knoll beside the one with the President's residence. The whole bush world was spread out before us beneath the setting sun, running on forever like a chant that never ends.

Chapter 31

BACK TO SCHOOL

Next day we visited Kawaza School. I rode there with Jo and the American guests Daniel and Elizabeth, with big Fred driving the Toyota. The road was much busier than it used to be. "Twenty years ago there were three bicycles, one car, and one shop. There has been a population explosion," said Jo, who had written a compelling article on how the global financial crisis, abbreviated locally to "The Global", was affecting lives here, just when some prosperity from safari tourism was trickling down to make things better for the local people. RPS themselves were not exempt: bookings were down, and the agencies squeezed their set terms and profit margins ruthlessly.

As we turned off the main road between the bridge to the Parks and the airfield, Jo told me that RPS were involved with two schools, Kawaza and Nsefu, plus two community schools, Kapita and Katapilla, which just taught reading to the third grade. They paid for 18 teachers and sponsored 48 pupils to continue their secondary education away in town; that cost $200 per year, while tertiary education cost an annual $2,000. Jo spelled it out: "Without secondary education, you are tilling the fields for the rest of your life." The number of children being educated in the chiefdom had risen from 500 to 1,640 via donations from RPS guests, plus time and effort from RPS staff. At Kapita, for instance, they had built, from scratch, three classrooms and two teachers' houses, at which point the government were willing to take over and provide two teachers. But there were not enough funds to complete a similar project at Katapilla as donations had slowed, again due to The Global.

This was no dry lecture. Jo Pope laughed a lot and rose to new heights of beautifully-enunciated obscenity, describing the unexpected pain she had suffered from knee replacement operations the previous year. It was just as well she was so full of energy as, in addition to developing RPS to its current award-winning status, and the work administering the schools, she had become involved with the domestic airline business. Life was hectic, but Jo still missed Robin fiercely when work took him away on safari a lot of the time.

The road to Kawaza was being improved. The first section was well-graded brown dirt and, traversing the humps of large drainage culverts, we reached the first stream and Fred got down to check the 4x4's hubs. The sandy approach was steeper than I remembered and the water a good 18 inches deep, enough to cover the Ariel's crankcases. The second stream, where women were doing washing, was deeper still, with a steep climb out. Not impossible but, as Clint Eastwood once observed, a man has to know his limitations. After the chilli-fence corner, the road surface got bad, and the growth pressed in on the single-track path.

At Kawaza School it was very lively indeed. There was a sports tournament going on involving soccer and netball, for nine schools, with kids colourful in tabards and strip, though all played barefoot. We met a young white volunteer teacher from the UK, Dorothy, who, smiling, said the tournament had a festival atmosphere, "like Reading or Leeds". She was also pleased about the food-sellers there, which meant she didn't have to walk to the shop in the village. We watched a bit of an extremely lively netball game which was real fun – very loud of course, with partisan roars and pitch invasions whenever anyone scored. I was reminded of my sports-writer father, Peter Wilson, who regularly visited African Commonwealth countries for sporting events, usually boxing matches, where the audience would not infrequently end up hurling their chairs into the ring. I also remembered him, home again after one of his trips, running a comb through his slicked-back hair and showing me tiny glistening fragments of windscreen safety glass. He was being driven away at night and they had hit a buffalo at speed, wrecking the car. In the Sixties he had been sure that within a generation or two African athletes would dominate athletics in particular, and he had been right.

Daniel, Elizabeth and I had a sit-down with headmaster David Mwewa in his dark office. Understandably, given the number of visitors, he didn't remember me or the book I had given him. The library seemed painfully depleted, despite various donations of material mentioned in the RPS newsletter. David said there were now 875 pupils at Kawaza. They ranged in age from seven to 17, and 435 were girls. Female attendance had risen over the previous five years. Of the 26 staff, 12 were supported by RPS. Most were men, but having eight women teachers at the school encouraged girls to stay on.

Pinned up in the office was the School Plan for the next five years, and this had real scope. It included a programme for supporting orphans and vulnerable children, recommending them for sponsorship. Forty boys and girls had been sponsored for boarding schools over the past three years – children whose parents, if they were alive, could not afford to pay. There was staff development, with a number of teachers on programmes and going to college in the holidays. There was school transport, with buses to take the children on trips so they could be experience other places. Most of the children walked to school, though in the wet season some came by canoe, or bicycled. There were also motorcycles, so that teachers could attend meetings/ workshops economically, and collect government supplies from the District HQ. I had spotted the well-used Japanese trail-bikes outside.

Teaching was in English from the second grade; in the first grade it was still in Chinyanja, the local language, which was also spoken in Malawi. The switch, said David, was a big challenge, as the pupils still spoke Chinyanja at home. The school had a wide remit. In addition to the national curriculum the children learned needlework and crafts; also conservation, the benefits of safari tourism, and the dangers of not preserving wildlife because, he said, the culture of hunting/poaching was still active. An adult education programme had begun, but not many people came. Really, it needed to go out to them. The adults were mostly learning to read and write in the local language, though there were also some former students whose progress in school had been blocked and who now wanted to catch up.

Kawaza had done well, but it needed more. More classroom space, because at present it was necessary to split the children into morning and afternoon sessions. David wanted to get more pupils to come in the morning when their minds were still fresh. (Dorothy also provided a reality check: in Class 8, attendance might fluctuate from 40 pupils on a Monday to 25 by the Friday. Their intentions were good, but then they had to work, or help at home.) David said a bigger library room was required; also more text books, story books and magazines. They needed a science club and, above all, audio visual equipment – computers.

A start had been made. Most country schools didn't have computers because they lacked electricity, but Kawaza had solar power. Two or three weeks previously, some computers had been acquired for the sixth form. Once the teachers had got the necessary skills, said David, classes would start. There would be no outside link yet, so no internet. Putting in a landline would cost 1.25 million kwatcha, or this could be done by the phone company who would sell them modems. The mobile phone network was good, so that would probably be the way to go.

But later Jo Pope professed profound reservations about abruptly exposing "farm kids to western grunge on the internet". She knew there was a power spike in Lusaka from noon to 2pm as office workers hit the porn sites. In fact she had several reasons for concern. The solar power itself was unreliable, and the room set aside for the computers was badly needed for other lessons; she had found that all the bulbs there had failed and not been replaced. Dorothy pointed out that the computer room needed more desks – also doors that closed properly to keep out the noise. "Spoon-feeding them may just corrupt them," said Jo. "They have to show initiative." There were always problems with Kawaza, she admitted. "Organisation here is a headache. David is so organised that everyone leaves everything to him."

We took Dorothy over to visit the second school, Nsefu, where another English volunteer was in football strip on the dusty playing fields with the lads, all barefoot except him. RPS had built all the classrooms bar the original one, and funded some of the ten teachers. The library was better than Kawaza's but classrooms were pretty basic, already worn and dusty, with window panes broken because the builders had used poor quality putty and the wind then blew them in. "But also there is crime," said Jo. "People do break in to steal things." A broken chair lay in pieces because there were no screws to mend it. "How did it all get so buggered so quickly," said Jo in frustration. But she knew that the schools would always be worn and dusty because the teaching was in continuous shifts. "With pupils in from the country, who live without running water, running around the school, putting their hands everywhere, bumping desks into walls – just like any other school in the world – of course the buildings are going to show wear and tear very quickly."

Back at the blue and white buildings of Kawaza, small children were sweeping dust off the steps with short brushes that looked like sprigs of lavender. Adults – parents? – wandered around. The classrooms with their tin roofs must have got hot but at least there were shade trees here and in the central compound area. From one of the trees dangled the "bell", a section of lorry wheel-rim hanging on a bike chain, which you hit with a tyre iron. There was a big well, a fallen tree trunk for a seat, chickens scratching around, sandy dogs and drums. (At Nsefu, hanging from the rafters in one classroom we had found a goat skin, which a teacher was curing to make into the skin for a drum.)

The Kawaza boys and girls, fired up by the sports tournament, were fierce, but at least they seemed to know what they were worth. I wondered aloud how diminutive Dorothy managed with a class of 40, but she said that, in contrast with the UK school where she had taught previously, "The kids here are all polite. If they do play up, you only need to tell them once; they want to learn." Jo Pope had another volunteer who spent three months analysing the effectiveness of the RPS schools project. Since RPS began their assistance, exam passes were up from 40 per cent to 80 per cent and, whatever the imperfections, you couldn't argue with the fact that "it's great so many children are getting a better education".

Chapter 32

WILD DOGS
AND ENGLISHMEN

Back at Nkwali later that afternoon, the others were off bundu-bashing on foot, and I went out with Melissa and Kiki. There was a surprise by the river for the walking party: a table fully laid with food and sparkling wine, although Melissa couldn't find any of the little purple wildflowers to decorate the table. We hid behind bushes and soon the tired walkers came on the table with gratifying astonishment.

That evening on the drive, Kiki manoeuvred us carefully up a wide track between bushes, and there at the end in the shade, sheltered from the heat of the late afternoon sun, sprawled three tawny full-grown lionesses, with legs akimbo and their swollen pale-coloured bellies uppermost (they had killed and eaten recently). They were motionless except for their stiff tails twitching at the flies. They ignored us completely as Kiki edged slowly to within 15ft. Later, at a distance in the dusk we saw the male lying on his own, and after dark we heard his never-to-be-forgotten snarling roar for 10 or 15 minutes, before the pride gathered and milled around at a path crossroads prior to the night hunt.

It was quite a drive because before that we had seen – another first for me, rarer than lion or leopard – one of Nkwali's two packs of wild dogs. In the last of the light, Kiki had found the eight dogs with their saucer-like ears and black-and-sandy spotted coats. The dogs' social order is a matriarchy; this group consisted of the mother and the seven surviving cubs from the previous year's litter of nine.

I knew they were formidable hunters, but off-duty they seemed relaxed and playful, just like, well, dogs. Kiki pointed out how one of them was lame, and after dark, when in a casual way they fanned out and trotted away to start hunting, we watched intermittently by lamplight as they began to run down an impala, and the lame dog could not keep up. The prey headed straight for the Toyota, the lamp went off and we felt the hooves of the desperate animal pass so close that our vehicle rocked on its springs. The impala got away, but later we would see the dogs, including the lame one, sharing food. Unlike hyenas or the big cats, the dog pack tolerated a disadvantaged member.

The following day was my last at Nkwali. Guests arriving meant that I would vacate Robin's House and sleep the last night in one of the well-appointed huts where hippos sometimes came up the bank from the river and munched on the grass in front. Our group was joined by a cool and elegant Canadian lady, Leslie, married to an American working in Lusaka, and here to check out Nkwali for her travel business connections. A story she told put in perspective the careful way we were always escorted around the camp. That day, for instance, there had been a family of elephants just the other side of the camp pond – they loved the pods from the winterthorn tree there. Leslie told us about a camp in Tanzania she knew of, where a guest's unsupervised seven-year-old child had been taken by a leopard (and how the camp was running down now as the parents prepared to sue).

I hadn't been sure at first about the Americans, Daniel and Elizabeth, but having spent a couple of Nkwali days and evenings with them, we were now close enough for me to ask Daniel, who was serious about his photography, if he could get images of the Ariel and elephants. I had mentioned this to Jo Pope and she had suggested coming to the lovely house the Popes had had built for themselves beyond the camp. There was a lagoon at the back of it, and she said that if I rode there around lunchtime, there was a good chance that ellies would come and drink.

First we all set off on a morning walk on the far side of the river, with Kiki leading and the taciturn old scout, Jackson, bringing up the rear with his worn but well-maintained .375 rifle. You tended to see less major wildlife when walking at Nkwali, but the compensation was the lack of buffering from being up in the vehicle: this was direct. Everyone had water bottles in white linen slings. Kiki carried a stick which he twirled like a majorette, stuck under his arm like an army officer or flipped at things he was explaining. The etiquette was that we took turns of a few minutes each with him walking at the front, and then dropped to the back as the next person/couple moved up. We walked steadily through the bush, past a set of puku whose ears all swivelled towards us like radar dishes. We discovered three trampled plover chicks: when we came on them someone asked the scout, "What are they, Jackson?" Jackson answered laconically, "Dead meat". With his stick Kiki pointed out hyena tracks and fresh elephant droppings as we walked through barren landscapes where a few petrified trees had died after the elephants had stripped their bark. Further on we had a proper opportunity to see passing zebra, and how incredibly effective their stripes were as camouflage against a bush background. In the distance I mistook black logs for lying down buffalo. We walked for a couple of hours, with the heat increasing, but at the end I felt better for it.

The truck was waiting, and we had tea and home-made biscuits at the base of a wooded hill beneath the Presidential Lodge, watching a large troop of baboons moving in and out of the trees. We drove on and came to a big herd of black buffalo, 35 or more, with some family groups, and luckily not disposed to charge that day. One stood off on its own so you could see the little white cleaner birds on its back and head. We also encountered a tame wart-hog who came quite close. Wart-hogs are nature's light relief, with their tails stuck up vertical and their hysterical air of being permanently on the verge of panic – they always raised the spirits. Kiki and Jackson called this one "Mugabe". His pal, "Robert", was missing, and later we heard that it might have been Robert inside those well-fed lionesses the evening before.

Further on, by a shallow stream, there was another perfect family group of giraffes: the big male with a ridged, knobbled forehead, the better to exchange head-butts with his rivals; the female stretching out gracefully to reach leaves on tree branches far above, some of which fell and floated down; and the gawky young one tenting its legs so it could reach its head down and drink. Back at the river we crossed in the boat with the outboard motor. Melissa was waiting to greet us at the top of the steps cut into the earth bank, and I handed her a few of the purple wild flowers we hadn't been able to find the evening before.

The others went for lunch, but I walked with Fred round to the workshop area where the bike, all cleaned up, was ready. Rob and the lads had done a great job, tapping a more substantial bolt into the rocker shaft and then sealing it with solder. I gave Fred a lift back, half on the short pillion and half on the rack. He really was a big guy, 6ft 2in tall and all muscle, and due to his weight the bike was basically unmanageable on the sandy tracks, with the front end going light and waggling about. At the office he stepped off and Jo came out, hopped into her Toyota and led me out to their house. She took me round the back and showed me where to set up the bike by the tree there, about 75 yards from where the ellies were liable to come and drink.

But back in the house Jo said abruptly, "I'm going downhill fast I'm afraid. I think it's malaria; I've been lucky all this time and never had it. I'm so sorry – I'm going to have to drive to the doctor. Have you eaten?"

"No, no! Melissa is keeping some," I said, flustered. Looking properly and seeing how poorly she seemed, I offered ineffectually to take her to the doctor myself, but she drove off and I settled down to wait for the American. Only it was Jo who drove up again, with my dinner; I guess she must have known I was diabetic. She told me to make myself at home and drove away again, but returned shortly afterwards with pudding and with the news that she had arranged for Kiki to bring Daniel over shortly to take the photos. Only then did she go upstairs to lie down as, wisely, she had arranged for the doctor to come to her. Was this the best hostess in the world or what?

Soon enough Kiki drove up with Daniel, who brought a couple of cameras and was also kind enough to take a few shots with my pocket rocket so I could send them in time for the next magazine article. Kiki sat on the Ariel and allowed that the bike felt as though it could be fun. Daniel found his spot in the shade beneath an upstairs veranda, while I had to push the bike back out into the light as the sun moved the shadow of the tree I was beside, and we waited. It was hot in the midday sun. After 20 minutes I began to think that nothing was going to come that day, but then sure enough there was a stirring in the trees beyond the lagoon, and a grey head appeared in the distance.

Elephants do things in their own time, and it was long minutes, with the bull standing still or wandering in and out of sight among the trees, before slowly, rhythmically, he came swaying across the parched yellow-brown grass towards the water. He stopped and flared his ears at me once, and then came on again. Behind me Daniel snapped away. The bull drank and I was feeling the satisfaction of it, when things got even better. A second bull appeared in the trees and eventually joined the first at the lagoon. It was very moving to watch, as they dipped their trunks in turn, taking their time, and finally, after long minutes, wandered off along the watercourse and back into the trees. It's a cliché, but it was a privilege, and all thanks to Jo Pope. You can see the photographic results on the cover of this book. Daniel did a fine job and I shall treasure those pictures for the rest of my life.

When we were done, I rode the Ariel back to the office and, fetching the tank bag, checked the spoke tension and tyre pressures. The day, however, was not over. I went on a last evening drive with Kiki and the others. Moving further into the Park, we drove along the new tarmac road for a bit; this felt intrusive and I didn't like it. Jo had told us how it had been built to government regulations as to width and so on, and also, thanks to consultants having been employed, featured road signs reading "Wild Animals Ahead". Well, yes, in one of the most famous game parks in the world, I guess there would be. South Luangwa until now had kept its prices for visitors high, to prevent the kind of tourist saturation that reportedly had spoiled parts of Kenya's parks and plains and, selfishly, I wanted it to stay like that. The road seemed to argue that things were going the other way.

We arrived at a wide, dry sand riverbed and saw why we had ranged wider than usual. In the light of the sinking sun, the pack of eight wild dogs lay sprawled asleep, utterly relaxed, resting up before the night's hunt. But the first thing we photographed, as did people in several other vehicles when they arrived, were not the dogs, but the occupants of the other RPS Land Cruiser already there. They were Americans staying in the spectacular Luangwa House, who appeared to be engaged in a "My-Lens-Is-Longer-Than-Yours" competition, with two of the guys pointing cameras with 4ft to 5ft protuberances. This scene was offset by one of their wives who was sitting beside them completely unimpressed, reading a book.

It was exciting to see these dogs so close, but they weren't about to rise and pose for photographs. Leslie, the travel lady, was itching to get a full shot of one, but she always seemed to be checking her elaborate camera gear as first one, then another dog rose and settled again quickly in the sand. Daniel and I developed a "Dog Up/Dog Down!" routine with her. Another vehicle arrived and one of its occupants let out a screech of "Hyenas!" which mightily amused Kiki. Then the most amazing thing began to happen. In ones and twos, and later in larger numbers, about a hundred yards beyond the sprawled dogs, elephants started to troop from right to left across the dry riverbed. In the end I counted over 40 of them, a living frieze – bulls, mothers and calves – slowly crossing the river of sand in the last of the light.

When night fell and the dogs roused themselves and trotted off, Kiki poked and hoped in the bush around, and eventually successfully anticipated where they would be, close to the spot we had come on them the night before. The sky was clear and, with a big moon that night, we hardly needed the lamp. After they assembled, several of the young dogs licked and nuzzled the matriarch's face, and eventually she regurgitated what she, the most experienced hunter, must have killed. The lame dog fed with the others.

Back at camp I enjoyed a last delicious supper with fine South African wine, all formally announced from beyond the circle of lamplight. I talked to Leslie a little about my trip, and about staying with Ginty. Her Lusaka, with charming fruit markets and diplomatic receptions, sounded like a different city from the one I'd seen. When I mentioned that in 1967 I had been living in the Haight-Ashbury, the part of San Francisco beloved by hippies, Leslie said, "Now, why I am not surprised?"

I turned in early and, despite having to do that bad road again tomorrow, slept well. Just before dawn I woke to the soft drums, dressed and pulled on my clean boots and carried my bags through the gap in the fence to where the Ariel was parked by the office. I had everything, with one exception; somewhere within the dark of the hut, after I had taken it off to shower, my little lucky Mnyame-Mnyame talisman still lay.

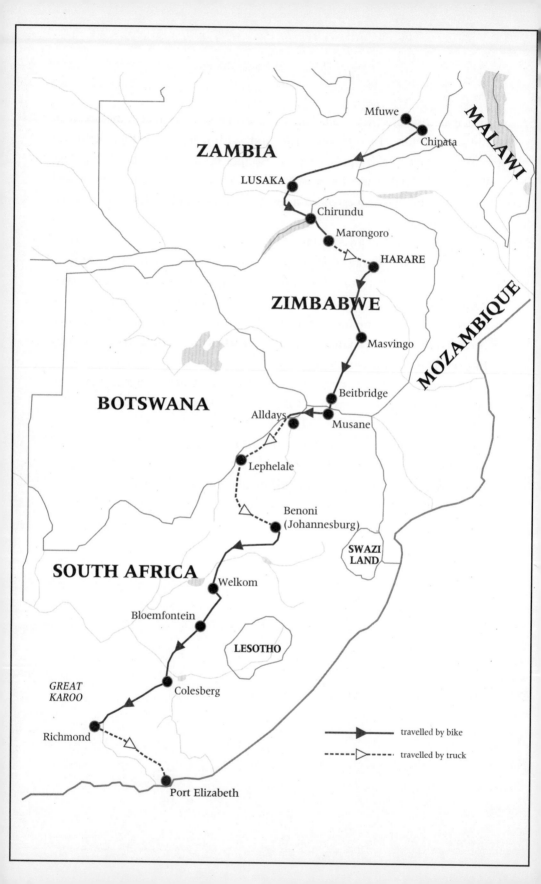

MALAWI

Mfuwe
Chipata

ZAMBIA

LUSAKA

Chirundu
Marongoro
HARARE

ZIMBABWE

Masvingo

MOZAMBIQUE

BOTSWANA

Beitbridge

Alldays
Musane

Lephelale

Benoni
(Johannesburg)

SWAZI
LAND

SOUTH AFRICA

Welkom

Bloemfontein

LESOTHO

GREAT
KAROO

Colesberg

Richmond

Port Elizabeth

travelled by bike
travelled by truck

PART FIVE

ZAMBIA – PORT ELIZABETH

"You don't travel to decorate yourself with exotic anecdotes like a Christmas tree, but so that the journey will pluck you, will rinse you, will squeeze you dry."
Nicolas Bouvier

Chapter 33

TYRED OUT

I hate it in two-wheel travel books when The Journey is interrupted by stretches on a train/lorry/plane. It doesn't matter why: Ted Simon having to fly home from India for a family funeral; the older guy in *The Last Hurrah* finally being overcome by his diabetes; or "Smith and Son's" erratic progress down Africa due to a combination of political upheavals and their Triumph Tiger Cubs. Whatever the reason, interrupted bike trips – even if in real life the problems themselves may result in rewarding situations – can make for less satisfying reading. So apologies in advance for what follows: there were to be three major interruptions on our journey back down to Cape Town.

That last Nkwali morning, in the pre-dawn light around the breakfast fire, I was given a picnic package with fruit and rolls. I said adios to Kiki, and then Melissa said, "Hey, you, listen…" and we hugged goodbye. I was by the bike, getting ready to leave and catch as much of the morning cool as possible, when Freddy told me that Robin Pope had arrived late last night, and that he and Jo wanted to say goodbye. So I rode to the house and parked the Ariel beside Robin's old Series I Land Rover. They came out, Robin with a quietness that could be mistaken for diffidence until you looked in his eyes, Jo beamingly happy to have him back.

After a sincere last "Thank you" for everything, I said I was sorry to hear about them retiring from Nkwali. Jo was quite put out that this was already general knowledge. Robin was scrutinising the Ariel and observed, "But it's leaking oil…" My only response was a feebly off-hand, "Oh, they all do that," which could scarcely have satisfied the perfectionist in him. But Jo just said she thought it was a marvellous thing to be doing, and how would Robin like driving the Series I all the way to Cape Town?

Jerry started second or third kick, and I rode off, more confident of the way now, shadowed by Fred until the junction where I waved goodbye. Back on tarmac I was glad of the early coolness. I stopped at the airport for a break before plunging into the bad road, but there was a bakkie-load of brash American hunters parked there so I didn't linger. And the first bit, back to the Wildlife sign and beyond, was better than I remembered. With that and the cooling breeze, and going at my own pace, I could more often ride the bicycle tracks in the dust on the road's edge. I covered 22 miles before the next stop and almost thought I had exaggerated the punishing road surface, but after that it all got really bad again, really bloody "Once-was-road". In some of the worst of it, riding under trees, on the wrong side of the road in a vain attempt to avoid the trashed islands of fragmented tarmac, concentrating hard, I nearly fell off the bike as out of nowhere and at almost twice my speed, a fully-equipped BMW came roaring past from behind on my left, the pillion passenger standing up on the pegs and raising both arms in the air as they disappeared into the dusty distance. It was the spirit of Ewan and Charley, come to taunt me.

Things didn't get any better. Twice I found myself saying out loud, "Thank you Ariel!" for the way the bike thumped me steadily out of deep slippery berms of sandy dust in the apex of left-handers. We took the beating, and the early coolness did make it a little less uncomfortable, but by the time we had reached the second short strip of tarmac, it was 10.15am and there were 25 miles still to go. I stopped, drank water and ate a biscuit. The bike had had no power on the tarmac, but I hoped that was just because of the efforts I had been asking of it. I checked the tyres, noticing idly for the first time that they had joints like hoops in the rubber of the tyre walls. A couple walked past. Soon it was time to go. Only a third more to do.

I must have gone another five miles or so when, on a straight bit of road with a village ahead, the back end rapidly began to misbehave. I whipped in the clutch because this I was familiar with – a rear wheel puncture. Coming to a halt the bike was awkward to manhandle with the flat, but I got it on the centre stand, and from the tank bag fished out the aerosol of tyre inflator/sealant foam. I screwed the tube onto the tyre valve and hit the button; even if the inner tube was split badly, it should get me to Chipata. But it didn't inflate. One of those joints in the tyre wall was gaping wide open. This wasn't just a puncture – the bad road had actually *split the tyre itself*. Which was not good news.

At that point, the first vehicle to pass drew up – and it was a two-stroke motorcycle with a young African guy and his pretty, fearless-looking girl on the back. Before too long he had agreed to try and fetch a bakkie from the next village, 10km down the road. His girl said why didn't I ride there? Well, the tyre was wrecked anyway, so why not? But 100 yards of wrestling the handlebars convinced me that I wasn't up to it, even if the bike was, so I got to the little village beyond the crest, turned in there, and hopped off. My new friends rode on, and I pulled the bike onto its stand in the shade of a low tree.

There were people about, and before long a retired teacher with a hoarse voice had come over and introduced himself. I told him about the ride and Kawaza School, and he had someone bring out a tiny chair for me to sit on. The problem was that the Ariel's tyres were 19-inch ones, while everything available locally would be 18-inch or less. So the first thing I did was phone Andy Legg in Lusaka (hurrah for cell phones!), and I was lucky enough to just catch him before he went off somewhere. I said I knew that Ginty had a 19-inch rear tyre which he had offered me the use of, and Andy said he would fetch this and try to get it on the newspaper truck that ran from Lusaka to Chipata overnight and doubled up carrying parcels. And he did it, too.

Meanwhile I draped all my kit on the bike, and settled down at Mkowe. There were young men and a couple of children, their clothes dirty but their teeth wonderfully bright, hanging out around the tree, and I joked a bit with some of them and shared the picnic, but there was no undue interest or attention on their part. One guy watched me make the call, take a drink from the Camelbak, and then slip out the camera from my waistcoat to take a snap, and said appraisingly, "You have everything". But it was just an observation, without resentment. Some black missionaries wearing shirts and ties arrived on bicycles and began circulating pamphlets, smiling brilliantly. There were cattle wandering about, including a Brahma-type bull, goats humping and bleating, and across the road a young boy was told off as a goat got into the sack of flour he was supposed to have been watching. The sun shone but there was a breeze under the shady tree, and the cadences of voices rising and falling.

After about three-quarters of an hour my friend returned in a smart white bakkie, bearing the logo of the Dunavant organisation. (This later turned out to be part of either Ginty's SeedCo or Andy Legg's Multicrop, so there was outraged laughter at this moonlighting use of the truck when

Ginty saw it in a photo.) One of the guys who helped load the Ariel was wearing a Harley-Davidson T-shirt celebrating the 2001 grand opening of an HD dealership in Elk River, Minnesota. For $20 they agreed to take me to Chipata, but we stopped after a few miles and unloaded the bike and luggage while the bakkie was used to ferry bales of tobacco down the road. However, I was in no hurry, and talked and exchanged e-mail addresses with the bike rider and his friend.

When we got going again it was a pretty hairy ride; these guys did not hold back speed-wise, whatever the surface – it was not "skimming from crest to crest" over corrugations, just pedal-to-the-metal and the hell with it. I phoned Ginty later and he got the idea (or liked the thought) that I had been astride the bike in the back. There were a couple of guys there holding it steady, but they had insisted I ride upfront, and that was terrifying enough. I finally understood that African driving could be somethin' else!

We off-loaded back at Mama Rula's, the camp where I'd stayed before, and I found Isabell and booked in for a couple of nights; the tyre would not arrive until 10 the following morning and then would have to be fitted, and I needed a full day to do the run back to Bridge Camp. But losing just one day was still a pretty amazing result. After freshening up I hit the bar again, where the only news on the TV all night and all next day was the death of the singer Michael Jackson. Not a favourite of mine, and it was a bit puzzling why Africa would be mourning someone who bleached his skin; but some of the clips did remind you how good he could be. There were new bus-loads of American girls, and a couple of the big black helpers off one bus were at the bar, drinking hard. They were extremely pally with the bubbly young things, but after the girls had gone, one man turned to the bartender and sneered with deep, bitter contempt, "They're *students*." It was one of the ugliest things I ever heard.

Next morning the taxi driver recommended by Isabell arrived, and we set off for the newspaper depot to collect the tyre Andy had despatched. The driver, Graham, was cool and bright. We sat listening to tapes of kicking Zambian music till the place opened at 10am, while Graham cleaned his nails with a toothpick. The music I liked best was *Not Guilty* by Dandy Krazy. Once we'd collected the tyre, I got the driver to sort out another bakkie to take the bike from Mama Rula's to the tyre place, as I didn't want to have to remove and, even more, to replace the rear wheel on my own. We plunged into the market area and at $10 got what we paid for, a decrepit truck that ground to a halt soon after the bike had been loaded. It was only lack of petrol, for which they wanted more money, but didn't get it.

At the tyre place by a big garage, outdoors in the dust men were setting about truck tyres with sledge hammers and monster tyre irons. I, Graham, the nervously energetic taxi man, and our tyre changer got the Ariel's wheel out quickly after some tense moments trying to make sure of the order in which the wheel spacer and chain would go back together again, and that nothing got mislaid. The tyre guy was obviously used to truck and car covers, but from Mike Coombe's lesson I knew what to do, and had brought the tools, tyre irons and inner tube. But it was still an edgy and chaotic business, and in the end it was only Graham who was certain of the reassembly order. He stiffed me for an extra $10, but after negotiating for the bakkie and staying with me for the tyre change, he'd earned it. I bought some 40 oil at the garage and, with the tyre inflated and everything feeling good, rode back to Mama Rula's.

That afternoon I had a good spannering session in the beehive shed, topping up the primary chaincase with the new oil, and spraying WD40 into the inlet rocker box. I filled a little plastic box with petrol from the tank and, soaking a rag in this, washed off the dust-caked rear chain, and then sprayed it with WD40 as a stop-gap until I could get more proper chain lube back in Lusaka. I cleaned leaked oil off the exhaust system and engine, and then discovered a *faux* chamois hanging on a nail, and gave the bike a full wipe over. This is always worthwhile because, while doing so, satisfyingly I found out that one of the nearside engine bolt's spacer was rattling about so I tightened its nut which, despite looking painted on, turned out to be quite easy to do, as it had been coming loose. I also did the right thing, loosened off the rear axle nut with the big adjustable spanner, and then bashed the wheel forwards so that the rear wheel spacer was more nearly touching the adjusters on either side; there had been a gap on one side, and now the wheel would be better aligned. Finally I tightened the wheel spokes. Despite having done this at Nkwali, many of the rear ones were loose again, thanks to that road.

Then I went and chilled with my book on the guests' lawn by the pool, by the ochre-painted, tin-roofed restaurant room, among coconut palms, fronds and mauve flowering plants. The place was the fruit of constant maintenance by a garden crew, leaf sweeping, watering and sprinkling the rough, broad-bladed but cut and regimented grass.

Chapter 34

BACK TO LUSAKA

I set off in good time back down the road to Luangwa Bridge, after a night spent worrying, with the wind in the leaves outside sounding like rain. I had hoped that Mama Rula's would swap dollars to kwacha for the road, but they didn't have enough change. However, the old proprietor said I would be all right changing money with "the Indians" at Nyimba. After 50 miles or so I used virtually the last of my kwacha to fill up at that nice-looking town of Katete. I wasn't sure about the feel of the rear end with the new tyre, and there had been a rattle that worried me, like piston slap. But new tyres take about 100 miles to settle down and this proved to be the case here. And when, noticing the Bakelite damper knob rotating, I tightened down the steering damper, the "piston slap" noise stopped; it had been the loose damper rattling.

The road surface got bad, but after the Bad Road I could tell myself it was *nothing* as long as it was tarmac. Soon the landscape became bush and forest, with conical mountains popping up in the distance. The side wind from the north was tiresome for a while, but then became a cooling breeze. There was the usual blissful scarcity of traffic, the only exception being fairly smart, fast, long-distance coaches. I stopped for lunch in a small lay-by and was lying sprawled back in the bushes, chewing biltong, when a pair of slightly-built, mild-mannered guys passed, carrying bunches of small green bananas, a mattock-like implement, presumably to cut the bananas, and a catapult to "shoot little birds" as they told me. "What kind of birds?" I asked. "Little," they said. They wished me a safe journey and walked on down the road, looking back from time to time.

The bike, despite one bout of rough running in 2nd and 3rd when slowing down for speed bumps in a small town, was plonking along all right. I had been passing people carrying sticks, who then gnawed on them: sugar cane.

But riding on from the lunch stop where I had dutifully poured in some oil to top up the tank, I realised that I had forgotten to re-secure the helmet bag in which I carried the oil bottle, so I rode with one hand behind me holding it on for a minute, looking for a relatively empty place to stop. The road was particularly thronged with Africans, including boisterous bunches of kids returning from school. I found a place half-way down the hill, fixed the bag, and the bike then would not start. With people coming down the hill, I bump-started it, but as it caught, the front end went into a violent wiggle. Oh no – *another* puncture, at the front end this time?

I stopped further down the hill outside a cluster of huts. People came out immediately. A slight guy with a wispy moustache and beard, as I apologised for parking without asking, said, "Welcome to my house." I put my helmet apprehensively on the grass to one side, took off my jacket as the throng thickened and pressed in. For the first time, probably because it was a long day, I resented them all, and kept my eyes down as I unfastened the bag again and got out my cheap, lightweight foot-pump, only to find that the nut on the end of its piston had gone AWOL. I swore and, after checking inside the bag, rummaged through the tank bag, found a packet of nuts and bolts, and miraculously the first one fitted the pump. But when I fixed it onto the front tyre, the pressure seemed healthy, and checking with the gauge it proved to be so. So why had the Ariel wobbled?

The guy, taking in the oil-streaked bike, was saying I should go to the mechanic at Luangwa Bridge, though he didn't know him. Pretty well talking to myself, I speculated that the steering head bearings might need grease – but everything had been fine up till then. I pulled my kit back on and told my adviser that I would ride slowly to the Bridge, but I must get there. They gave me a push downhill and the head-shaking wiggle was fierce. We tried it one more time, with the wiggle still there, and then suddenly it was gone. I shouted thanks and rode on, carefully at first, until I had worked it out; the only thing I had done different was tightening the steering damper. I loosened it off a turn, and the problem went away, though from then on the loose damper would be an intermittent bother.

I stopped at Nyimba as advised to change money and buy petrol. But this was where I had noticed the mosques on the way in, and the "Indians" turned out to be fundamentalist Islamic. When I was led from the petrol station into a back building, looking like a gunship pilot with my boots and helmet, the guys sitting at tables there with full black beards and *kufi* prayer-caps stared flatly and told me, deadpan, that kwachas had run out. So I was going to find out if the Ariel, with a theoretical range of 280 miles, could do the nearly 270 miles from Katete, where I had filled up, to Chongwe, 30 miles this side of Lusaka, as there wasn't any petrol in between. Soon after this I spotted one of the number plates that African bicycles often had, reading "THALIBAN" (sic) "FIGHTER". Further on, a large schoolboy on his way home scooped up a stone and, as I ducked, buzzed it at me with good force. The last time that happened had been on the first Greek trip, when village kids had thought we were German.

I enjoyed riding the wonderful hillside bends to Luangwa Bridge. At Bridge Camp, Lindsay and Will were away, but the staff saw to me. The meal was good again, with pancakes for pudding filled with cut-up oranges and liqueur. Across the river in the dark there was a crackling sound, and I looked round to see two patches of fire on the black hillside opposite. There had been burnt verges and bunches of charcoal by the roadside as I had approached the bridge.

The next day I rode the 110 miles to Chongwe, with the only problem being bad pot-holes, which were sometimes signalled with cut bush branches, stacked on the road like warning triangles (Ginty called them "tree-angles"). It was also hard to find somewhere away from population to stop. The more you looked, the more villages and hut clusters were almost continuously lining the road to the hub, Lusaka. I ended up parked by a quarry, and even then there was a village about a quarter of a mile opposite. I quietly watched people coming and going, and some kids playing with a billy-goat, until it got up on its hind legs at them and they ran away.

I was first to arrive at Chongwe, and had filled up by the time Andy and one of his sons arrived on Harleys, with Ginty on the Monster, complaining about the side-wind. I felt pretty good. I had succeeded in reaching my goal, which had not disappointed, and, in a 900-mile loop, had coped with whatever came up.

We rode back to Ginty's. It was the end of June. I had a month to get down south.

Ginty put me in Kate's Corner again, though Kate herself was away in Harare and would remain so for the rest of the week. Our mission (and again, Ginty gave unstintingly in terms of time and effort) was to get the missing cap nut for the rocker shaft replicated, and bring the lights back by sorting out the dynamo. It was good that Ginty went at this with his usual energy, because I was feeling tired to the bone, after the intense time at Nkwali, and the alarms and excursions on the way there and back.

The first morning we drove to The Castle complex on the way in to town, to replenish food and whisky supplies, which I was happy to pay for. The Castle, with its mock battlements, was a one-stop where there was a post office as well as the all-purpose supermarket, and the Indian owner changed some of my dollars to kwachas. As we parked the bakkie up, an African drove in and stopped, straddling the lines that marked out parking spaces. Ginty had a go at him verbally, and after a long moment he backed up and re-parked.

The next night the maid was also away, at a funeral. Ginty said these could go on a bit and that he was lucky Cholo had turned up, as some didn't, since the previous day had been their monthly pay day and "they get pissed and stay away". So he cooked us an excellent supper of bream and fresh spinach, but before that we sat with a drink and talked about the Rhodesian war. He had already told me a good story about a truck full of his platoon being ambushed and them responding as per training, not by going to ground but by fanning out with all guns blazing. This had succeeded in making their attackers fall back and, as they did so, the Rhodesians had heard, between bursts of gunfire, one calling to another, "I *told* you they were not Administration!" By the end, he admitted, they were all smoking dope and taking benzedrine tablets, and, when exhausted, were given Pethodone injections to perk them up.

But that evening, Ginty gave me another perspective. "You'd be spotting a village where there were definitely terrorists, you could see kids wandering around, goats. Then you'd call in the Canberras, and those Cans were loaded with serious shit, Willie Peter, white phosphorus. Afterwards there would be nothing left. Nothing. It was terrible, but ... it was so exciting, I loved it." Later when I asked him what had been the worst thing, he said that, while losing mates had gradually changed his feeling about fighting, the hardest moment had been at the end, handing in his FN rifle, his weapon. His side had lost, not militarily but politically due to the tides of history, and they had lost not just a war but, as Mugabe took over, their country.

We were both hung over the following morning, driving into Lusaka, and chasing round different workshops. We eventually hit pay-dirt, with an engineer Ginty knew called Peter Mostert (Dutch for "mustard") who lived up to his name in taking the fabrication of a replacement blind nut for the inlet rocker shaft as a personal challenge. Using the capped nut on the exhaust shaft as a pattern, the blind thread on the inside of it was found to be an unusual one. Peter had a book of period thread charts and believed it to be British Standard Pipe. We drove back to Ginty's, where he delicately ground off the cap of solder put there by Nkwali's workshop to seal the bolt they had inserted into the end of the shaft, so we could remove the latter and take it back to Peter. But though in the end Peter never found an exact match (one theory was that it had been Gas Thread), he had an exact replica milled from solid bar, and would take no payment for doing this. For a while, we had an oil-tight Ariel.

The news on the dynamo was less good. After two places had turned us down, we ended up at an auto specialist run by Mauro, a patrician, venal-looking Italian. I watched nervously as an older black mechanic dismantled the dynamo and tested it on an enormous machine. They said that the problem was failure of the armature, and Andy Legg believed he could provide a replacement. Ginty said that Mauro, as he had shrugged and walked away, had muttered something about only fools not riding a Ducati! But it emerged that the armature had overheated and spat all its solder out of the commutator, causing a big short-circuit and effectively wrecking the instrument. Back in the UK this would be replaced without question free of charge, but that didn't help us then, and the trick battery was now also shot due to lack of charge. Ginty provided a Chinese-made substitute plus a charger for it, but was then frustrated to find at the very last minute that the rear brake light still wasn't working, because the inaccessible wiring had been disturbed during our tyre-changing capers.

Ginty devoted two whole days to these endeavours and, at the end of the second afternoon, decided we needed haircuts. He drove us to the Lusaka Intercontinental where, in a fragrant unisex salon, in the company of a Chinese courtesan having a re-style, strong black hands massaged my scalp deliciously prior to a No.3 buzz-cut which looked warry, but also exposed a certain asymmetry to my protruding ears. I told them I felt a changed man, which made everyone laugh. We proceeded to a session at the Gymkhana

Club and then, with a friend of Ginty's, dinner and more drinks at an Indian restaurant which I sprung for. Afterwards Ginty initially had some trouble finding his way home. In the night my bottom dropped out – Indian food again?

I spent the next couple of days before departure writing the month's story for the bike magazine, which Ginty's daughter Debi, between power cuts, helped me to send with the necessary pictures. I also caught up with my e-mails. One thing that emerged was that Ginty had been sending disparaging accounts of my various misfortunes to Bruce in Cape Town, Mike Wood in Port Elizabeth and others. Stuff like "maybe (Steve) lost his virginity in a similar fashion, waiting, thinking that 'something will turn up'…"

I was too embarrassed to raise this with Ginty then and there, as the mails had been between him and the others, but what particularly annoyed me was that he relayed as fact his speculations about how I had been feeling ("not in good spirits…" "not in the best of spirits, again, what's new…" etc). Whatever else, I hoped I was not a mope. When, a month later, Ginty got wind of my unhappiness about his messages he wrote immediately to apologise. I told him those speculations were a bit like picking someone else's nose for them in public, and that on at least one occasion when he had reported me as low, I had actually been feeling rather chuffed about having worked round a problem.

However it was typical of Ginty that, as well as firing off the mails, he had apologised unreservedly. "We have a way out here … unfortunately we are often insensitive to others' feelings and the further north one goes, the worse it gets…" He was a mass of contradictions: a Bulawayo boy who had bedded down on the porch of the family home with his brother and other apprentices, worked as an apprentice printer himself, and then a bank teller, while pursuing his passion for motorcycles, including speedway, and track racing in the company of local men like future champions Gary Hocking and Jim Redman. A Main Street Cowboy who on Fridays would ride his AJS single 500km from Choma to Lusaka, strip the bike and race it over the weekend, then ride 500km back to work on Monday morning. A guy who, despite his views, after Zimbabwean Independence, at the age of 40 had attended an all-black post-graduate college in Texas, where he got on fine as he'd been in the Rhodesian baseball team, playing short-stop. Even if, in terms of the movie *Platoon*, he had been the Bad Sergeant on this trip, I was still glad to have known him.

On our last evening we had a good steak dinner with a nice bottle of wine. That afternoon we had watched TV as the British Lions, who had already lost the three-match series, played the Springboks for the final time, and won decisively. I rarely watched or took an interest in sport, but was overcome by an excess of patriotism as the Brits, with their dependable hands, outmanoeuvred the brute strength of the 'Boks. I think the defeat had not sat well with Ginty.

I woke, with a numb feeling, from a fantastically powerful dream about San Francisco. I found Ginty already outside, cutting up a reflective jacket and fastening it to the Ariel's headlamp and to the loaded bags at the back. It looked scruffy but I was to be glad of it further down the road. He was curt that morning. I was subdued but made an effort not to be ("It *is* quite parky...") for fear he would trumpet it about again. (He did! "I think Steve left with a good deal of trepidation...") But at least that time it was true.

We rode out before 9am, with Ginty's Triumph Speed Twin sounding good but smoking from the offside cylinder. We drove across the road to a monster garden centre and waited for the others. It was Sunday morning and there was a public holiday until the following Wednesday, so Andy Legg was off on a trip but, from his work, in a bakkie, came David Woods, an ex-Southern Rhodesian who was serious about his shooting. It was good of him to pitch up, and he had some really useful input, as I was headed for his country, Zimbabwe.

Chewing it over, I had been disinclined merely to reverse my previous route and go back down through Botswana. The original plan to head west to Namibia was history in view of Jerry's record on reliability. Looping round east through Mozambique would mean extra miles and a long stretch out of touch with useful contacts, so Zimbabwe it was. Also, with less than four weeks to go before my departure back to the UK, it was the shortest route south. I had been told by Ginty and others that the situation there was much better following the coalition government and the adoption of the US dollar as currency. Even so, the night before, I had put black tape over the tiny Union Jacks on my Belstaff gauntlets and tank bag.

I had planned to stop the first night at a hotel in Karoi, some 80 miles over the border, and proceed the next day to the capital, Harare. This would have given me time that first day to ride down to the Kariba Dam, but David Woods had news that the place in Karoi had closed, so we re-jigged the route to avoid the Kariba dog-leg. He also drew me a map of Harare, and gave me his girlfriend's number there. (Rash!) And as an afterthought he gave me the name of a Senior Warden he knew with the Zimbabwean Parks and Wildlife service, in case I had any problems around the National Parks on the far side of the border. I had been told that for communications in Zimbabwe I was going to have to buy a whole new cell phone rather than just a SIM card, which I might have been able to get at the border. So I would be out of touch on the road until I got a new phone, and any contacts were welcome.

A guy on a BMW and an Afrikaner in full business-like rig on a big Harley rolled in, and it was actually quite touching to have some company as I left Zambia – though Ginty was probably coming to make sure I was finally gone! We got underway. Jerry's front end was playing up at low speed now that we were fully loaded again, despite having given away more stuff, including the mallet, to Ginty. The bike also felt marginally unstable in the quite strong side winds, but we were rolling, and it was a bright day. We negotiated lumpy, industrial Katine, where a VW van had just been front-ended. As I was using my last kwachas to fill up at the petrol station, Len with the Hinckley twin drove up in a restored metallic blue/green TR4A roadster. The others turned back, but he, Ginty and I drove straight on, past where the road turned to the right back towards Livingstone, and a few miles on pulled into another petrol place.

Ginty said a gruff goodbye but then went on talking for a bit, and it was Len who said, "You'd better be on your way". It was 10.30am, we had done about 40 miles, and they reckoned it would take me about six hours to reach my destination. And there were the Zam and Zim borders to negotiate as well. So off I went.

Chapter 35

TROUBLE IN
ZIMBABWE

I felt bleak at first and managed to hit a couple of pot-holes, but then the wide, generally well-surfaced road began to climb and dive through forested hills – good stuff – and I became absorbed. Warning triangles signalled several broken-down trucks as the road climbed. After over an hour of that we descended, and by midday approached Chirundu and the border. The frontier post was medium chaotic, with trucks everywhere and no signs, but a guy indicated for me to go back into a compound, so I did, and parked doubtfully outside the large passport control building. There were crowds of dudes hanging about, including a loony who looked at the bike, and laughed and laughed – takes one to know one, I guess. Once I had gone in uncertainly, he began polishing Jerry with a rag. I went out again, but another man told me that this guy did it all the time, and put a finger to his head.

Inside again at the desk, the news was not great. I had forgotten that my visa had only been for three weeks and had expired two days previously, meaning a $220 fine. I was suitably downcast. The uniformed official, steady-eyed, called his white-shirted superior. I suggested a reduction since the delay for this tourist had been caused by genuine, unavoidable mechanical difficulties. $100? "This fine has to be receipted, and we cannot do that," said the white-shirted one. There was impasse. I kept repeating, "This will be very difficult for me to pay," but they didn't seem to be budging. Finally I was ready to cough, though it would have left me severely short, but I must have been looking particularly old and pitiful that day, as at that moment the seated one handed me back my passport. That was it? "I do this," he said seriously, "on humanitarian grounds." I thanked him sincerely.

Outside among a crowd of scoffers, I tipped the one who had looked after my bike and gave the rest of my change to the loony. The Ariel took its time about starting, but 300 yards further on, the motor vehicle shack, surrounded by grumpy baboons, could not have been more helpful with the *carnet*. It had all been a fitting farewell to Zambia which, of all the African countries I visited, I liked the best, mainly because of its people. Then it was across the bridge over the Limpopo river, dodging an ABNORMAL wide truck coming the other way, and riding slow for half-a-mile up a hill to the big compound for Zimbabwean Customs. I parked the loaded bike prominently in the huge truck park, and guys gestured to me, showing the way in to the building. I went to the car park loo, and it was clean.

Up some stairs, the passport official, inaudible behind glass but somehow satirical, mocking, passed me through a form to complete. Colourful ladies and sporting dudes crowded around and invaded my space, as they will do. When I had filled in the form, the official gave me a torn square of paper and waved me off vaguely across the hall to get it vouched for by 'Police', but in the meantime he did give me my passport back. I tried a window opposite where the guy was asleep, but politely, under the circumstances, sent me to an office round the corner. The police detective in plain clothes there again was somehow satirical, joking in the Shona tongue with a guy who came in while gesturing at me and sarcastically interpolating the English words "our beautiful country". For the first time I was asked for the vehicle registration document, but soon enough he wrote on the square of paper, which turned out to be the Gate Pass, and sent me back to the inaudible passport window.

There I paid $55 for a visa and got sent to the motor vehicles window, where they processed the *carnet* with no problem. As an afterthought, at a private office on the way out, I bought $21 of third-party insurance; if I did get stopped by Zimbabwean law, I wanted everything in order. Back out in the lorry park I ate biscuits and the last of the Port Elizabeth biltong, and sucked some water from the pack, turning down a young man selling Coca-Cola ("It is good for a journey, and you are going on a journey"). I negotiated exiting the gate with the engine still running, and rode out past lines and lines of lorries parked on both verges, and onto the flat road through the forest, with occasional baboons and monkeys crossing and re-crossing ahead.

I had gone nearly 15 miles when I began to worry a little about how the engine was feeling. A couple of miles later there was definite roughness: I went onto full alert and changed down. After a while in 3rd, I tried to change up to 4th again, and there was big distress. Looking down, I could see that the separate gearbox was leaking oil from the screw holes that held it together, and visibly shaking, so I changed back down to 3rd and kept going, my mind curiously crystal clear, knowing that the situation was not good due to the lack of communications via cell phone now I was in Zim, and looking for a safe place to stop and investigate, as the occasional lorry thundered past me from the border behind.

I kept going at perhaps 30mph in 3rd for a few miles, until we reached the base of the Zambezi Escarpment. A couple of hundred yards before a manned Tsetse barrier there was an apron of tarmac on the left, with a track running off it to the Parks and Wildlife barrier before the bush, and some buildings set off to the right of the track. I stopped, got off, and looked at the gearbox. The outer case's top fastening screw, the one that my Swiss friend Martin had found was coming unscrewed the first time at Mama Rula's, and which I had checked since, now came out easily: almost all its threaded portion was missing. Obviously, I thought, it had broken in half, fallen into the gearbox and was jamming the works.

I became ambitious and determined, though the situation wasn't good – I was about 60 miles from the nearest accommodation, and it would be dark within a couple of hours. I got tools out from the panniers and from the tank-bag, rags and a little plastic box which Mike Coombes back in Oxfordshire had advised me to take for keeping bits safe during work. At that point a Land Rover with its truck-bed full of jolly male and female Zimbabweans, some with cans of Castle beer, turned into the track. Someone giggled, "How are you, sir?" and when I replied, "Fine, and yourselves?" they all cracked up. They dropped someone off at the buildings, and went off through the barrier. I positioned the little box to catch the gearbox oil, undid the different length screws fastening on the outer casing and laid them in order on the rag, removed a nut so I could take off the gear lever and gear indicator, then the kickstart which, when loosened off, whanged forward, so there was a spring involved. I worried briefly about the box's gasket, but the outer casing, though partly off, still wouldn't come all the way free. Meanwhile I had pushed the big screwdriver, which had a magnetic tip, down through the gap and probed about, hoping to pick up the threaded bit of screw. No luck, and I realised that it was the right-hand footrest that was stopping the outer casing coming off. The big adjustable spanner was too long to use in the available space, but the second-largest one from the double-ended set did, with difficulty, enable me to get the footrest nut loose. But by then I had realised that the exhaust was going to have to come off as well, in order to get the footrest removed.

I did not like the thought of that. So I levered the outer casing out as far as I could, hoping something would drop out of the bottom, although part of me by now had worked out that the threaded portion was likely to have dropped out into the gearbox proper, behind the outer wall of the inner case. Then, as the outer casing came a little further out, there was a sickening Boing! It was the sound and feel of springs unwinding and thrusting outwards, and that meant game over for me. I invoked a quote from W.C. Fields which I had been holding in reserve: "If at first you don't succeed, try, and try again. Then give up. There's no need to be a damn fool about it."

I fastened the casing loosely back on and reattached the levers, securing all the little bits in the plastic box. Inside, the tired part of me was thinking that this was enough. Still, I'd had a go. I walked down the track to the huts, where a dusty young toddler wearing just a torn T-shirt was scratching its bottom. A young woman came out, unsmiling and apprehensive, scooped up the child and called over to another hut, where an older, diffident, but friendly African with a moustache, wearing a Park Ranger's ribbed green sweater, came out and greeted me.

I deployed the name of Norman Monks, David Woods' friend in Parks and Wildlife and, though he was evidently based elsewhere, it did the trick. The moustached guy's name was Shakita. His radio was not working but he was very eager to oblige. He said I could leave the loaded bike out of sight behind the house and someone would come along and take me up to the P and W station at Marongora, at the top of the road up the escarpment ("7 KMS OF SHARP CURVES").

And come they soon did, in the form of a Land Rover which he flagged down. So, taking the Camelbak with its water, food and my journals, I got in the open flat-bed with several young Africans, and an AK47 assault rifle clattering about on the metal floor. The Rangers, as well as supervising the wildlife, turned out to be a paramilitary force to counter the armed gangs of poachers who penetrated the safari area. We hurtled off up the twisting escarpment road at hair-raising speed, and were soon exchanging shouted remarks about England. When I said things were not so good there right now, a clear-eyed young guy said he still wanted to go, "because of the lifestyle". Another laughed and called "Sandwich!" as we got stuck behind one truck with another close behind us, but then there was some hairy overtaking on a bend and we were clear.

Marongora Parks and Wildlife station was a smart place, with a wrought-iron name sign, whitewashed edging, and stone steps up to the main building. It stood in landscaped grounds with flower pots, an ornamental pool and nice trees and bougainvillea; there were diesel and petrol pumps, and flags on tall poles. And the African Ranger, standing behind the counter beneath the obligatory portrait of Mugabe and the stuffed head of an enormous eland, could not have been more helpful. Norman Monks could only be reached by radio, but there was a working phone, so I opted to call the contact Ginty had given me in Harare, a Dane named Karsten Nielsen, who ran an agricultural machinery repair business, and with a friend had ridden Yamaha 600s overland from Harare to Belgium.

The uniformed Ranger made the call, and after a long wait said, "Hello, yes," and handed me the phone. I introduced myself to Karsten, who sounded quizzical, after I had explained about the gearbox problem, asking, "What is it exactly you are wanting?" Then he said he would set off at 6am the following day from Harare in a Toyota Hi-Lux, and should be with me around 10 to 11 o'clock. And also that "I expect we can find someone" to fix the box. Major result. Ginty would later e-mail Karsten that "the guys in South Africa asked me to congratulate you on being the newest member of SWAT (Steve Wilson Assistance Team)."

It was nearly 4pm by then, and the Ranger at the desk had already said I could sleep there with the night watch. I thanked him and told him that food would be no problem (I had bought some more biltong in Lusaka), and that I had a sleeping bag back down with the bike (childishly, I was delighted that carrying the bag around was finally going to be justified). We shared a Polo ("the mint from England"), and then I settled to wait on a chair in the corner. The impulse to sleep was strong, as the last hours had been exhausting, but people kept coming and going, so I worked desultorily updating the journal. One guy said I would be in a nice tent, and we laughed as I queried the lion situation. Then a young, bright-faced Ranger in civvies came in with his little boy – who stared at me wordlessly, unblinking, for minutes on end – and with an older driver. The young man, Brighton, asked me what I would eat? I said tea, but he asked about "rice and sweety potatoes"; I rejected the latter, as I thought I would be cooking for myself.

Brighton said we would go down and fetch not just my sleeping bag, but the bike itself. We got into the Land Rover and I sat with the driver as we bumped up the single track opposite, and drove to Brighton's compound, to fetch fencing wire to help secure the Ariel, and the food in a plastic bowl. Then we skirled down the main hill again, with the driver and me praising the Land Rover's ability on "bad, slippery roads". When we arrived I greeted Shakita, offloaded all the luggage from the bike, and got out a couple of tie-down straps which I had brought along to secure the Big Bag if the going had got rough enough to disable the bungees. These straps held down the bike on its side stand, so the fence wire was not necessary. With the Land Rover's tailgate removed, and stood upright with the spare wheel, the Ariel was lifted onto the flatbed and, with three guys steadying it, we climbed back up the escarpment at more moderate speeds, and wheeled the bike off at Marongora onto a raised bank by the petrol pumps.

Chapter 36

TRAVELLING
MERCIES

Then Brighton said that I would come and spend the night at his house, so my gear (there was so much of it!) stayed in the back of the Landie, and off we went again up the hillside opposite. His single-storey home was inside a wildlife-fenced compound on the wooded slopes. Brighton said that two others nearby used to have fences, but the elephants had broken them down. Softly spoken and sincere, he told me that the park there was for licensed hunters – from the US, some Europeans, and South Africans – but there were other parks nearby for camera tourism. He stressed more than once his belief in the importance of conserving wildlife for future generations, and he evidently was prepared to battle for it; the militarily-dressed Rangers were anti-poachers, with a policy, if I understood him right, of shooting dead anyone other than licensed hunters found in the park with a gun. As well as the AK47s, he said the Rangers had FN and SLR rifles, the previous two generations of British Army weapon. But Brighton extolled the AK's ability to work even if it had been dropped in water.

It was getting dark fast now, and the power was off as Brighton showed me a room with a single and a double bed, with clean washing strung above it. I was unclear whether I would be sharing the room with the family. He showed me the bathroom and loo, and offered to heat water for a bath, but I didn't want to trouble him. The house was a long bungalow, with the rooms set off a single, wide veranda-like corridor with windows that looked down the hill. Now he took me to the end room where, in the shadows, his wife Esirida was working over a mopane-wood fire. I had learned about these from Kiki, and how slowly the dark wood burns. Chairs – a deck chair and a camp chair – were brought in, and we sat watching the fire, a great pleasure and relief. Brighton had his vocal two-year-old daughter Constance (who, due to the usual interpretation/deafness problems on my part, I thought at first was named Cornerstone) on his lap, while his son Philanthrop sat silent beside him, watching me intently, as he had in the office.

After a while, tea was ready – no rooibos leaves here, but regular tea bags with powdered milk. The brew tasted faintly smoky, but not unpleasantly. There was no chimney so the smoke just stayed in the air, eventually stinging your eyes, though when Brighton asked if it was a problem I denied this; I would rather have died than admit it. He said it was cold, and we pulled our chairs closer to the fire. We talked, the conversation interspersed with "OK, OK," from Brighton, spoken with many different inflections, as he processed what was said and cast around for new approaches. It was good talk, broad strokes mostly, returning again to the need for conservation for future generations, but we did speak for a while about the political situation as well. Brighton was quietly hopeful, believing that people saw that the opposition leader, and now Prime Minister in the Coalition, Morgan Tsvangirai, was genuine, and that things would go better for his Movement for Democratic Change at the next elections, which would not be faked up like the last ones. It was very moving to hear the hope in Brighton's voice, in some way against all odds, as he sat there with his family around him.

I told them a bit about England, and they seemed really interested, about the green of the countryside because of the rain. But when Brighton asked about computer technology, I said that at home people often stayed in their own room with their own TV and laptop, and ate separately, so that family scenes like this were endangered; and how people were trapped in mortgage repayments and the consumer lifestyle on credit, so that they had fewer children, and later. Brighton said that their own problem was population, as a man could have two or three wives, with three or four children each.

When we ate, it was big plates of white rice, with packet minestrone soup as sauce. I had offered biltong, but Brighton had said, not today. Before eating, we washed our hands, as the kids had, with a basin of water and a tin mug to pour it over, holding the basin for each other. The food was very welcome to me. The cooking had been done on open flames, with the wood/fire contained on a foil base circle, and expert feeding or damping down of the flames by both of them. Esirida's skill was to balance two cooking pots and a kettle on the wonky wire mesh set between stones, keep the fire right, *and* look after Constance and Philanthrop, stopping the little girl from falling in the fire/spilling stuff/unpicking the mat they were sitting on. Voices were never raised, and across the room Esirida was an occasional brilliant smile in the smoky darkness. I told them it was a privilege to be there, and meant it.

After we had shovelled down the food, I cleared it with the parents and dished out to the children from a waistcoat pocket the two remaining boiled sweets from the Wimpy at the Desert Sands. These went down well, though Constance became stridently vocal shortly afterwards, no doubt as the e-numbers kicked in. The parents made more tea and Brighton built up the fire into a glowing pyramid, which was lovely to look at. He initiated most of the conversation, on global warming and the changing weather, for instance, and with English as his second language, this must have been an effort. It was funny to listen to the couple talk together in their native tongue and then hear the odd English word like "motorcycle" or "gearbox" interjected.

When we had finished our tea, it was only 8.30pm (Brighton had a watch which he kept in his pocket) but I was flagging fast, so I got led back to the room which was evidently to be all mine. Brighton produced, from a large sealed transparent packet, one of those big synthetic coloured furry blankets that I'd been rather sniffy about when I saw them for sale in markets. Brighton said I would not need to use the sleeping bag, which suited me as I was not sure I could get it back so neatly into its stuff-sack. I ended up using it as a (hard) pillow, and the blanket, folded double like an open-sided sleeping bag, was wonderful. I went to the loo by torchlight, and when I couldn't work the flush, which was a bog brush hanging from the overhead cistern, poured in a bucket of water. I had taken an Imodium to pre-empt night emergencies, and two sips of the sweet brandy flask. Then, with a full moon shining outside the uncurtained windows, I went straight to sleep for six or seven hours, despite the onset in the meantime of power and the bare bulb illuminating. Brighton had deliberately left this switched on, I never did find out why. I slept well, with good dreams, until 6.10am, by which time it was light outside.

I was dressing when one of the lads, a relative I think, came in, anointed his head and ankles from a bottle, and went off again. Out in the passage, seeing a stripped-to-the-waist Brighton going into the bathroom, I stepped outside, walked to the fence and took a long, satisfying pee, hoping I wasn't letting the side down. Breakfast was tea, plus last night's supper, taken on chairs outside in the passage looking down over the forest. Then we drove back down to Marongoro. After unloading my kit, I said goodbye to Brighton, taking a chance and palming a $20 bill to him ("for the family") as we shook hands; he did not seem displeased. I would not like to exaggerate a brief encounter, but Brighton's manners, patience and unconditional hospitality meant that I left their home feeling nourished by more than the food, as the generosity and warm family life made me sense that for a moment on my journey, I had touched a true heart of Africa. Once again, an apparent misfortune had turned into a blessing.

ABOVE: *Off alone again to Luangwa Bridge.*

BELOW LEFT: *Guardian Angels. Daniella and Martin Haenz from Switzerland, tapping a thread to seal the open end of Jerry's rocker shaft.*

BELOW RIGHT: *Ariel on the Bad Road from Chipata to Mfuwe.*

ABOVE: *Hostess Melissa, head guide Kiki, and Jackson the scout, at Nkwali.*

BELOW: *Rough Eden. South Luangwa at sunset.*

ABOVE: *Steve at Kawaza School with headmaster David Mwewa (right) and sports tournament kids.*

BELOW: *Sleeping lionesses, possibly full of 'Robert' the wart-hog.*

ABOVE: *Give way!*

ABOVE LEFT: *Robin and Jo Pope at Nkwali.* (Robin Pope Safaris)

LEFT: *Giraffe stretching for lunch at South Luangwa.*

ABOVE: *Village life. Split tyre at Mkowe.*

RIGHT: *On the road back to Luangwa Bridge.*

BELOW: *Ginty, Andy Legg and Steve back at Chongwe, outside Lusaka.*

ABOVE: *Jimmy Whyte, in Harare, rebuilt Jerry's gearbox.*

LEFT: *Zimbabwe remains a most beautiful country.*

ABOVE: *Tys Pottas' private museum. Are Steve and Jerry the latest exhibits?*

BELOW: *Last morning. Tys (left), Frank, Steve and Bertus, by the Bella Vista Hotel.*

ABOVE: *End of the line. Not much traffic in Richmond that morning.*

BELOW: *In borrowed helmet, Steve says a final 'Thank You' to Mike Wood and fellow Kickstart members.*

Chapter 37

BOB'S TAKEAWAY

I had nearly three hours before the SWAT cavalry was expected, so I settled down on the porch outside the building and worked at the journal. On a small level area further down the hill, Rangers, both male and female, fell in for a spot of square-bashing. The close-order drill and the way the NCO's voice rose to a screech were all traditional British Army, well familiar to me from the School Corps. When the drilling was over there was immediately loud chatter and laughter, the buzz of talk continuing as they were fallen out, some going on to lectures. One of the guys from the previous day walked past and asked me why I was all the time writing, so I told him about the book and how they would all be in it. "Everything about us, eh?" he laughed, walking on. Later a yellow lorry full of wheelbarrows and workmen, singing, pulled in. After that a white man and a black one arrived with an old elephant skull and tusks, which for the first time I discovered were hollow. Marongoro was never dull.

The cavalry, in the shape of Jimmy Young, arrived at 11.30am. He said he had "left late" from Harare, at 8.30am. Jimmy was a 72-year-old ex-policeman from the war days, who for 30 years since then had worked as a quality controller for SeedCo Zimbabwe, as well as now working part-time for Karsten. He was a lean, tough *hombre* and would have driven the full six-and-a-half-hour round trip in one hit.

With unsolicited African help as usual, and Karsten's plank, we loaded the bike, tying it down with just my two straps, and were away. It very soon emerged that Jimmy, though mildly spoken, was a bitter and angry man, which was a sharp contrast to the ambience of Brighton and his family who I had just left. But he had cause. Jimmy was one of only two white guys left at SeedCo, where they now had prayers at board meetings; he had recently been given six months' notice and, despite his long service, the chronic

Zimbabwean currency devaluation meant that his pension was now worth about 5 US cents a week.

After an hour or so we had come down out of the hills and were driving through the ultra-fertile farmland leading to the Great Dyke mountain range. Through his work Jimmy had known the farmers there personally, and named them as he pointed out the weeds, the derelict irrigation machinery, the roadside place where one farm used to have wildlife fences and wild game on display, all eaten now – the sorry, skinny remnants of formerly big cattle herds, and the huge long rows of tall grain silos, all currently empty. The majority of farms had been taken over by Mugabe's "war veterans" (or "wovits," as Peter Godwin said they were known) and run into the ground. The theft was quite brazen. Jimmy said the country's finest dairy farm had been taken and given to a wife of Mugabe. It was sobering to see first hand how the "bread-basket of Africa" had been reduced to a place where starvation had become a reality.

There were many police checkpoints along the way, but we were never stopped. We did halt for fuel, but as Jimmy turned briskly onto the forecourt he had forgotten about the bike, and it toppled; there was no damage except for a possible extra ding in the tank, which was so distressed already that it made no difference. Jimmy would have driven straight on, but I pleaded a diabetic's need for food, and we went next door into a formerly smart café, now in African hands. There was a fine long mirror in the entrance hall, only it had come off the wall and now just reflected our shoes. The smart restaurant was empty. We asked the lady for something quick, and all that was available was a toasted egg sandwich, but in the end it was untoasted as the power was off. When we came out a cluster of African evangelists were at the truck, asking for a ride into the next town. Jimmy took six or seven of them, standing in the truckbed with the bike and my gear.

We drove on, Jimmy entertaining me with tales like the time, as a policeman during the war, when a game warden had asked him to help with a couple of cattle-killing lions, and he had ended up shooting one dead with his FN rifle. The hairiest moment of our trip came when a gesticulating red-bereted sergeant appeared on foot in the road in front of us, and then a jogging squad of troops, with more frowning and cursing NCOs trying to get Jimmy to drive the laden truck into the ditch to make way for them. Jimmy, serenely ignoring them despite their weapons, swung wide of the column and drove on steadily, murmuring, "Wait till one of their government friends comes round a corner in his brand new 4x4 at 200kph". Later I remembered that the North Korean-trained 5th Brigade, who had carried out the massacres in Matebeleland, had been distinguished by their red berets. All in all, the journey left a bad taste that would linger.

We crossed the Great Dyke, and Karsten Nielsen's workplace was before Harare itself. Jimmy delivered me and the loaded truck and, after a beer, said goodbye. Karsten proved to be a somewhat sardonic but extremely nice Dane, slightly weird-looking, with protruding ears and bulging, almost hypothalamic eyes, which he rolled to comic effect as a commentary on stuff going on around him, particularly in relation to his wife Linda. He proved a hoot to hang out with. He drove us in the truck to his extensive home compound in the Harare suburbs, and already it was clear that, with its wide avenues and abundant trees, despite deterioration Harare was still a beautiful city.

Then I met Linda, a trim lady with dark curls in a thick, tight, late-70s perm. She proved interested in books and cultural matters, and I was able to continue reading Peter Godwin's *Mukiwa* in her copy, which had been signed by the author. There were two nice daughters, Tina (15) and Rebecca (12), as well as an adopted son, 18-year-old Devon. Karsten, who reputedly was always doing things for other people – he certainly did for me – had taken Devon Rooschuz in after his mother died of cancer and his father had been killed in a car crash with Devon on board. He too was an extremely pleasant, fair-haired young man, with an excellent gift for doing impressions of the girls, and I enjoyed the family interplay. Devon had to share his room in the guest cottage with me, and despite the age gap we got on all right. That first night I slept only intermittently due to the cold. Finally, there in Zim, I came to realise that it really was winter in Southern Africa, with their July the equivalent of our January. Extra bedding from Karsten fixed that.

The mornings were cold too, though under blue skies. On that first one, Karsten drove me in the loaded bakkie into Harare, with its wide grid layout and beautiful trees. The African girls on the streets were the prettiest so far too. Down Second Avenue he pointed out, among the shining high-rise buildings ahead, a bank where he remembered seeing Russian-built helicopters lowering the air-conditioning units onto the roof. This bank was known locally as "Bob's Takeaway," due to the Presidential habit of spiriting money from there out of this broken country. Despite the capital's grand appearance, the traffic lights were often dead because of the regular power cuts – Jimmy Young had said these were because Zimbabwe "hadn't paid the bill" to their supplier, South Africa. Also, the road surfaces were deteriorating.

The exception to this was the two-lane road running past Saint Georges, the impressive English-type public school Devon was attending, and on past the Presidential Palace. The penalties were that the traffic on the other side of the road had to stop dead when the Presidential motorcade drove out, and that the road was closed from 6pm to 6am. Pedestrians fared no better. Devon told me that one of the nurses from his school had been walking past the Palace's outer walls when she had tripped and broken her leg. She had been immediately surrounded by armed security who held guns to her head, screaming that she couldn't stop there, she had to move. As she had dragged herself away, she had thought she was done for.

We proceeded to bumpy Coventry Road, aptly named as it was home to several light industrial plants, and to TT Motorcycles, which was run by one-eyed Superbike champion road racer Chris Whyte, who had won world-class events in South Africa. Karsten said hello to him in the busy yard. TT were the concession holders for Chinese-built Honda 125 replicas, virtually the only motorcycles you saw thereabouts. We walked into the showroom where a white-haired man in shorts went to slap Karsten. This was Jimmy Whyte, Chris' father and a former TT racer on the Isle of Man, and the mock slap was because Karsten had recently beaten Jimmy and his cronies at a feet-up trials event they had organised themselves. Karsten told him about my trip and Jimmy called me a brave man, which I told him I knew was shorthand for stupid, and we laughed. I filled him in on what had happened with the gearbox, but when I said I thought the broken bolt might be inside the inner box, he said peremptorily that he was not going to remove and dismantle the box. That did not seem to bode well.

But he appeared well disposed towards the crackpot/adventure side of my trip, though in Africa he had been an early convert to Bavarian reliability for touring, and told me with a grin that I should have done it on a BMW – had I heard that before? He had the Ariel wheeled onto his workbench, which was not in the workshops but located more comfortably in the showroom. It was surrounded by a collection of reassuringly well-restored British classics, including a BSA A10 and Matchless G85CS, which Jimmy had rebuilt himself. Despite his reservations, the luck seemed to be running good, because he was probably the best-qualified guy in the country to rebuild Jerry's Burman BA gearbox.

Then Karsten and I drove on bumpy roads out of the city, to a business appointment with a fellow Scandinavian, first name Ajs, pronounced 'Ice'. Ajs lived on one of a complex of four or five dairy farms owned by his family. They had stood up, successfully so far, to official attempts to take these, fighting the government/"wovits" through the courts – a success which emphasised the contradictory situation in Zimbabwe, where the rule of law had not been completely abandoned. The family was offered the compromise of handing over just some of the holdings, but had refused – "you take it all, or you take nothing," as Ajs expressed it. On the ground there had been a price: his father had been knifed in the head during an attack by "wovits" and lost an eye, dying not long afterwards in Denmark.

On the road out, there was a hut that Karsten said would soon become a toll-booth taxing all traffic, a newly introduced version of a medieval notion. We turned off; the farms were set at the end of a long single-track strip of tar, which Karsten negotiated expertly, smoothly dodging pedestrians and cyclists, and putting one side of the bakkie's wheels on the gravel verge to miss the worst of the pot-holes. The council would not fill the holes, Ajs had to do this himself, and it was a long road.

We turned again, driving past good-looking, properly fed herds of dairy and meat cattle, called "mombes" out there. The farmhouse was nice and spacious, built by Italian POWs with an arched, discernibly Italian inner court, though the sloping roof was not red tiles, but corrugated tin. Ajs came out with his Rottweiler-cross dog; he was a tall, rangy man, energetic but tired around his red-rimmed eyes. His wife, understandably, lived at their town house. "Yes," he joked, "I'm a Lone Ranger."

The night before he had got up at 1am, rather than the easier 10.30pm or dawn options, to check the guards, and had found them all asleep. There was a saying locally for deep slumber, "Sleeping like a security man". He had taken the radio and torch off one of them, put a bucket over his head and when he still hadn't woken, hurled something metal at it. The guy had come to, instantly denying that he had been asleep. Ajs had then had a run-in with his own dog, who had sat where he shouldn't have in the truck's crew cab, and, although friendly, would normally have resisted if told off. But Ajs, big and angry by then, had got him by the scruff and hurled him out, to run off yelping. But the dog now lay amiably by our feet while we sat out in the sun, as it was too cold in the shade.

The meeting concerned getting hand maize-choppers fabricated, for making silage. These would be for the seven small African-run dairy co-operatives which, as his suppliers, Ajs tried to encourage; many of the workers' wives had jobs at his cheese-making dairy, so these people had a strong incentive to resist the "wovits".

The experts arrived, bearded John and his son Richard. John had set up a metal-working company, one which Karsten said was proud of doing a good job, after he and Richard had been kicked off their farm, so they also knew about silage etc. The hope was that they could make new and possibly improved versions of the derelict hand-grinder Ajs had found and, with the cost of fuel soaring, this would make good sense. Interestingly, however, when we visited the co-operative HQ, the African farmers politely expressed a preference for a diesel-driven grinder, their lives presumably being labour-intensive enough already.

Karsten would get 10 per cent of whatever John earned if the deal went down, for putting Ajs and John together. I realised that business was Karsten's real thing. He was happy to stay in Zim despite the situation; he and Linda had once gone back to Denmark and got jobs for six months, but then one morning they had looked at each other and come back to Africa. If the worst came to the worst (a Mugabe-centred coup) they could go back to Europe, as Karsten was a qualified industrial electrician and could always get work, but they didn't want to. They liked the people, the Shona majority at any rate, who – unlike the Matebele – were not war-like or aggressive, but nice-natured. Like Brighton, I guessed.

As we drove back in the afternoon, I rang Jimmy Whyte to check what he had found, but background noise made him virtually incomprehensible. Back at home Karsten showed me the 600 Yamaha single he had ridden up through Africa, and told me about the time his friend had been fixing their 11th puncture in the middle of nowhere, when an American in a lavish 4x4 had rolled up, taken in the scene and asked, "Why didn't you take a plane?" That had become their catch-phrase. When Devon came home from school, he set me up on the computer to email, and I contacted Ginty and my step-brother, as well as home, where the great news was that the dog was much improved.

That evening I took the whole family out to a Chinese restaurant called the Shangri-La, which was excellent value at $74 for all six of us plus beer, though Linda brought along a bottle of good wine which she and I drank while we talked about books. The only loser was daughter Tina who found even the blandest dish too spicy, though apple fritters and whipped cream afterwards were some compensation. And she may have had a point. Karsten and I had chilli sizzling stuff, for which I would suffer during the night. It felt slightly odd that the waiters were African not Oriental, but we enjoyed watching the adjoining tables of Chinese, adulating a solitary child (presumably due to the one-child policy), puffing away at fags over their grub, and popping up and down to do toasts.

Karsten was unimpressed. As well as his 20-strong company's main work, servicing agricultural machinery in Zambia and Mozambique, he had developed a sideline, solar water-heating panels, manufactured by a medium-sized company he had selected in China. He had spent a week in overalls working on their shop floor, to crack the problem of building the panels so that they could be packed horizontally, to make container loads more economical. His current stock was being held by him in a bonded warehouse, as there was news that the government was very likely shortly to reduce import duties, which were currently standing at 55 per cent. He told good stories about out-drinking the wily Orientals, who tried with multiple toasts, using smaller glasses than their guests, to get Western business folk drunk early in the day. This was a tactic which reportedly had been successful in the early 2000s on representatives from MG-Rover, helping lead to the loss of the last independent British volume car manufacturers. Karsten the Dane said contemptuously, "But Chinese beer is weak!"

The following day, Wednesday, Devon drove me round to TT Motorcycles to check on progress with Jimmy Whyte. As we drove I told him the black girls here seemed the prettiest in Africa. HIV/Aids was a compelling argument for keeping it in your pants, but had he ever been tempted? He was completely surprised – inter-racial liaisons were right off his radar. I had asked the same of Mike and Rialet Wood and faced the same incomprehension, but had thought it might have been different with a younger generation. No, said

Devon, if he ever brought a black girl home to his parents, it would be the same as if he had turned up with another boy (which also gave an idea of some of the difficulties of being gay in the region). There was, said Devon, just no attraction.

At TT Motorcycles, Jimmy Whyte was very cheerful and chatty. He had already fixed the gearbox problem, which had been partial seizure of the selector forks, due to lack of lubricant (though the oil had been changed at Nkwali less than 600 miles previously, and topped up since), and to looseness. To that end, Jimmy had replaced some of the cheese-head screws holding the back-plate on. "You can never keep them tight enough for long," he said, "it was a problem with all British gearboxes." Presumably he meant in the harsh conditions of Africa as, apart from the powerful Norton Commando's over-stressed box, I had never heard of or experienced trouble like that with a pre-unit gearbox. Instead, he had used two Allen-headed bolts, and three ¼ head, ³⁄₁₆ ones. He had also turned up a suitable case bolt to replace the broken one. He had found the fragment of bolt, but it had done no damage.

So that was sorted. But in the process Jimmy also discovered that the primary chain was utterly knackered – for the third time in 5,000 miles! – with plates missing. He had also found out why: its two sprockets were ⅝ inch out of alignment with each other, and he had remedied it by machining and fitting a spacer. But even after removing a half-link, he still could not get a new O-ring chain to fit. He was on his way home (which was not nearby) to hunt up a good second-hand Renolds one, which he swore by and which he said would get me home. In the event he found and fitted a new one, not the easiest item to come by in Harare. He would, he said, definitely get me on the road again by Friday.

We were feeling pretty chuffed driving away. But on the way home Devon was pulled over at a police check. The cop said he had no reflective stickers on the rear of the vehicle. Now Devon was a bit more street savvy than I had been at his age. He talked to the guy in Shona and had nearly joked him out of it, lack of money, poor student etc. When the guy suggested I pay the $20 fine, Devon quietly advised against, so I pulled the poor tourist, only traveller's cheques etc. We were nearly clear, when we were called over by a nasty, narrow-eyed and officious female officer. She told Devon with a sneer, "You think every day is Christmas – well it isn't". She took his name, address and phone number. Devon at least got his licence back, in case he was stopped again on the way home, but though the original guy, smiling, was now advocating just a caution, the female cop insisted that Devon turn up at his local police station at 1pm with the $20.

After we left, I gave Devon the money and offered to go along to the station with him, but he said not to, because the presence of a foreigner would possibly provoke matters further. At the station, they got him in a back room with six detectives as well as the female cop, who wanted to handcuff him. Devon, who was braver than me at any age, said afterwards that you had to show them you were not intimidated. He told them he was there with the money as requested, and that the cuffs were ridiculous. He got the sympathy of the officer who went out with him to inspect the car, which now sported not only the rear reflectors but ones on the door edges as well, as Devon had been advised at the garage that without them he might get done all over again. But the officer was junior, and when he spoke up for Devon he was told to shut up and sit down, which he did, with his head hanging, as if he had been told off by his mother. Devon walked free, but the whole thing again left a very nasty taste indeed.

Chapter 38

GET ME
OUT OF ZIM

The morning I left was a bit jangled. Karsten had brought the bike home in the bakkie the evening before, and I had test-ridden it. But that morning, with Karsten watching, it flat-out would not start. This caused a lot of kicking, cursing and sweating. When the engine eventually caught, it soon spluttered and died. Finally the answer proved simple: for the first time on the whole trip I tried using full choke, and instantly all was well. There was frost on the grass that morning; the engine had just been cold. Then a rat had run into the kitchen, and through into one of the empty bedrooms where I shut it in, and the family's drink-prone gardener came with a stick and did for it. In my superstitious mind-set, I took this for a bad omen.

Jimmy Whyte had refused all payment for two days' work and more, except for the price of the parts. So I followed Karsten, who was leading me out of town in the bakkie, back first to TT Motorcycles. There, as Karsten had suggested, I presented Jimmy with some fine wine, plus the largest bottle of good dark rum we had been able to find, before saying thanks and goodbye. Then one petrol place wanted paying in advance – I didn't know how much a full tank would be, so I couldn't – and at the station where Karsten had waved farewell and peeled off, they made a fuss about me going to the correct side of the pumps, and then the attendant half-heartedly claimed to lack the necessary $1 change. I plucked the bill from his hand.

I rode out on the same route we had taken to Ajs's farm, and though the sunshine was warm enough, the morning's events so far had done nothing to lift my mood now that I was back on my own again. I was headed for Masvingo, roughly the half-way point on the 400-mile run to the border crossing with South Africa at Beitbridge, and home to Ginty's nephew Errol. Shopping with Devon had produced a working SIM card for my phone which was very reassuring, but so far I hadn't been able to contact Errol in advance. On the road my confidence grew a little bit as we thudded on through cattle country. There were frequent roadside police checks, but I took my cue from Jimmy Young and rode on through, on one occasion doing the wave to a guy who was holding up his hand.

At the next one I came unstuck, as I hesitated a little too long behind a stationary bakkie full of Africans. A very tall, closely-shaven African officer, with a pistol on his belt and a sharp face beneath his peaked cap, stalked over and asked for something which I took some time to understand was my licence. I pulled over, stopped the engine, and extricated it. He asked what I was doing and I told him I was a tourist from Britain. What had I brought with me? I paraphrased Oscar Wilde and replied, "Nothing, just myself". I sketched out the journey and he snorted, gesturing at Jerry, "You do all that on *this* thing?" "Certainly." "Aah, because you love cycling!" "Exactly, yes!" On this note of mutual comprehension, we parted.

But the day was wearisome. While the gearbox now seemed to be back to normal, the emerging worry was the front end. The steering damper was still rattling unless it was tightened down, and on ridged, tramlined sections of this relatively busy road, the front felt edgy, which caused me to tense up and make things worse. And both the engine and I were tired. Despite the rest in Harare, I was feeling at the end of my strength, and I thought that if something happened I would not have any reserves left to cope with it. I found myself praying: just get me out of Zim.

Karsten had said there would be no petrol until Masvingo, but there proved to be stations open at Chivhu, the half-way mark, though foolishly I failed to heed the rule and stop to top up when I could have. We rolled on, with cows in the road becoming a regular hazard. Stopping further on in a lay-by to eat, a guy strolled back down the slope ahead from a broken-down flat-bed truck, munching on a roll, and I instinctively stashed my food after only having a mouthful or two. He was a bit shifty, and only interested in talking and asking about ways of making money. I paid for my stinginess, as later I discovered that the best biltong, the stuff from the Gymkhana Club, had fallen out of the partially open Camelbak. I stopped again by one of the many big stone outcrops, a *kopje* (pronounced 'copy' – there had been much quiet mirth from Jimmy Young when I had sounded the 'j'). I was sitting eating in the shade of the rock, some way from the Ariel, when the sound of voices from down on

the road made me pack up again in a hurry, as I had left my jacket on the
bike. It was only a harmless old geezer with a stick and a younger companion,
and we chatted a little, but the disturbed moment said as much about my
state of mind as anything else.

Thirty miles further on we flogged into Masvingo at around 3pm. I
spotted the Toyota place where Ginty's nephew worked and turned in, but
the receptionist told me that "Mr Edwards" was at another dealership in
town. I rode in, slowly, and just as well, as it was a 40mph limit and there
were police with a hand-held speed gun. I tried for petrol at the first
station, but fuel there was to be had by voucher only, and the next two
places had none at all, though a friendly younger guy had said he had seen
a Shell tanker go through, so I might get lucky later on.

The bike was being awkward about starting, and I was still getting a
disconnected signal on Ginty's nephew's cell phone, so I located the dealers
I had been directed to. There I met the nephew's son, Brandon, who told
me his dad was away in South Africa, but was very helpful and considerate
indeed. He suggested several options for staying the night, gently warning
me off the nearby town hotels which I had inclined to as I was so tired, and
giving me a voucher for the first petrol station. I filled up with "Blend"
petrol, all that was on offer, had a cold drink and a pie, and met an African
old vehicle enthusiast in a Mercedes who asked if I knew about a US
Henderson-4 locally, and shook my hand.

The bike started first kick and we rode out around 10km south to
Panyandas Lodge, which Brandon had recommended. But at the
gatekeeper's hut, before a mile of dirt road leading to the Lodge itself, I had
to stop the engine and then Jerry asserted himself, resolutely refusing to
start again under the sympathetic eyes of the gatekeeper and his pal, who
even gamely tried a kick or two himself. It was the last bummer of the day,
but after a few minutes' wait and a change of the very sooty spark plug, the
Ariel started first kick.

At the Lodge there was no power, but the androgynous young African in
charge was nice, the beers from the bar were cold, and my cabin was
comfortable. There was only one other party there, a large South African
family with "Montana Meats" on one of their bakkies. They seemed pleasant
enough, but at dinner all smoked over a baby in a pushchair, and the meat
man, playing macho to a young boy, told an extremely unpleasant story about

cattle-prodding fallen beasts at the abattoir. But later the boy told me how to work my shower, and it was hot and good. I had been funking the unreliable one at Karsten's, and my scalp was itching.

I began reading my last book, Rose Tremain's *The Road Home*, and hoped that the title would prove appropriate. I slept well and, standing on my veranda early the following morning, I slowly realised that quite close, in among the tall trees on the far side of a game-fence, a graceful giraffe was gently browsing the leaves. It was to be my farewell to wild Africa.

Chapter 39

LEAVE HERE NOW

I had about 175 miles to go to the border with South Africa, which now to me represented an unlikely sanctuary. We slogged south, and the country at first was outstandingly beautiful. On a straight road before the first town of Ngundu, to the right of the highway wonderful tall rock outcrops rose from the red earth. I saw an African in the flatbed of a truck saluting one, and did the same mentally myself. In warm sunlight, pale dry riverbeds and fine forests punctuated the way. Zimbabwe, if nothing else, was beautiful.

But Jerry, as if sensing my desperation to get out of the country, acted up. The engine began losing power and pinking on even mild inclines. My initial reaction was to flog it, "just get me there," even if Avis had to take over in RSA. Then I saw the folly of that, and began to let the bike find its pace more, and that was better for a while, though it was still pinking at the top of slopes. The probable culprit was the "Blend" fuel, and I could see a lot of debris in the fuel filter, despite having cleaned it out at Karsten's. I stopped to rest the engine among some particularly lovely wooded hillsides, but soon a young guy came walking past with his girl and began to call out ironically in a falsetto voice, spoiling it.

Underway again, the front end problems re-asserted themselves, not aided by some terrible rain-groove/tramline surfaces. With about 65 miles to go I stopped again to rest the engine and myself, as it was seriously hot now and I was beginning to feel a bit dizzy. We rode on, counting the miles, but things got worse. The country had gone to flat and barren bush, with plenty of cows and some goats ambling across from the unfenced edges of the road. The only features were some fine baobab trees along the way, and plenty of lay-bys, though most were unshaded. The bike was now vibrating badly as well as pinking, and with about 35 miles to go – I couldn't believe this, we were so close! – it began to slow and falter after the pinking had worsened. I pulled in the clutch and coasted for a while. But as our speed slowly declined, deciding this was not the place to stop I let out the clutch – the engine was still bad – and changed down into 3rd, which inexplicably felt and sounded OK. So we crept onwards in lower gear, counting the miles, willing the bike on.

After eight or nine miles like that I decided cooling off was the wiser course, and pulled into a lay-by on the far side with a sliver of shade from a baobab tree. I trickled forward over the dust till the ground underneath felt firm enough for kick-starting on the stand, then stopped the engine and turned off the petrol. I took off my helmet and jacket, putting them on a concrete table a little way away. I checked the gearbox temperature and oil level, in case something had gone wrong and it was that top gear thing again, but the box was cool and full of lubricant. I poured a little fresh oil into the oil tank. I cleaned out the fuel filter. I changed the plug – the one in there had little silver scratches on the electrodes. All this took about 15 minutes, and it was now around 2pm.

At that point, a white bakkie carrying two Africans pulled in, honking once in greeting. The driver wanted to know if I was in trouble. I began to sketch out the story but he interrupted, "Does the bike run?" I said, "Yes, but not very well." "Then leave here now," he said urgently. "It's not safe, they will take your stuff. Two weeks ago I left one of my truck drivers here, I told him to wait, and by the time I was back from Beitbridge, he had been attacked; he was stabbed."

I threw up my hands in probably inappropriately mock horror. "Do not stop here," he said seriously, "or the next lay-by, or the third." And then he drove off. Feeling like Mole in the Wild Wood, I kitted up, and luckily the Ariel started fairly easily. There was less than 20 miles to go and top gear now felt OK, though the engine was noisy. I passed the other two lay-bys which were as empty as the land around. I felt the urgency. After all the warnings from white friends, it had taken a concerned black to really get to me. I nursed Jerry along, willing him on, past lay-bys with people selling carvings, and finally the first sign for Beitbridge came into view.

I poked and hoped on for a couple of miles, through some rough bits of road, past lorry parks, with all the Ariel's front end troubles and everything else forgotten in the need to negotiate this last hurdle. There were, of course, no signs, and I had to guess, and ask once, about the way to customs and immigration. I finally pulled up by some parked bicycles in the shade outside a big, busy, likely-looking building. There were too many people hanging around outside filling in forms, so when two kids offered to watch the loaded bike, I accepted.

Then I plunged in, jacketed and carrying the helmet. Inside it was like an old-fashioned bank. I went to a window at the counter, paid $5 for the privilege of leaving, got a gate-pass form, got sent to the immigration window, who were not interested in the *carnet* but did stamp my passport, paid for the gate-pass and got its first stamp, got sent down the corridor for its second stamp, but there was no one at the window I thought they had indicated, so went back to the first window and got sent to customs, another, smaller adjacent building, for the *carnet*. Miraculously, after waiting for the guys to finish in front of me, the official there did the *carnet* business with no problem. Big relief. I thanked him warmly. Back to the original window to pursue the gate-pass, they again sent me down the corridor but this time made it clear that what I needed was not a window but a table in the corner, which I'd thought was money-changing. The lady there scrutinised the Ariel's log book uncomprehendingly, but stamped the gate-pass – and then sent me back to the first window for a final stamp.

But that was it. Outside, I gave the boys a dollar each, pushed the bike a little way away, put the pass half in the tank bag and stuck the gloves down my jacket. Jerry started fourth or fifth kick, and at the gate before the bridge back over the Limpopo I handed over the pass while keeping the engine going with my left hand, and a young gate guy grinned, "You are an Easy Rider!" It was a plus note to be leaving on. As I moved off, a taxi-bus abruptly pulled in nose first across the lane, but I rode round him and sailed over the river.

Customs on the South African side was predictably more organised. An Afrikaner family I got talking to said that a few weeks before this they had been coming through, and on the Zimbabwean side, when a log-jam had developed in a doorway, an official had come with a stick and started whacking. When one of his little boys started playing up, the man threatened to put the child on the back of my bike. At Customs I got an extravagantly hair-curled, traditionally-built African lady who was flummoxed by the *carnet* – oh no, the South African problem again! – but she consulted a colleague and soon got it right. Yes! I had cleared the last hurdle on that one.

Outside on the road again I was mildly confused as the N1 dual-carriageway came up quickly, with signs indicating it was a toll road – should I have turned where it had said "Residential Area," to get to the border town of Musina? But then there was a sign indicating that the town was 10km further on. I nursed the bike along again, pulling left over the yellow line to give way to cars speeding up from behind. The town, when I reached it, rambled, and included an unpaved section of road, but there were some promising-looking eateries, an Avis sign, and even a train station, complete with locomotive. Eventually I booked into the clean but noisy Limpopo Hotel, which also had secure parking, with an electronic gate, around the back. The doll-faced but almost completely unhelpful receptionist would not take dollars so I had to pay by MasterCard; in all the excitement I had omitted to change dollars to rand at the frontier, and it was now 4.30pm on a Saturday night, so the banks were closed.

Though stupid with fatigue and only wanting to crash, this meant a further odyssey onto the streets of Musina after dark, and it was not the safest town, with beggars, people going through the garbage cans, and some Africans with attitude – one called to me mockingly, "How are you, my baas?" But I badly needed to eat and nowhere was taking plastic. I asked about changing money at a petrol station, who sent me to the next one on the far edge of town, where they directed me to the fruit- and veg-selling ladies on the forecourt, but it was no dice with them. Walking back, I tried the last one, a Shell station. There was an older lady swaddled in rags, with a skirt of many layers, some of them sheets of plastic, lying against the back wall of the forecourt behind a rampart of bananas and tomatoes. And she did it, for a not great rate, 7.50 when it was more like 8.50, but where else was I going to go? She sat me on a plastic drum while she went across the road and got the money, then inspected my $100 bill closely before doing the business.

So I could walk back to the diner by the hotel pool, where the proprietors were half-cut, but the Windhoek beer was cold and the pizzas delicious. At the bar I fell in with a raw-boned, hatchet-faced Afrikans ex-enduro rider who said he had once, racing a 535 KTM, suffered a heart attack in the middle of an event out in the bush. But after an hour, when the support vehicle eventually arrived, he had been conscious enough so that, like a 19th-century English fox-hunter, he wouldn't let them cut off his boots, and he had woken up in hospital in just his underpants and his R600 motocross boots. How was it, I thought, that even after the day like the one I had just gone through, other people's stories always had to gazump mine?

I slept for six-and-a-half hours, until woken at 4.30am by the African neighbours talking, laughing and going in and out of each others' rooms, before departing two hours later. If I'm honest, African voices – would jabbering be too strong a word? – had been getting on my nerves for the past week or so. That morning I was at the end of my strength, mentally and physically; things like pulling on a shirt required disproportionate effort. I was played out; the thought of riding on into another breakdown on another empty road was insupportable. I just wasn't prepared to face the long roads with a bike like that anymore.

In daylight, Musina disappointed. The Avis place only rented cars, the train hadn't left the station for many days, and I failed to drum up a rental bakkie at any price. But I did revive the phone with its previous South African SIM card, which still had credit on it. I rang Andy Legg in Zambia, as we had discussed a fall-back plan of loading the bike onto one of his company's south-bound trucks, but nothing was coming through for a while. I talked to Mike and Rialet Wood in Port Elizabeth, and when I told Rialet about the previous day's incidents at the lay-by, she said, laughing, "You must have eight angels looking out for you!" Then when I confided earnestly to her that I no longer trusted the bike, there were peals of laughter as she cried, "At last!"

Finally, reluctantly, since he was a virtual stranger, I called Pierre Cronje, the Classic Club President in Johannesburg, 300 miles to the south. He had phoned me at Port Elizabeth and generously offered assistance should the situation arise, but I'd had no personal introduction to him. I was cold-calling to ask for help – which was readily forthcoming.

Pierre said he would sort something out transport-wise, and immediately offered to work on the bike once I had reached his home in the eastern Johannesburg suburb of Benoni. After some confusion (on my part) about what was going to happen, early on Monday morning I rang one of my potential helpers, a Classic Club member named Bryan Hunter from

Lephalale (formerly Ellisras – another example of the name changes that irritated the white tribe). Bryan said it would suit him best if I could meet his bakkie at Alldays, a town about 130 miles to the west of Musina, where I was, and he would then take me to Lephalale, where an employee of his was leaving in a truck for Jo'burg early on Tuesday morning.

This was too good an offer to miss. I packed up, fiddled with the bike rather than doing a real check, loaded it, fired up first kick, opened the parking gates electronically, gassed up at the nearest petrol station and asked its friendly proprietor to keep an eye on the bike while I returned the keys to reception and got my $10 deposit back. Riding off again, I found my way out of town. There was a more direct route to Alldays, but on the map it looked as if it might turn into dirt, so I opted to run the road west, parallel to the border, and then turn due south. The great endless emptiness of the place hit me again, but the bike seemed to be doing all right after a day's rest.

The long straight road, with hunting lodges occasionally indicated to the south of it, was leavened by some amazing rock formations and outcrops alongside. We found the turn south at a T-junction, and thudded down to Alldays. It was about 300 miles from Musina to Jo'burg. With the bike running OK, should I have taken a chance on it, I was wondering? Then, just one mile short of my destination, despite a tank full of fresh unleaded hopefully having flushed through the dreaded "Blend", the bike did its thing again – the engine faltered badly in top gear, almost ready to die. I downshifted and crept into town, grateful that my luck had held, and grimly satisfied that I had made the right decision.

Alldays in the late morning sunlight was a small place but civilised after Zim, with some shops and well-stocked stalls, white faces, many of them young, and the Africans not looking desperate. I parked Jerry prominently outside the Delicious Café, a nice rather arty place next to the petrol station and, in a spirit of satire, ordered a strawberry milkshake. I sat outside and phoned Pierre who said Bryan Hunter was already on his way! I had only told him I would *try* to get there. Contemplating the bike, I realised with a shock that the battery Ginty had given me was gone. It could have been nicked when I was parked in Musina, but I suspected that, shamefully, it had fallen off somewhere on the road that morning.

Bryan Hunter had arrived by the time I finished my milkshake. He was a very tall, moustached, bluff Afrikaner, but pleasant. We got a couple of the garage guys to help lift the Ariel onto his bakkie, and Bryan then lashed the bike down with black and white ropes, very effectively. It felt a little weird and unrighteous to be riding in the comfortable bakkie, but our next stop was the bottle shop for two six-packs of Hansa and Windhoek draught, my shout. Two-and-a-quarter hours, 150 miles, three beers each and a piss stop later, we had completed a long loop to the south west and rolled into Lephalale.

We parked at Bryan's store. This dealt in pipework and pumps, mostly for the nearby opencast coal mine, which had recently come into its own as the ones round Bethal (where I had stayed on the way up) were getting worked out and there was a power station locally. Coal-fired power stations, drink-driving, and smoking everywhere – this was indeed an unreconstructed world.

In Bryan's showroom were the classic bikes for use in his favoured event, the DJ Rally (Durban–Johannesburg) for machines made no later than 1936. There was his twin port 600cc BSA single, and his magnificent scarlet and chrome Ariel Red Hunter 500, Jerry's girder-forked father from the model's glory days. There was also a friend's 1934 Panther 600 single. One of these rugged Yorkshire-built singles had always been on my wish-list, but I had had trouble starting them, even though a diminutive girl biker friend of mine never had any problem with hers. Bryan showed me his way. With the bike on its stand, you ignored Panther's patented "half-compression device", put the bike into 2nd, reversed the rear wheel by hand till it wouldn't go any further, then put it into neutral, set the advance/retard lever at about the half-way mark, tickled the carb, and kicked. It started first time.

Bryan and three friends also rode modern Hinckley Triumph Tiger 900 bikes. They had done big journeys together, and Bryan swore that the Triumphs beat their BMW equivalents (they were faster, 50kg lighter etc). After loading the Ariel and a generator onto the bigger truck that was going to Jo'burg the following morning, Bryan took me back to his house and showed me his Tiger, and his wife and daughter kindly gave me supper. After that I spent a short night in an expensive B&B next door, as Bryan's driver Corné arrived at 4am. I had expected a redneck, but in the bumpy darkness he and I talked amiably about cars. On the N1 toll road we stopped at a smart service station. As the power was out in the Wimpy sit-down section, we got burgers and coffee to go. The sun came up and, after about an hour on the dual carriageway N1, we started hitting traffic around the northern fringes of Johannesburg.

We passed the airport, reached the eastern suburb of Benoni, and were soon at Corné's drop-off, just as – thanks to cell phones but still impressively – Pierre Cronje rolled up in a flatbed truck, towing a wide trailer with a hydraulic tilt facility. As I said goodbye to Corné and transferred my luggage to the cab of the flatbed, Pierre was loading the Ariel, securing it expertly with pukka tie-downs. Then we were away. It had been 300 miles from the border town of Musina to Johannesburg and, since I had ridden over 130 on the dog-leg to meet Bryan at Alldays, I had not taken too big a chunk out of the trip on that bakkie stage.

Chapter 40

PIT STOP

Pierre Cronje was as friendly and soft-mannered as he had sounded on the phone, with much facial hair and a bit of belly. When we got to his home in a gated suburb, there were three dogs (two Staffies and a Jack Russell), Pierre's very nice wife, Gwyneth, who was proud of her Welsh origins, his pregnant daughter and his large son, all of whom worked from home in his computer business. There was also a good painting on the wall, of an unmarked DC3 dropping a stick of paras into the bush. "Yes," said Gwyneth, "that's what Pierre used to do."

The most obvious surviving trait from Pierre's military past was his energy. Right away he got the spanners on Jerry, after first displacing his own beautiful engine-in-frame stage rebuild of a 1939 Triumph Speed Twin from his hydraulic workbench. The first job he did was tightening Jerry's slack magneto drive-chain. As Ginty had noted, the Magdyno drive arrangement on the VH was unusual, and had been necessary because of Ariel's thoughtful policy of mounting the Magdyno on a platform on the frame of the machine, rather than on its vibrating engine where, as on BSAs, the Magdyno could be gear-driven. Writing in the magazine, I later described Pierre as "moving the platform backward", for which, quite rightly, I was picked up. What he actually did, as per my little Pitmans handbook, was loosen the two set bolts which held the Magdyno onto the platform, and slide the instrument itself backwards, thus maintaining the chain-line and the oil seal at the back of the chaincase cover.

This was all within an hour of my arriving. To test the efficacy of what he had done Pierre wheeled out his pre-war ES2 Norton 500 single, which he said had twice let him down on the DJ Rally (which he was organising this year) but which had a great deep crackling exhaust note. I was in a 3.30am waking daze and not too keen on all this activity, but went slackly along with it. One reason was that I got the impression that there was an underlying drift here, of which I approved. In the Vietnam war book *365 Days*, the theory was explored that the best way out of combat fatigue/ burnout, which might otherwise blight a soldier's life for decades, was – after a short period of recovery – to return him to his unit and the line as quickly as possible. So I felt that, although I was genuinely welcome to stay with Pierre, and maybe take part in the local rally he was organising at the weekend, he also thought I had best be back in the saddle and away as soon as possible. Inside I agreed with him. But that morning I could have done with a lie-in.

We drove round to another nice elderly restorer – we'd already stopped at one on the drive back – with a rack of tasty motorcycles in his garage, who said to me gently, "It would be a shame to give up now." Unfortunately, as we were leaving, Pierre's Norton kicked back on starting, leaving him with a painfully crook ankle for the next few days. We then rode at a brisk clip through traffic, Pierre leading decisively as the car drivers were not giving much quarter, to the town centre of Benoni, and what Pierre called "my engraver". This was a Muslim Indian who looked bemused as Pierre brought him out to the street and I sketched my journey to him. When Pierre asked me what I called the trip I got the picture, and before long he was presenting me with a Classic Motorcycle Club medallion engraved with "Short Way Up" – an extremely kind gift, which I have cherished.

Then it was straight back for more spannering. Pierre addressed in turn each of my concerns, like the front end/steering damper. He dismantled the latter, which we found had been over-lubricated and was not working; and from his extensive spares' stock, substituted a fresh disc for the one with too much grease on it. He checked the oil in the forks, which if anything was over- rather than under-filled. He reconnected the wires to the rear light, an extremely fiddly job as it involved removing and replacing the back of the rear mudguard, and he gave me a second-hand battery to replace the missing one. The old exhaust valve lifter cable had been crushed under the tank. He made up a fresh cable from my 'blank' – Hurrah! I had finally used one of the complete set of spare cables I had been carrying – and, after adjusting its arm, got the exhaust valve lifter working again, so that once more I could stop the bike without having to stall it.

Anything I mentioned, Pierre set about. I was reduced to standing there dumbly, fitfully cleaning oil off the bike. In the workshop out of the sun it was cold – my mockery of "It's our winter" finally bit the dust – but I couldn't even rouse myself to go in and get my fleece. Eventually, in a diabetic low, I had to ask for something to eat.

Later that afternoon Pierre, Gwyneth and I went round to visit a neighbour, Jack, who had restored an MGA. We had first stopped at the bottle shop so I could buy us beer and wine. There we were offered free samples of cane brandy and, since we had gone back for seconds before they told us it was 80 per cent proof, the session at Jack's was uproarious, with an importunate golden Labrador, and an allegedly depressed friend whose wife had left him and who wanted to *go back to Scotland* which, as a cure for depression, struck us as hilarious. Back at Pierre's, Gwyneth cooked a curry. That night turned into a cold one, but they had given me enough extra blankets in the spare room, and they had all three dogs sleeping on their bed.

The following day brought more spannering, despite Pierre groaning frequently from the discomfort of his ankle, and taking many calls about the weekend rally. He said numbers were down – as they were for most events, due to "The Global" – and, given the amount of effort these events involved, he was inclined to do fewer of them in future. He called everyone who rang "Mein heer", pronounced "Mineer", which roughly translated as "Sir" or "Monsieur". And he invariably flattered callers by telling them "You be good now" as he said goodbye.

That second day's work centred on a recommendation from one of Pierre's older cronies, 81-year-old "Uncle" Hew Hollard, aka "Mr Ariel", who had recommended a de-coke as a possible cure for the sooty plugs. So off came the seat, tank and cylinder head. But before the cylinder head had been fully removed Pierre found a washer lying in the inlet rocker chamber and, in the exhaust rocker chamber, one of those little Alfa Romeo-sourced caps off the end of the valve stem. The combustion chamber was not really coked up, but Pierre cleaned it anyway, with a wire brush on an electric drill, while I checked the exposed bore and piston, visually and manually, for play or scars, but there was nothing that I could see or feel.

Pierre then reassembled the head and set the valve clearances, putting back the valve stem cap and reassembling the inlet rocker shaft with the washer back in place, as well as with cork packing to deal with an irritating clacking noise. Finally, having seen me trying to get burnt oil off the silencer, Pierre removed it and used a polishing wheel and fluid to restore its finish. Phew!

In the afternoon I did a short interview with their neighbour Jack, complete with constant interruptions from his boisterous golden Lab, and took photos of his restored MGA in a neighbouring park. Together they would plump out my next piece for the car magazine, based on stories from the engineer Reg Morrey in Lusaka, which had been fascinating, but light on pictures. Then I took the re-assembled Ariel for a test run round the block. It did seem to be going well now, but the test was a good deal longer than I intended, as I immediately got lost and didn't even have Pierre's address or phone number about my person. In the end it was Jack's dog that saved me as, after many circuits of the neighbourhood, I spotted him outside his gate and knew that Pierre's place was just around the corner.

That evening, another chilly one, Pierre, Gwyneth and I went out for a farewell Chinese dinner, with the warming Won Ton soup particularly welcome. It was a good evening, though with a bizarre moment when a drunk/crazy man stopped by our table, and he and Pierre tried to work out where they knew each other from. After he had gone, Pierre reckoned he hadn't known him at all, and as we left, the guy was getting into it verbally with a takeaway customer.

Next morning they gave me a good cooked breakfast and, though I was a bit trepidatious and tired in myself still, I knew this was the right thing and felt considerable gratitude to Pierre Cronje for getting the Ariel as right as it could be in such a short time, and for stiffening my resolve again. It was around 900 miles direct from Jo'burg to Cape Town, though I expected to ride over 1,000 to avoid, where possible, the monotony and unvarying higher speeds of the arrow straight N1, which would not suit either machine or rider. This was the last long leg, and I was just about ready for it.

I loaded the bike, fired up, and Pierre and Gwyneth led me in their car out to the start of the road down to Heidelberg, where I was to turn west before heading south again. Off on my own in the sunshine, I rode through what on the map was coloured in as part of Jo'burg but in fact was open fields through which the straight road soon ran on into rolling hills. I missed the township of Soweto, which lay somewhere off to my right. I had been dismayed to read somewhere recently that before the 1960 shootings at Sharpeville, another turning point in the anti-apartheid struggle that had left 75 dead, the crowd had been buzzed by F86 Sabre fighter planes, one of my childhood aviation icons thanks to their exploits in the Korean War.

It was a cold day despite the sunshine. Up till then I had always been OK riding in just a jacket, waistcoat and shirt, but now I was soon feeling it. I was also a bit out of practice and, with the bike running well, approached the robots at a crossroads too fast to stop when the lights changed, and shot over them as I had back home at the Dead Man's Gulch junction, only getting away with it now thanks to the light traffic. I rode steadier after that and, following one brief unnecessary turn into a town and back out again, got on the right road south through pretty country with fields of white grasses. After about 50 miles, tackling an incline, the engine did its dying-in-top thing again, but there were no signs of distress, just a momentary hesitation, so I carried on, though it did make me nervous every time a bad bump jarred my throttle hand and the engine's drone wavered.

At the next large town I stopped to gas up. I talked to a guy about the trip as I did so, and next fumbled my fleece out of the Big Bag, put it on and thawed out with coffee and a pie in the station's café, then bopped on, luckily having got directions from a second interested party, as the way I wanted out of town was far from clearly signed. We ran along a stretch of highway under construction, but it was not too bad, and by lunchtime we had crossed the N1 to the west of the highway, and reached the town of Parys. As its name suggested, the place boasted a mild air of affluence and artiness.

I parked and, squatting down, checked the bike over (tyre pressures, rear chain tension) under the smirks of a couple sitting in the sun outside a coffee and pancake shop. They turned out to be the proprietors and the guy wanted to know what year the Ariel was. I sat out in the sun, watched the town go by, drank decent coffee and ate the nondescript savoury pancakes and over-sweet cheesecake. When I was done, the bike wouldn't start, but I wheeled it out of direct line of sight, changed the plug and it was OK again.

By mid-afternoon I had covered about 150 miles, and reached a Shell station outside Kroonstad. The station was big and busy, with a large modern shop, but with its own bantam-type chickens dodging the traffic in the car park. I had another coffee and, sitting on a low wall outside, phoned Tys (pronounced "Tace") Pottas, who Pierre had set me up to stay with that night. He had said Tys owned a private motorcycle museum and I would probably be sleeping in there. Perhaps as an exhibit?

Tys told me that his chicken farm lay exactly 50km down the road towards Welkom, and I told him I would be there in about an hour. After some dual carriageway getting clear of Kroonstad, it was a straight country road with convenient 1km distance posts along it. I figured I would smell the chicken place before I saw it, but a couple of kilometres short of 50 I spotted a bike ahead, U-turning in the empty road so that he was facing the same direction as me, and realised that the red-helmeted rider was probably Tys. I fell in behind his Brit single, noting gratefully that there was no showing off or excessive speeding. I thought the bike was probably a Matchless, but it turned out to be a pre-Featherbed-framed 350 Norton Model 50, its owner's pride and joy.

And Tys was a guy with a few machines to choose from, because his museum turned out to be a large, tall-ceilinged building with a wealth of well-organised memorabilia and machinery on display. There were over 15 British bikes, including an iconic 1927 BSA 1000cc V-twin, on which he did the DJ Rally every year – Tys favoured BSAs, sound fellow – and three modern Hinckley Triumphs, plus many BMWs and, lined up against them, a row of classic Japanese machines, mostly sports bikes from the Seventies and Eighties. Clearly the chicken game was profitable – and it was not Tys's only business. Before this he had had a Ferrari phase. I found it more than a little surreal to wheel in the travel-stained Ariel and park it centrally, with a drip-tray for the oil leaks, amidst all those gleaming motionless two-wheelers. Passing in a moment from real life to waxworks.

Various bods came and went, including Tys's son and his brother-in-law, a swarthy, bearded man with a broad Afrikaner accent. Tys was an attentive host, though his conversation was mostly "send", about the growth of his bike obsession and the virtues of his peerless Model 50. These '56–'58 models were in fact under-rated machines, their swinging-arm frames, though eclipsed by the legendary Featherbed adopted after that, were more than adequate for the 350's lowly 20bhp output and, unlike the later Featherbed models, they featured magneto ignition, as well as the superlative AMC gearbox. Tys said his would cruise tirelessly all day and it was the favourite of all his Brits. The only detail imperfection, he said, was the lack of the little round Lucas badge for the top of the headlamp, which I duly noted.

I wondered if there was a Mrs Tys. It was hard to be sure, as they were all Boers speaking Afrikaans most of the time. I thought there was, and that they probably lived in the house opposite the museum, but I was confined to the all-boys compound. The beer soon came out, and I met Tys's friend Frank Korbe, a very pleasant pharmacist who I did manage to talk to about my trip. It was only the following day that I found out he had lost a leg riding an Earles-forked BMW, when a truck had pulled out and run him off the road while he was overtaking it uphill. Tys had gone onto the whisky by the time I had parked my gear in the windowless brick sleeping room, but I could forgive the place anything, because there was an old-fashioned electric fire to combat the night chill.

I was fairly zonked after the near 200-mile day in the saddle. Before long, however, we were off in a car to the town of Welkom, to the clubhouse of the local chapter of the Ulysses Club whose badge, with indecipherable lettering and a cartoon bearded guy with a big conk, I had seen on Ginty's jacket. I believed they were a Southern African biker organisation for the over-40s. On the way Tys explained that Welkom was a gold mining town and hence prosperous until quite recently, when the gold had begun to run out. The next day we would see the bare pale earth, scarred with long open-cast spoil heaps but somehow not too much disfigured. Tys said the Ulysses mob did a *braai* on club nights and we would participate.

There were mostly customs and cruisers parked outside the club bar where, inside, the atmosphere was friendly, with a couple of reasonably nice-looking girls. But, thanks to fatigue and the general weirdness in myself, I was skating over it all and did not connect with anyone in particular, though I did notice that one of the younger guy's cut-offs carried a brand-new red and yellow swastika badge, perhaps as per the late far-right Boer leader Eugene Terre Blanche. This was Boer heartland, with the Voortrekker Monument to the original pioneers in nearby Winburg.

After a couple more beers, Tys came over and said that club politics had done for the *braai* that evening, so we left and drove on to a motorcycle-themed restaurant – though the showcased vehicles inside were a moped and a scooter, so it was not exactly Jack Rabbit Slims. We were a large party and convivial enough, with one older guy in particular taking the trouble to talk to me in English, but though I remember the steak was good, the evening kind of dissolved into a blur of beer, wine, fatigue and loud Afrikaans. Weird as it was, I was glad eventually to be back alone in my cave at the cold museum, in front of the warm, nostalgic glow of the two-bar electric fire.

Chapter 41

LEADER OF THE PACK

Next morning, Tys announced that he and a couple of the others would ride south with me that day. I was not quite sure how I felt about that, but there was no way to say no, so I just made sure that the ground rules were clear. I was not prepared to over-stress the loaded Ariel, and would cruise at around 50mph (estimated, because the speedo was still U/S) and stop to rest the bike not more than every 50 miles. In the event, we were to be a fairly well-matched party, with Tys on his beloved Norton 350, one-legged Frank riding Tys's sprung-saddle plunger BSA 650 A10 Golden Flash (and it was gold-painted too), and Bertus Geldenhuys on his older, Earles-fork BMW, with any advantage it had in terms of stamina being lessened by the fact that he was running-in its rebuilt engine.

We gassed up on the outskirts of Welkom, with the older guy from the night before driving in to say goodbye. Then we rode out through town, staying to the west of the N1 and taking the R30 down towards Bloemfontein where, after 100 or so miles, we would briefly converge with the highway. It was certainly less lonely to be riding in a small group for once, and I settled down to a good comfortable speed behind Tys, who looked stylish on the black and chrome Norton, in his metallic red flip-up helmet, tight black leather jacket and baggy white chinos. But as we approached the R30 we were three not four: Bertus, bringing up the rear, was missing. Tys and I waited in the sunlight on the grey dust of the roadside as Frank took off back down the way we had come. After a while he returned with Bertus. Ironically, that day it was not Jerry or any of the other Brits that hit trouble, but the BMW which, with its still-tight engine, had nipped up a couple of times already. With regret Bertus decided to turn back and ride it gently home, hopefully joining us later on something more modern. The three of us rode on; for once I didn't have to navigate, just follow the leader.

The road south was undergoing a lot of improvement, so there were two or three places where we had to wait at lights and then ride up over ramps and onto long stretches of rolled rubble, and I tried not to tense up as I followed Tys's black bike, which kept steadily on the pace despite the surface and the sometimes mildly chaotic repair crews, with heavy plant turning and men walking up and down the sections. So it was a relief mid-morning to turn into the town of Brandfort and call on a pal of Tys called Chris, who ran a towing and repair business.

We swept into the big yard behind his garage and parked up, as Chris and his young son came out. Tys, ever-stylish, produced a metal flask with four metal cups, full of ruby red Muscadel, a sweet, warming wine that made the perfect stirrup-cup. We stood around drinking and talking for a while, with the boy looking on, and then took off again, refreshed. Tys pushed on the remaining 40-odd miles to our designated lunch-stop, at a big cafeteria/ restaurant on a bluff north of Bloemfontein, overlooking the N1 curving its way around the city. On the climb up to it, the Ariel faltered for a moment in top, but again recovered well.

As we entered the restaurant parking lot and prepared to park up in a spot where the bikes would be visible from the panoramic viewing window above, a short, red-faced bearded man came bustling up and, speaking in a thick accent, tried to direct us down to the far corner of the lot. Tys ignored him, while Frank mildly argued the toss. Later from the waitress we learned that this parking warden was strictly self-appointed, a wanderer who would take off for Namibia, so he said, for months, and then pop up again. We settled down in the tower-like restaurant at a window table, ordered burgers and enjoyed good talk, watching the cars pass silently below on the N1. Half way through the meal Bertus Geldenhuys turned up again, having got home, swapped the older BMW for a more modern Beemer, a Paris-Dakar R80G/S from the Eighties, and run down the N1 to meet us.

Back outside, after glancing round for the "warden", I got a plug and spanner from the tank bag, to see if a clean plug would help with the motor's hesitation. But as I pulled off the plug cap it came away in my hand from the HT lead. With the others helping, we stripped back an inch or so of the lead's insulation, made a secure connection to the plug cap – and that was the end of the engine faltering, for good. It's always the little things…

We had decided against visiting an older rider in Bloemfontein, and to get round the city we now hit the N1 which by-passed it to the west. As we did so there was a big green road sign with distances, and my eyes locked onto "CAPE TOWN 1000km". That was only just over 600 miles! I felt my heart leap. Through all the previous difficult days, it felt like I had been riding the Ariel balanced on a tight-rope of stretched chewing-gum. Now – 600 miles – we really might make it.

We rode steadily down the dual carriageway, and I followed them off at a junction south of the city. Tys and the others disagreed about the way to get back on the B roads and in the end we had ridden down the slipway nearly back onto the N1 to ride on to the next exit, when they had a change of mind, U-turned and rode back up the slip-road (there was no traffic and the bikes were narrow enough to get away with it even if there had been), then turned right at the top and navigated successfully onto a minor road running parallel with the N1 down to Edenburg. There I invoked the "stop-every-50-miles" guideline, riding up next to Tys and gesturing for us to pull in at a petrol station. There was a tiny store nearby where we got cool drinks and, in the heat of the afternoon, passed ten minutes in the shade.

Then we pressed on, down to Tromsburg and west there to Philippolis. I stayed tucked in behind and slightly to the right of Tys, whose metallic red helmet glittered in the sun as he hammered on aboard his 350 Norton (reg. 4044 OKE – I had memorised it by the end of the day), all the long afternoon. For me it turned into some of the best riding of the trip – rolling in a pack through the empty farm roads and winter sunshine conjured 1950s California, and the restless energy of the flawed but seminal movie *The Wild One*. The Ariel felt tireless and we rode together through lightly rolling countryside, over level crossings, past cattle, across creeks, on to the small town of Philippolis. Then it was down, completing a long loop and crossing the Orange river in the process, finally pitching up at Colesberg, just off the N1 again, and riding through to the Bella Vista Hotel, an old-fashioned building standing on its own between the town and the highway. The sun was sinking and it was the end of a day of well over 200 miles, so by then I was very ready to rest.

The place was big, clean and old-fashioned, but pretty well empty. I think the improvements in both vehicles and the highway, allowing higher cruising speeds, meant that fewer and fewer people broke their journeys at mid-way places like this. Tys was known there, and they all three joked with and tickled a tiny old *San* maid. As mentioned, Tys was a seriously wealthy guy and I don't think the other two were on the breadline either, so I was shocked and surprised to discover that they had booked just one room for all four of us. They said it had two single beds and a double, and it then became a discreet race to make sure I was early up the stairs and into the room to bag one of the singles. Which I shamelessly did, telling myself that I hadn't been consulted about sleeping arrangements and that these guys knew each other and were clearly keen on the stench of comradeship. Tys got the other single, leaving Bertus to bunk up with Frank, who during the night would prove himself the undisputed winner of the snoring contest that developed.

The rooms were unheated, naturally, and as the sun disappeared outside the big metal-framed west-facing window, the temperature plummeted. I lay down, fully rugged up, under a blanket to wait for dinner-time, ostensibly reading but soon nodding off. The others did likewise, except Tys who was restless and soon went off downstairs. I was comatose by the time Bertus's cell phone rang. "It's Tys," he laughed. "He says, tell the Englishman that I'm sitting in the bar next to..." (what, I wondered – a magnum of Champagne? A couple of hookers? Ewan and Charley?) "...a HEATER!" That did it. In a couple of minutes I was on my way down.

The brown wooden bar was fairly busy, and we sucked down more than one beer before it was time to eat. On the way through there was a framed document with points of interest about this part of the Orange Free State. These included the fact that Vincent Van Gogh's brother Cor had come to South Africa in 1890 to build trains for Dutch South African Railways. When the Anglo-Boer War had broken out in 1899, he had served under General Villebois Mareuil against the British, been captured and fallen ill and, a sensitive soul, had taken his own life (at the hospital in Brandfort, where we had stopped that morning) just as his brother the artist had done in 1890.

In the dining area I made the mistake of ordering Karoo lamb steak, a local delicacy which I had missed at Cradock, while the lads went for that night's special, big racks of rib like a Barnsley chop. My lamb was good but the rib-racks had it on volume alone. I tried to ignore it when the others' conversation threw up the occasional word like "Jewboys". By now

Chapter 42

ENDGAME

After breakfast next morning, under a brilliant blue sky, we mustered outside for a last photo opportunity. I had lubricated the chain and topped up the oily engine's primary chaincase and, when Frank discovered I would need some more 40 oil, to save me time he rode down to the petrol station and came back with a tin. When I went to settle up for the room I found that Tys had already done so. All he wanted, he said, was a copy of the book I would write. I said goodbye to them and rode off alone with some regret, but mainly buzzing about one fact: by my reckoning I only had around 500 miles to go. It was 18 July. In two and a bit days I should be sliding into Cape Town, with a long week before my flight home to chill out and finalise arrangements for shipping the Ariel.

I was taking a last long loop on empty country roads, with just the occasional bakkie or cattle-truck passing, riding through the sere yellow grassland sometimes dotted sparsely with cows. We crossed the deep, tree-lined bed of the Seekoei river, a tributary of the big Orange, bumped over the railway at the tiny junction of Hanover Road, and rode the last few miles into Hanover, which signs proclaimed was "Half way to Cape Town" – 700km, or about 435 miles. We'd done about 80 miles and it was warm now, a quiet Saturday, and on the outskirts of town I pulled into an empty diner attached to a general store, like in a Western, but also decorated with religious homilies. The burger and coffee were good travelling mercies in their way.

I felt strange, internally unwilling to consider that I might actually make it, tip-toeing superstitiously around that notion. I stopped a little further on at a big service station to gas up before rejoining the main N1 road, which then ran for 40 miles without a break to the next town, Richmond. As I approached the highway, there was a sign indicating another road forking off left to Middelburg, Cradock and Port Elizabeth, which was 411km south.

I felt a brief tug of my friends there, but then headed the bike onto the N1: at that point, the shortest way seemed the wisest.

The wide two-lane highway ran arrow-straight for long miles through the Great Karoo desert. There was very little traffic, but what there was came up fast from behind, a grey blur in my mirror, often 4x4s pulling trailers. Soon the distances and monotony, broken only by red and white radio masts away from the road, were literally dizzying, and I began to feel weird even though I had eaten and taken my pills. I found it helped if I swung my head from side to side, to prevent getting locked onto the furthest horizon, the vanishing point.

The bike was still pulling strongly. Gradually the miles passed and the road became a little less monotonously flat and straight. I was passing the time trying to work out mileages, which to my mind were out of whack on the odometer, so I wondered if the long monotony had disoriented me (I had actually just mis-recorded the mileage at the last petrol stop by one digit – 100 miles). We were cresting a slight incline, with just a few miles to go to Richmond, when abruptly a loud knocking noise started coming from the engine.

Providently, a little way further on there was a lay-by with trees on the other side of the road. I pulled in there and rested the engine in the shade, feeling completely calm. I checked the oil level, looked for loose fastenings, and finally checked the tightness of the rocker spindle, in case it was a repetition of the trouble at Luangwa Bridge. In myself I think I knew exactly what the problem was, but I was going to try to cover all the possibilities. After quarter-of-an-hour or so I started up and moved off again, and the noise didn't seem so bad at first, but by the time we rode slowly into the service station at Richmond, the deep knocking was bad enough to turn bystanders' heads. I parked up, got a cold drink and sat slumped on a raised pavement. I'm sorry to say that when a couple came up with a friendly enquiry about the bike, I was off-hand with them. Because I was pretty sure that, with just 350 miles or so left to go to my ultimate destination, the big end bearing was finally letting go.

I crept into Richmond in the early afternoon. It was a small town with wide streets laid out in a grid pattern. Looking for lodging, one place eventually turned out to be full, but that worked for me, as a block further on there was the blue and white sign for the two-storey Victoria Lodge Guest House. I knocked on the fine etched glass of the door and a diminutive black maid answered, dressed in the South African equivalent of an Edwardian parlour-maid's outfit, and showed me a beautifully-furnished room fronting onto the street. The Victoria did what it said on the label; it had recreated as closely as possible a period lodging house, but with abundant hot water and television. The stout goateed owner, Conje (pronounced Connie), turned out also to deal in antiques. He had family members staying for the weekend but could not have been friendlier or more helpful, directing me round the block to the garage at the back of his property where we squeezed Jerry in safely among the other antiquities for the night.

The Ariel was starting and running perfectly well, but with that infernal ACK-ACK-ACK noise coming from the engine. Back in my room I considered the options. I could have pressed on next day, hoping the oil-starved bearing would make it to Cape Town. But I did not fancy a blow-up on those desolate highways or, if the bearing did go, taking the bike back to England in kit form with the prospect of an expensive open-ended rebuild if the head and barrel were damaged, rather than the relatively simple job of big end replacement. Only I felt the frustration of failing to finish, and the shame of having to call for help again. The gearbox trouble and the business on the border had at least been stages on the journey, but I was now, undeniably, failing at the last. Jerry had finally got the better of me.

Still, back in the room, I got the phone out and called Bruce Kirby, my original benefactor in Cape Town, and then Mike and Rialet Wood in Port Elizabeth. Mike said he had a classic bike restorer and colleague who lived in Middelburg, less than 60 miles away from Richmond – but he would turn out to be on holiday in the Kruger National Park at the time. All the SWAT crew were involved via email by then, with Bruce joking, "Not sure how Steve does it – how on earth does this machine keep breaking?", and Tony Lyons-Lewis offering a bed again if I was going to ride back from PE to Cape Town.

Meanwhile, feeling numb and exhausted, I drew the blinds in the Victorian room and tried to get a bit of rest. But some locals chose that moment to congregate, shouting, outside the Richmond Drankwinkel bottle store opposite. It sounded like a riot, but they were eventually told off and dispersed by a firm female voice. I could not settle. As darkness fell I took a bath (a bath!) and then sat on the edge of the bed. I looked at my faithful black boots; one photo I really regretted not having taken was of them standing, lop-sided and covered with red dust, on the veranda outside my room at Mama Rula's. I nipped at my remaining Wellington brandy in a tooth glass, until it was all gone. Something was going to happen. I felt it through the layers of dull resignation.

The old house was silent. In its chill perfection it reminded me of another beautifully recreated Victorian dwelling where I once had stayed, in the Melbourne suburb of St Kilda. The owner, and particularly his wife, had striven to get every detail just right; even the stacks of books on occasional tables had been arranged in artful spirals. But one morning on the floor of the passage, I had watched in silence as ants, in a curving double column, had dismembered the body of a beautiful dead moth and carried it away, piece by piece, over the cold marble. A year later we heard that the owner, beset by business worries, had killed himself. I was not really surprised to learn from Conje the following morning that the original creator of the "Victoria" house at the turn of the century, after over 20 years of struggle to get it built in the teeth of wars, material shortages, economic downturns and natural disasters, when it had finally been near completion, had also committed suicide in one of the upper rooms.

It was dark now and I roused myself to go out and eat. There was a good, stylish restaurant within walking distance; as it turned out, that too was owned by Conje. It was a cold night, and since I was early I could choose the table by their open fire. The food was excellent, and into the hollow inside me it went, along with a couple of glasses of wine. As I was eating, a large cheerful group of affluent whites came in and sat at the table opposite. The prettiest woman in the party held my eyes and gave me a smile. I finished with an Irish coffee and walked back through the empty streets. Then Mike Wood called; he had borrowed Tony Barlow's trailer and he would drive up with Rialet, aiming to leave at around 6am so they should be with me around 10. In the end I did sleep.

Next morning after breakfast, served by the two costumed maids in an old-fashioned dining-room, from my window I watched as the landlord Conje and his departing male relatives stood silently in a circle by the vehicles, their heads bowed in prayer. After they had gone, I got Conje to open up the garage, walked down and rode the Ariel round, parking it outside at the front for Mike to see. I also checked that Conje would not mind my bringing a chair out to the porch. He encouraged me kindly to do so, and soon I was sitting in the sun on the raised, tiled porch, behind its wrought-iron railings and under its corrugated canopy, separated from the sidewalk by a deep culvert to carry rain away, with Conje's little brown dog at my feet for a while, working on the journal and watching the world go by.

I felt like Wyatt Earp with the chair tilted, keeping an eye on the Drankwinkel opposite (mercifully closed), as church bells rang and much of Richmond's African population walked past, amused by the Ariel and staring covertly at me. Then a black man came begging – "I am on the road, I am very 'ungry" – but I was not very generous and, after counting the coins, he returned to ask for more. Next came a couple of smiling Orientals who wanted to take a picture of the bike. I asked if they were Japanese but could not understand their reply. Conje told me later that they were some of the team of Chinese workers laying cable on contract. They kept themselves to themselves so that, unlike with Mike Wood's crews of radio mast workers, there were no by-blows remaining among the locals after they left.

I sat there writing in the sun. Mike and Rialet rang, getting near, to check my exact location. Then I just sat and waited in a passive, washed-out mood, summed up by the Bob Dylan lyric, "She knows there's no success like failure/And failure's no success at all". The whole town was still now, the street completely empty.

Then, down by the trees of a small park, I saw Rialet's car and the trailer driving in. I got to my feet as they swung round in the wide road and parked with the trailer behind Jerry. I didn't know what to say as they got out of the car. Mike, smiling, came up the steps onto the porch. He peered at me and said, "That looks like a man who could use a hug."

This was no New Man correctness; there were no ironic reflections on Freudian overtones, no queer fear. I responded from the depths of my being and exchanged a tight bear hug with my good friend and brother.

Chapter 43

LIFE'S
JOURNEY

There was not much more to tell. We loaded the bike and proceeded south-westward, stopping before the town of Graaff-Reinet and climbing into the hills to walk in the beautiful Camdeboo National Park, and look down on the Arizona-like Valley of Desolation, with its tall pillars of reddish rock. We ate KFC companionably in the car and pressed on, driving into Port Elizabeth just after dark, past the Missionvale township and back to 5 Ralston Road. Mike and I unloaded the bike and, eager to explore the problem, he kick-started it, switched on the bicycle lamps and rode off, engine clacking, down the dark road.

By then I had half-convinced myself that I could have made a mistake, and that it might turn out to be valve seat trouble, and maybe remediable. So it was a shock when Mike returned shortly and confirmed decisively, even with slight satisfaction as his prediction was fulfilled, that it was the big end letting go. He lowered a screwdriver into the oil tank and showed me how clean and golden the oil still was, ie in nearly 1,000 miles it had not circulated properly round the engine. I was in shock because if he was right (and later Stewart Fergusson would confirm that the crank-pin mis-aligned in the flywheel and cutting off oil circulation had finally taken its toll), that was it, my journey was over.

I spent a few more days in Port Elizabeth, arranging for the bike to be shipped home from there, and borrowed Tony Barlow's little Suzuki for one last Kickstart group run out along the coast. On a fine windy day we stopped by a memorial with cannons retrieved from a ship-wrecked Portuguese galleon and, with whales spouting far out to sea, Mike made a short speech of congratulation to me, and we shook hands.

Mike's last piece of good advice, as he dropped me off at Port Elizabeth's modest airport, had been to make sure I got a window-seat that afternoon on the flight to Cape Town. In the event that was no problem as the plane was half empty; there was no-one next to me as we took off and I finished the last few pages of Rose Tremain's *The Road Home*, with its excellently muted ending. Then I looked down out of the window. This flight was very different from that one in the Piper Cherokee from Mfuwe which had set everything off. Today we had flown at first over wastes of sand, then rumpled grey-brown hills with vast expanses of sea off to the south. I had no impulse to ride across this country, though I had done so. As the man had said to Karsten Nielsen and his friend – "Why didn't you take a plane?" Looking back, the wing tip sliced over the land, and as we approached Cape Town the packed buildings of the townships below made the shapes of indecipherable letters.

My journey, too, was a mystery to me for months, and in some ways remains so. I have thought about meaning, or the lack of it, a lot while writing this book. In so many ways it could stand as a Tour de Farce, a model of how not to do a trip like that – the excessive luggage, the untried machine etc – and I had been old and experienced enough to have known better. But eventually one thing I did conclude, perhaps surprisingly, was that I was grateful to have failed at the last: that had been the final Travelling Mercy. Convenient, eh? What it meant was that I had not been able to file the journey away as just another dinner party anecdote. I was forced to think about it.

I could not deny that setting out, as well as the charity fund-raising, I had wanted to be admired. The Lone Rider! So a lack of reaction to the articles in *Real Classic*, and some negative feedback, were a disappointment. I believe it stemmed mainly from irritation with the constant breakdowns and my lack of mechanical skills. Before departure Tony Page had warned that very few riders, despite their dreaming about it, would ever actually undertake a trip like this, and that you needed to emphasise things you might have in common, to get them onside. I would add that perhaps if you were living other people's dreams, it might be better if things went as well as people imagined they would, in those dreams.

But for myself, the stripping away of that "Lone Rider" illusion, while painful to the pride, was a necessary piece of even partial self-knowledge. There is a Norman Mailer short story in which the protagonist, an Army cook, concluded that "he was no longer so worried about becoming a man ... but in his heart he wondered if he would ever learn the language of men". I was what I was; it wouldn't mean much to be admired as something that I wasn't, as one of my masks. And in the end it was more important that, with all the different kinds of help I had received along the way, the journey had made me more ready to face the rest of my life.

Meanwhile my friend, the writer Carey Harrison, saw the trip, gleefully, as essentially a role reversal. "Perhaps the key ... is the contrast between the seemingly tireless and unbreakable human beings ... and Jerry, who silently epitomises everything that old age actually brings ... it's not the man but rather robot Jerry that ceaselessly manifests the pain of life's journey on an extremely bumpy road. Jerry groaning, *I was not made for this!* and the rider, *Oh yes you were, keep at it,* as though you were twin souls ... you the spirit, egging Jerry on, and Jerry, the aching, fallible body."

I love the speech of scholars, but in fact I rarely felt like a "twin soul" with the Ariel, which was mostly just a Bad Bike, end of. Afterwards I did try to remember Jerry's strengths and his finest moments: riding fully-loaded down into the muddy trench and onto the Zambezi ferry. Or the time on the Bad Road when we powered up out of the deep ditch. But then I would recall how *Cycle World*'s Peter Egan, spot on as ever, had cautioned against complimenting a British bike, even mentally, on its reliability. "I swear," he had written, "an old bike can sense patronising approval. Especially if it's not backed up with the required hours of meticulous maintenance. Even a trace of sloppy sentiment turns the bike instantly into a lightning rod for trouble." Amen to that. Although it was hard not to remember riding the road beneath the mountain ramparts of Lesotho, or through the forested slopes beyond Luangwa Bridge, those moments had been few and far between.

The images that did keep coming back to me, however, were from Zambia's Great East Road, from Bridge Camp to Chipata. So often there was a stream of human traffic along its verges, Africans with sometimes grossly overloaded bicycles, but mostly on foot – children, men, and women with babies on their backs and loads on their heads, each one moving in his or her own particular way, but always erect, always proud somehow. Even in rags, even with nothing, even close to physical defeat by age or infirmity, something about their posture said, "I am".

They strolled, they shuffled, they strode, they hobbled, they marched, they strutted – they capered, they limped, they skipped, they danced – yes, the young ones sometimes danced, marvellously, no iPod, just dancing to the exuberant music in their bodies and their heads. Corpuscles in a bright stream of black blood, each one distinct but united by the pathway, the road. The road had been built and they came to it. They came along the road.

EPILOGUE

"I've seen things you people wouldn't believe. Attack ships on fire off the shoulders of Orion. I've watched C-beams glitter in the dark near the Tannhauser Gate. All those moments will be lost in time, like tears in the rain."
Ridley Scott, *Blade Runner*

A few weeks after my flight in Graham 'Corkie' Corke's Piper, news came that he had crashed one of his planes in the Karoo. He badly broke both legs, with multiple fractures, but at least came through it alive, and reportedly in good spirits.

The *Short Way Up* charity efforts ended by raising just under £2,000 for Kawaza School, and Haynes Publishing's generous decision to contribute 50p per copy from the sales of this book should at least double that.

Meanwhile the conclusion of the researcher who Jo Pope had set up to look at the RPS school sponsorship had been that a full-time administrator was necessary to take forward the work with Kawaza and other local schools. Since the seven other Safari Operators of South Luangwa also liked the idea, late in 2010 Project Luangwa was born out of the former Kawaza School charity, to bring the various community projects under one roof, "ensuring the people of the Luangwa Valley gain the full benefit from tourism by investing in education and business development".

The aim is to create an effective, co-ordinated approach to helping local communities improve their long-term economic prospects while avoiding a negative impact on the environment and wildlife. The charity believes that by developing and improving schools, creating a vocational training centre and supporting the micro-financing of small businesses, it can help families to have the chance of a lasting and sustainable income.

If you are interested in helping, go to www.projectluangwa.org and click on the 'Donate' tab to check out the different ways to give; these include a Direct Bank Donation option. Or, if you're a techno-boob like me, you can still post cheques made out to 'Project Luangwa – SWU', to: Kathy

Archibald, Administrator, Project Luangwa, Enterprise House, Meadow Drive, Hampton in Arden, West Midlands, B92 OBD. The positive bottom line remains what it always was: breaking the poverty trap for these young people, while at the same time helping to preserve the wonderful wildlife.

Jo and Robin Pope did indeed retire, sort of, to a new house outside Lusaka. Ironically, after all the years in the bush, Jo finally succumbed to malaria, but it does not seem to have slowed her down. She is very happy with the new house, and particularly with the garden.

In August 2009, Ginty Melvill wrote that the Zambezi Bikers had just suffered two fatalities, both Zambian members and both riding Honda FireBlades. In September, Ginty himself, during a Sunday ride-out on the Ducati to Luangwa Bridge, hit a pot-hole on the bad bit of road about 100 miles out, bent the front wheel-rim and punctured the front tyre. This provoked a "tank-slapper", where the handlebars wrench with uncontrollable violence from side to side, but Ginty managed to stay on, and was subsequently picked up by the recovery vehicle.

At Christmas he also wrote about the Zambezi Bikers' successful "Toy Run" charity appeal. The previous year, donations in cash and kind had gone to the Chilanga Hospice and the Mother Teresa Lusaka Orphanage in Kalingalinga, including five million kwacha towards a badly needed new bore-hole for the hospice.

Zoe, our black Labrador, was much better by the time I returned. Though her back end was never the same, she could jump in and out of the station wagon and walk for a couple of miles every morning, sometimes once again up onto White Horse Hill. Both she and the terrier adapted well when the family home was finally sold early in 2010, and Molly and I separated, though our new places were close enough that we shared the dogs. Zoe lived happily for another year and a half after her crisis, and then in her 13th year her health quite suddenly deteriorated, and it was time to say goodbye. We were with her to the end. She was a good dog.

In Bill Crosby's London Motorcycle Museum there is a Royal Enfield Bullet that had been ridden all the way down through North and South America. I once asked whether the owner was going to do another trip on it.

Bill told me that the guy never wanted to see the bike again, let alone ride it. I couldn't believe that. But I can now.

The Ariel arrived back in Blighty in August 2009, and was taken to Reg Allen's, where the plan was for Bill Crosby to replace the big end, and then sell it on. But Jerry continued to be Jerry. First we had to find a big end assembly. The foremost Ariel specialists said they had one, but then they didn't. So I went to the Ariel Owners Club magazine editor, John Mitchell, and for £125 a club member came up trumps with a genuine new-old-stock Ransom and Marles assembly, rather than a replacement item from Alpha Bearings. The oil-feeds to the Alpha one both go in at the same angle, where the original's holes had each been in a different plane, and this was less likely to cause weakness in the same spot.

So we had the parts but then, sadly, Bill suffered a stroke. I'm not saying that this was related to his working on Jerry, but it does make you wonder. Bill is made of tough stuff and came through it well, but naturally things had been slowed down. When he started working on the bottom end again in the summer of 2010, he discovered that where there should have been a spacer between the inner roller main bearing on the drive side and the flywheel, to control the end-float, there was none. That explained how in Port Elizabeth we could move the crankshaft from side to side. That, and the absence in addition of shims where there should have been some.

Bill remedied this and fitted the new assembly, but at this point, with the recession deepening, his potential buyer had evaporated, and a classic dealer local to me had expressed an interest. As ever, I needed the money and, with Bill's agreement, their driver collected the bike from Reg Allen's. But they hadn't realised that the engine was still only partially assembled and, since their original interest, the market had gone bad for them too. So they passed.

Tearing my hair, I got the wizard mechanic Lee Peck to collect Jerry in his van and finish the job. But – Lee's marriage had just collapsed and, due to one thing and another, contact was lost with him for six weeks. Would 'jinx' be too strong a word? Before that, he had expertly reassembled the engine, first confirming that the oil was now circulating as it should; but also finding that the exhaust valve had been partially burnt out, probably due to that troublesome valve lifter. When we re-established contact, Lee delivered the bike to Mike Coombes, who helped me to get it through its

MoT. So the last time I rode Jerry was a short, very careful run to and from the Forge Garage for the MoT test, and I did not regret that this was it. Shortly afterwards, as advised by Mike, a mutual pal from a reputable auction house carried the Ariel away to the North, for their final auction of 2010. Even then, dragging his heels to the last, Jerry only just scraped in on his reserve price...

🏵 In the months following my return, I scratched around and found and dispatched a number of things to the people who had helped me. Bruce Kirby got a pair of tank badges for his AJS single. Melville Price received my book *Harley People* (he'd said he never read, but it featured some great Garry Stuart photographs), as well as a replacement for the vital little dynamo nut he had given me off a B31 engine. I sent Tony Lyons-Lewis a copy of Captain Trevor Hampton's little book about a solo sailing trip he had taken post-war down to Spain and back, to amplify Tony's understanding of that unique individual who by coincidence had touched both our lives.

For Ginty I got the Haynes book on motorcycle electrics, as my dynamo problems had made him want to know more. In Jo'burg, Pierre Cronje's 1939 Triumph Speed Twin rebuild had been short of a rear number plate/rear light holder and, impressively, Bill Crosby at Reg Allen's was able to provide the correct item off the shelf. I sent Tys Pottas the one thing his so-original Norton Model 50 lacked, the little circular Lucas lion badge for the headlamp shell. Finally I gave Mike Wood my original Ariel rider's handbook, as it also covered his side-valve VB sidecar tug, and a lush black T-shirt embroidered with the Ariel logo.

None of these things came anywhere near repaying the individuals in question for the help and hospitality they had shown to a perfect stranger, but it was a way of saying thank you. The same, I hope, goes for this book, a blurry snapshot of themselves at a particular moment in time.

🏵 Meanwhile Bruce Kirby of the Cape Town TOC had written in their magazine,

"...this trip was also a catalyst that integrated the classic bike movement more tightly across the regions. For that I thank you, Steve. Through your gallivanting I too have met a whole lot of new people and built up stronger relations with others. Amen."

🦉 Our daughter Rosie, now 16, in the summer of 2010 flew to Madagascar and took part in a study undertaken by the Earthwatch organisation, counting and studying rare species there. She remains committed and working hard towards her goal, born in Luangwa, of qualifying as a zoologist.

🦉 Mike and Rialet Wood's story continues a happy if hectic one. Mike's early retirement was approved, and from December 2009 he started working himself "to a frazzle" (his words, and no exaggeration – he lost 8kg/17lb in the process), putting the house in Port Elizabeth to rights before it went on the market. The place was duly sold, and in spring 2010, they moved to their new home, 'Mammamia', in the West Cape at De Kelders, a seaside hamlet with beautiful views over to Hermanus across Walkers Bay – that's the next bay along, eastwards, from Betty's Bay, where I had stopped during my first day on the road.

Within two weeks Rialet got a social work job down there, and Mike hurled himself into building work, necessary a) because Rialet's 86-year-old mother was living with them, and b) because he needed a triple garage with a guest flat over it – for cars, the bikes, and a workshop for the many projects he has lined up. Mynka the Alsatian loves it there, with "regular walks and lots to sniff and bark at". Rialet has finally been happy to join Mike on two wheels – well three actually, riding in the Ariel VB outfit. But the best news of all was that late in 2010, within a month of one another, the wives of their sons, Michael and Philip, presented Mike and Rialet with grandchildren, Sarah and Michael Edward respectively.

🦉 All over Southern Africa, as one problem with Jerry had been followed by the next, men speculated with relish about the conversation I was going to have when I got back, with the guy who had built up the Ariel for me.

I did visit John Budgen's workshop once more, to return the unused spares, and pay him the £38 for the ones I had used. Happily his wife Pearl had made a partial recovery from her crippling shingles. John had no comment to make on the Ariel's problems, which he had read about in the *Real Classic* articles, although he did say that the engine and gearbox he had hauled out of his shed might not have been a matching pair to begin with. He had no explanation for the out-of-whack timing marks or any of the rest of it, and we did not pursue the matter.

I could hear Ginty's lip curl.

GLOSSARY

(Words in italics are Southern African)

airhead (BMW) Older versions of the German twin-cylinder motorcycles, with their protruding cylinders cooled by air only.

AJS abbrev. Albert John Stevens, British motorcycles owned from 1931 and manufactured by Associated Motor Cycles (AMC) at Plumstead, South-East London, alongside Matchless.

allen bolts Fasteners containing a hexagon head and requiring an appropriate 'key'.

alternator Generator of alternating current (AC) electricity. On British motorcycles, its rotor was usually mounted on the end of the crankshaft.

ammeter Instrument for measuring electrical current.

Ariel British motorcycle marque based at Selly Oak, Birmingham, and from 1944 owned by the BSA Group.

armature That part of an electrical apparatus, such as a dynamo, comprising the electrical windings in which a current flow or a magnetic field is generated or excited.

bakkie Pick-up truck.

BDC Bottom Dead Centre (which see); point at which piston is nearest the flywheel.

bearing Any part or surface which supports another part, although the meaning is usually restricted to parts which are moving relative to one another. Sometimes the bearing surface is formed by the parts themselves, but where high loadings or high speeds are involved, another material is placed between the two, and usually a film of oil is pumped in to avoid 'solid' friction. There are numerous types of bearings, from plain bushes to multiple row taper rollers, as well as shell bearings, roller bearings and ball bearings.

bhp Brake horse power, the power output of a working engine.

big end Lower part of the con rod at its point of location on the crankshaft.

BMW abbrev. Bayerne Motoren Werke, leading German motorcycle manufacturer, with bike production originally based in Munich, Bavaria.

bore Diameter of an engine's cylinder, usually measured in millimetres.

braai Barbecue.

braze To join two metal parts by heating them and adding brass from a metal rod as a filler. Weaker than welding but requiring lower temperatures and not melting the parent material.

breather A vent to atmosphere, particularly from an engine compartment which might be pressurised.

BSA abbrev. Birmingham Small Arms, motorcycle marque based at Small Heath, Birmingham. Also gun manufacturers and major industrial conglomerate, eventually owning Ariel and Triumph.

BTDC Before Top Dead Centre – see Dead Centre.

Burman British manufacturer of gearboxes.

bush Plain bearing, or lining to a bearing.

cam A rotating body with an eccentric protuberance which, as it moves, imparts a linear or angular movement of a cyclic nature to some other component of a machine. Frequently used in engines to operate the pushrods/valves (which see).

camshaft A cam in the form of an eccentric, rotating shaft with nodes, generally for the operation of pushrods/valves.

capacitor A condenser (which see), usually of large capacity, performing a smoothing role in batteryless current generation.

cc Cubic centimetre

chaincase Casing protecting a transmission or other moving chain from dirt, and guarding against the chain doing damage.

coil Electrical device for converting low-voltage current supplied by the battery to the high-voltage necessary to provide ignition at the spark plug (which see).

commutator The end of an armature (which see) against which the pickup brushes rub, so that electricity generated in the spinning armature may be collected in the proper cyclic manner for delivery to the main circuitry.

condenser Electrical device able to store electricity and particularly to release it very rapidly.

con rod abbrev. for 'connecting rod', which connects the piston to the crankshaft. The bearing which carries the piston is called the small or little end, while the one mounted on the crankpin (which see) is called the big end.

contact breaker Mechanically-operated switch in the ignition-system for rapid interruption of the low-voltage primary current to the coil (which see). This interruption induces the high-voltage secondary current necessary for the ignition spark.

crankcase(s) The structurally strong chamber in which is carried the crankshaft (which see). In British motorcycle engines, usually made in two non-mirror image halves to form a pair.

crankpin The eccentric journal which locates the con rod. Part of a built-up crankshaft (as opposed to a one-piece type), along with flywheels (which see) and mainshafts. These components are then pressed or bolted together.

crankshaft The shaft which is driven by the piston(s) (which see) to provide the engine motive force. The main bearings, which are supported in the crankcase, are all in line, and the crankpins are offset. Thus the crankshaft turns as the con rod and piston are pushed up and down.

Craven luggage Strong, well-made period British motorcycle luggage systems, including racks and panniers.

cubic capacity An engine's total displacement, usually measured in cubic centimetres, eg 350cc.

cush drive A shock absorbing part of the transmission.

cylinder A parallel-walled circular cavity, usually containing a piston. It is bounded at one end by the crankcase (which see) and at the other by the cylinder head (which see).

cylinder head End piece closing off the blind end of a cylinder (which see). It is bolted on top of the crankcase, and normally contains the combustion chamber and the valve gear.

damper A device which slows down or inhibits the movement of a part. In suspension systems, for quickly arresting oscillations.

Dead Centre The two positions at each end of the piston travel, BDC and TDC (which both see).

de-coke Slang for decarbonise, to remove accumulated carbon and other deposits from the combustion chamber and exhaust tract.

die Component used to form parts in metal and other materials. It comprises a female mould, and can be used to cut male thread forms. See also 'Tap'.

drive-side Side of engine on which drive-line from crankshaft to rear wheel is located. On British motorcycles normally the left side if viewed by rider seated on the saddle.

dynamo Generates direct current (DC) electricity. Its function is to keep the battery charged. The power is developed in windings carried on the armature (which see), and reversing polarity is kept constant by connecting the windings to a commutator (which see) with brushes placed so that one is always positive, and one negative. This low-tension current is then transformed into high tension by passing through a separate coil.

Earles fork Form of leading-link front suspension devised by British engineer Ernie Earles, used on some prototype Ariels, and on production BMWs.
end-float In and out (axial) movement along the length of a shaft.

Featherbed Superlative duplex cradle swinging-arm frame designed by the McCandless brothers for Norton's racers and roadsters.
female thread The spiral screw-thread in a hole or socket bored to receive the corresponding 'male' thread (which see) of a screw or bolt.
flywheel A weight attached to the crankshaft whose inertia is sufficient to keep the engine turning between power strokes.
four-stroke A type of engine cycle made up of four phases: intake, compression, ignition, and exhaust (colloquially, suck, squeeze, bang, blow), each one taking a full stroke of the piston (which see), and two turns of the crankshaft (which see) in all.

gasket A seal, usually soft or compressible, placed between two mating surfaces. Paper, cork, copper or composite material is commonly used.
gearbox Either the housing containing gearwheels and shafts, or the whole assembly. 'Unit' gearbox assemblies are built in a common housing with the engine shafts, 'pre-unit' or 'separate' gearboxes have their own housing.
G50 Famous Matchless single cylinder 500cc ohc (which see) racing motorcycle.
Gus Kuhn Well-known South London Norton and BMW dealership.

Hepolite A branded British range of pistons etc.

ignition Firing of the compressed fuel/air mixture in an engine's combustion chamber(s). In a petrol (as opposed to a diesel) engine, it is achieved by a high-voltage electric spark.
ignition timing Arranging for the contact-breaker (which see) to open at the correct position in relation to the piston's position.
IoM Isle of Man, home of the TT (Tourist Trophy) and MGP (Manx Grand Prix) motorcycle road races.

Jampot Proprietary fat rear suspension units used from 1951 to 1957 on AJS and Matchless machines.

lekker Good, sweet.

magdyno Magneto and dynamo (which both see) as distinct units but mounted together and using the same drive.
magneto A self-contained device generating electrical current for the ignition (which see) spark, by being rotated from the engine, usually at half speed. Current has to be at a tension, or pressure, of several thousand volts, to jump the spark plug (which see) gap over which it passes; it is transformed into a high-tension current by passing through coils of wire which are incorporated into the magneto, or by a separate coil (which see). A contact breaker (which see) incorporated in the magneto automatically causes the circuit to be broken and thus sends a charge of high-pressure current to the spark plug; in the type which carry the coils (which see) on the armature, the power to the spark plug is taken off from a slip-ring (which see).
main bearings Bearings supporting an engine's major shaft assembly – normally the crankshaft.
male thread The spiral on a screw or bolt cut to fit the spirally-bored circular socket of the 'female' thread (which see).
Matchless British motorcycle marque produced by Associated Motor Cycles (AMC) in Plumstead, South-East London, alongside AJS equivalents.
mushi Good, nice.

needle roller Type of roller bearing in which the length of the roller is much greater than the diameter.
Nimbus Swedish in-line 4-cylinder motorcycle.
nshima Also *mishima*, a maize-based porridge-like food.
Nyloc A nut with a nylon insert covering about half its depth and standing proud of

the threads. When fitted to a bolt, the latter cuts its way into the nylon, making the nut a very tight fit and preventing it loosening under vibration etc.

ohc Overhead camshaft. An engine in which the camshaft (which see) is carried in or above the cylinder head, operating the valves directly or via short rocker arms.
ohv Overhead valve. An engine in which the valves are carried inside the cylinder head. The camshaft is usually located closer to the crankshaft, and the valves are actuated by a system of pushrods and rockers (which both see).
o.i.f. Oil-in-frame. Design where the engine oil is carried not in a separate tank but, to save weight, within the tubes of the frame. Adopted by BSA and Triumph for most 1971-on models.

Panther British motorcycle marque based in Cleckheaton, Yorkshire.
pinion Strictly, the smaller of a pair of gears, but colloquially, any gear. See 'Sprocket.'
pinking A tinkling noise from an overloaded engine under open throttle. Caused by detonation, the explosion of mixture in the combustion chamber rather than its controlled burning. Very destructive. May be confined to the end gases or may involve the whole charge.
piston Bucket-shaped component that is a sliding fit inside a cylinder. In an engine, it is driven down by the expansion of burning fuel/air mixture to transmit driving effort to the crankshaft (which see) by way of the con rod (which see).
piston rings Thin, gapped bands of metal that fit into grooves around the piston to make seals against the walls of the cylinder (which see).
plunger Crude type of rear suspension achieved by undamped springs in pairs of twinned containers mounted on each side, above and below the axle.
primary chain Chain that transmits power from the engine to the gearbox.
pushrod A rod or tube used in compression to move a part such as a valve or rocker (which both see), or a clutch pressure plate.

rear chain Chain transmitting power to the rear wheel.
Renolds Principal British manufacturer of chains for transmission.
rocker A pivoted arm, used mainly to transmit motion in valve gear. The pivot might be at the centre or the end of the arm. Also, a greasy biker.
rocker box Housing or compartment which contains the rockers and adjustment for the valve gear, either with an inspection window or a detachable cap to provide access.
Royal Enfield British motorcycle marque based in Redditch, Worcestershire. Production of their Bullet singles began under licence in India in the 1950s, and now has survived the original company.

san The people formerly known as Bushmen.
scrambles The fast off-road motorcycle sport now known as 'motocross'.
shona Language and people found in Zambia and Zimbabwe.
side-valve, sv Engine configuration in which the valves and ports are carried in the cylinder block, not above it. Generally less powerful than equivalent ohv (which see) engines.
single An engine with one cylinder only.
single leading-shoe, sls Type of drum brake in which the operating cam only bears on the leading edge of each shoe.
slip-ring A rotating part of a magneto (which see), on the armature (which see), to which current is channelled and from which it is collected by the pick-up brush.
spark plug High-voltage electrical device for igniting the petrol/air mixture in the cylinder (which see), by arcing an electrical current, as a spark, between two electrodes. This assembly, inserted in the combustion chamber, is detachable, and mounted in a threaded hole.
sprocket A toothed wheel to transmit an engine's power by chain drive. The larger of a pair of gears, also termed the 'gear wheel'.
Square Four Type of Ariel motorcycle with engine designed by Edward Turner, featuring four cylinders arranged in a cruciform layout in a single block, with one pair behind the other. Was produced in various capacities, and as both ohc and ohv.

steering damper Friction discs (or a hydraulic damper) which provide resistance to the front forks moving too freely from lock to lock.

stroke The linear travel of an engine's piston, between the highest and lowest point.

swinging-arm Type of rear suspension in which the wheel is carried in a fork or radius arm pivoted in front of the wheel, with spring-and-damper units mounted on the fork.

tap A tool for cutting female thread (which see) forms, eg in a casting.

TDC Top Dead Centre (see 'Dead Centre').

thread Helical groove cut into rod (male thread) to fit a similar groove cut inside a hole of the same diameter (female thread). The shape and depth of the thread form, together with the pitch (the number of threads per inch measured along the length of the bolt etc) have been standardised into different types such as British Standard Whitworth (BSW), British Standard Fine (BSF) etc.

timing The point at which an operation (such as ignition, or a valve opening) takes place in relation to the position of the crankshaft when it happens. Usually measured from the TDC or BDC positions, and expressed as degrees of crank rotation before or after TDC; or inches/mm of piston movement before or after TDC.

timing gears Gears driving valve mechanism or ignition equipment.

timing-side Side of an engine on which timing gear is located; opposite to drive-side (which see). On British motorcycles, normally the right side of the motorcycle if viewed by rider seated on the saddle.

torque Turning effort exerted by or on a revolving part, measured in lb ft. For an engine, the mean turning effort exerted on the crankshaft by the pistons, and available for propelling the vehicle.

transmission Means of taking power from the source, to the part to be driven; may be by chain, gears, shaft etc.

trials Off-road, feet-up motorcycle sport involving specialised bikes negotiating difficult observed sections.

triple An engine with three cylinders.

Triton Classic special, normally made up of a Triumph twin engine in a Norton Featherbed frame.

Triumph Most successful British motorcycle marque post-war, based at Meriden outside Coventry, and surviving today after a 1990 rebirth at Hinckley, Leicestershire.

turbo cabbage Marijuana.

twin An engine with two cylinders.

two-stroke Engine cycle which gives a power-stroke at each revolution of the crankshaft (eg for every two strokes of the piston).

valve A device which can restrict or open a passage to control fluid or gas flow. In post-war British four-stroke motorcycle engines, poppet valves were the norm. These are mushroom-shaped, forming a seal at their widest diameter in a circular port (seat), and are opened by lifting them off this 'seat'.

valve lifter A device to partially lift the exhaust valve, spoiling engine compression so that the motor may be turned over easily. Also called a decompressor.

valve timing The point at which the valves open and close in relation to crankshaft position.

VMCC Vintage Motor Cycle Club, largest and best organised old motorcycle club in Britain.

V-twin A piston engine with its two cylinders set at an angle (usually less than 90 degrees) to one another.

Wankel Type of engine with a rotary piston.

weld To join materials by heat and sometimes pressure. Many different methods of welding have evolved.

Woodruff key Slip of metal (the key) fitting into grooves on a shaft and into a wheel, gear etc on that shaft, as a means of locating it. The key may be tapered, straight or curved on one side.

INDEX

Folio numbers in italics refer to colour plate sections